Directed by Clint Eastwood

Directed by
Clint Eastwood

Eighteen Films Analyzed

LAURENCE F. KNAPP

McFarland & Company, Inc., Publishers
Jefferson, North Carolina, and London

British Library of Cataloguing-in-Publication data are available

Library of Congress Cataloguing-in-Publication Data

Knapp, Laurence F., 1965–
    Directed by Clint Eastwood : eighteen films analyzed / by
Laurence F. Knapp.
        p.   cm.
    Includes bibliographical references and index.
    ISBN 0-7864-0271-7 (library binding : 50# alk. paper) ∞
    1. Eastwood, Clint, 1930–   —Criticism and interpretation.
I. Title.
PN1998.3.E325K63   1996
791.43'0233'092 — dc20   96-31358
                                         CIP

Manufactured in the United States of America

McFarland & Company, Inc., Publishers
  Box 611, Jefferson, North Carolina 28640

To Moyenda, my best friend,
soulmate and wife —
no film could be as beautiful,
complex, and extraordinary as you

Table of Contents

Preface

If there has been an American filmmaker who has been misunderstood and taken for granted, it is Clint Eastwood. Although Eastwood has directed 18 films, he is seen as a star and an American icon, not a filmmaker with a distinct style and world view. Eastwood has been the subject of innumerable books, essays, and interviews, but the depth and scope of his directorial work is rarely acknowledged or discussed. Critics and journalists tend to fixate on Eastwood's venerable persona and to ignore Eastwood's craftsmanship and cinematic technique. Eastwood's persona is an integral part of his *oeuvre*, but it is not as "Eastwoodian" as Eastwood's immanent presence behind the camera.

Directed by Clint Eastwood is not a biography or a filmography — it is a chronological analysis of Eastwood's filmic syntax and vision. That syntax and vision can only be found in Eastwood's 18 films as a director, not the spaghetti westerns directed by Sergio Leone or the 16 other Malpaso films produced by Eastwood and directed by Don Siegel, Michael Cimino and assorted members of the Malpaso production crew. Eastwood's Malpaso star vehicles reflect his affinity for blue collar humor and low-key narrative (*Every Which Way But Loose*), but they lack Eastwood's unique and integrated use of editing and mise-en-scène. From *Play Misty for Me* to *The Bridges of Madison County*, *Directed by Clint Eastwood* traces and examines Eastwood's style as he redefines his persona (*High Plains Drifter, The Outlaw Josey Wales, The Gauntlet, Sudden Impact, Pale Rider, The Rookie, Unforgiven*), reconciles the battle of the sexes (*Play Misty for Me, Heartbreak Ridge*), dramatizes the mixed blessing of being an artist (*Bronco Billy, Honkytonk Man, Bird, White Hunter, Black Heart*), and the mysteries of being human (*Unforgiven, A Perfect World, The Bridges of Madison County*). While Clint Eastwood the man is unknown to us, we do have access to his films, which are full of rich insight, wit, emotion, and humanity. That art is the focus of this book.

Introduction

I love acting and intend to continue doing it. But I must admit
that the satisfaction of directing goes deeper than any other facet
of filmmaking. In direction you are responsible for the entire
concept of the telling of a story; in acting, you are mainly concerned with your own interpretation of one of the characters in
the plot. But I suppose that my involvement goes even deeper
than acting or directing. I love every aspect of the creation of a
motion picture and I guess I am committed to it for life [Dou-
glas, 1974, p. 117].

Of all the film theories that have congealed since the 1930s, no other
has taken the critical drubbing of the auteur theory. Fashioned by the new
wave essayists of *Cahiers du Cinéma* in the 1950s to account for the aesthetic
and thematic consistencies of such directors as Alfred Hitchcock and Jean
Renoir, the auteur theory contended that the filmmakers most worthy of
praise and study were the ones with an identifiable style and *Weltanschauung*. The directors who expressed themselves in a personal and consistent
manner were considered full-fledged artists, worthy of the respect given to
the fine arts community. Quickly adopted by cineastes, the auteur theory
helped to differentiate craftsmen from journeymen, popularize obscure or
adventurous directors, and define overlapping movements in world cinema.
It also fell prey, however, to a certain arbitrariness based on personal prej-
udice rather than on consensual analysis or agreement.

With the rise of the semioticians and structuralists in the late 1960s, the
auteur theory came under intense scrutiny and calumny. Authorship became
anathema. A central quandary arose: in a collaborative, commercial art
form that involved the close interaction of thousands of skilled technicians
and performers, who should be credited with being the author? Can a director have that much autonomy? Can he or she be that omnipotent? To the
post-structuralists and deconstructionists, the true author of a film was
either the cultural system that produced it or the viewer who invested the

"text" with meaning and syntax. The director became less and less of an architect and more and more of an unwitting bricklayer. The auteur-cum-bricklayer meant less than the political, sexual, and cultural "signs" that made up society and cinema.

Refutations aside, the auteur theory has always naively presumed that a director can be credited for the content of his or her work. That naïveté compromises any auteurist expedition into the American studio era, but in discussing the Balkanizing of the studio system and the rise of independent production in the 1950s, the auteur theory gains considerable worth and credibility as a means of classification and analysis. Even with the iconoclasm of the post-studio era, however, the quandary of authorship remains. If there is one group of filmmakers that affirm the basic assumptions of the auteur theory, it is the small number of star-auteurs (or, as I call them, "starteurs") who have emerged out of the morass of feature film production with their independence intact.

Equally present both on and off the screen, the starteur represents the unique triumph of the individual over the collectivity of filmmaking. Not only do starteurs have financial and personal control over their careers, but they determine the nature and character of their on-screen personas as well. Starteurs should not be confused with the numerous stars who have formed their own production or distribution companies (for instance, Mary Pickford, Kirk Douglas or Steve McQueen) or with actors who have occasionally directed (Robert Montgomery, Charles Laughton, John Cassevetes, Paul Newman, Jack Nicholson, Warren Beatty, Sidney Poitier, Robert Redford, Barbra Streisand, Thomas Chong, Danny DeVito, and many others). Starteurs have a self-reflective relationship to their work; their films are an extended dialogue with their screen personae, an attempt to shape, reshape, and break the mold that gave them their initial creative and commercial independence. The most successful and resonant starteurs are those who have an interdependent — not codependent — relationship with their personae. With great delicacy and insight, they are capable of making successive films that deconstruct or circumnavigate their personae without reducing them to bathos, parody, or caricature. Their longevity and singular status comes as a result of a direct understanding of themselves, their craft, time period, and archetypal appeal. As they mold and reconstruct their personae, they develop unique themes and compositional motifs that are wholly their own.

Starteurs, on the whole, enjoy a brief, delirious period of autonomy and notoriety before they lose their commercial and cultural appeal. There have been a precious few: William S. Hart in the mid-1910s, Charlie Chaplin from the mid-1910s to the early 1950s, Erich von Stroheim in the late 1910s, Buster Keaton in the 1920s, Jerry Lewis in the 1960s, and Woody Allen and Clint

Eastwood from the late 1960s to the present. Von Stroheim departed from the screen after sabotaging his career with such extravagant projects as *Greed* (1925) and *The Wedding March* (1928); Keaton capitulated to MGM, the sound era, and alcoholism; Lewis repeated himself ad nauseam until his persona became intolerable; and Allen allowed his screen self to degenerate as his public self took on a much greater significance. Only two starteurs have managed to stay professionally and culturally viable for the majority of their careers: Charlie Chaplin and his modern equivalent, Clint Eastwood.

Like Chaplin in the 1910s and 1920s, Eastwood stands as a breed apart from his peers — an Olympian among Danaans. He, like Chaplin in his heyday, is a towering megastar-director-entrepreneur with his own distinct iconography. While Chaplin represents the sentimental hopes, bittersweet dreams, and melting-pot frustrations of the early 20th century, Eastwood embodies the tensions and anxieties of the late 20th century. Chaplin and Eastwood represent the sanctity of the individual against an ever-encroaching modern world: the Tramp's brushes with industrialism, poverty, and penology in *Modern Times* (1936) form a continuum with Eastwood's struggle against corruption and conformity in *The Gauntlet* (1977). Both Chaplin and Eastwood are inveterate nonconformists — the Tramp's mere existence is an affront to the status quo; Dirty Harry has no qualms about talking back to his superiors and taking the law into his own hands.

A consummate filmmaker, Chaplin ran his own studio from 1918 to the 1950s, overseeing all facets of production. Eastwood achieved the same feat. He toiled for nearly ten years as a studio contract player, television cowboy, and Italian cinema prodigy before wresting complete control over his career and burgeoning persona. Eastwood's Malpaso Productions — a cottage-industry sized production company that Eastwood has presided over since the late 1960s — is the modern equivalent of Chaplin's studio. Eastwood, like Chaplin, had a substantial role in the creation of his persona. Chaplin's clowning in such early Mack Sennett shorts as *Kid Auto Races at Venice* (1914) and *Mabel's Strange Predicament* (1914) resulted in the guise and muse of the Tramp; Eastwood's sojourn to Italy to film *A Fistful of Dollars* (1964) led to the overnight phenomenon of the Man with No Name. Like Chaplin, Eastwood gained mastery over his persona and swiftly adapted it to the texture and tenor of his own films, pushing his persona into cinematic directions only Eastwood could have conceived.

That persona, the instantaneous signifier that enabled Chaplin and Eastwood to thrive, metamorphosed into a mixed blessing as both tried to test the boundaries of their on-screen selves. While Chaplin strove to politicize and finally atomize the Tramp with *The Great Dictator* (1940), *Monsieur Verdoux* (1947), and *Limelight* (1952), Eastwood pushed toward a minimization of his own adamantine persona with such films as *Honkytonk Man*

(1982); *White Hunter, Black Heart* (1990); *A Perfect World* (1993), and *The Bridges of Madison County* (1995). Many of Eastwood's more personal and eccentric projects such as *Breezy* (1973), *Bronco Billy* (1980), and *Bird* (1988) have met with the same popular and critical consternation that greeted Chaplin's *Monsieur Verdoux*. Like Chaplin, Eastwood has angled for a body of work in which his physical presence is not the sine qua non of his films. Both have an identifiable style that unifies and distinguishes their work — not only is their corporeal presence evident, but their directorial presence is just as noticeable. Their efforts to retire their screen selves while remaining active filmmakers have resulted in a fascinating struggle between the commercial demands of their persona and the need for personal expression. Both starteurs serve as excellent test cases for the auteur theory — without Chaplin and Eastwood's artistic input and physical presence, their films would have no context, no meaning, and no guiding spirit. As Eastwood himself has said, "To me what a Clint Eastwood picture is, is one that I'm in" (Johnston, 1981, p. 138). How can Eastwood be deconstructed from Eastwood?

1

Clint Eastwood, "Starteur"

Without sounding like a pseudo-intellectual dipshit, it's my
responsibility to be true to myself. If it works for me, it's right.
When I start choosing wrong, I'll step back and let someone else
do it for me [Cahill, 1985, p. 23].

You are probably talking to the one person in Hollywood who has
never even tried cocaine. Beer is fine for me [Clinch, 1994, p. 179].

Eastwood's quip quoted on the previous page ("what a Clint Eastwood
picture is, is one that I'm in") is a prime, if tongue-in-cheek example of Eastwood's self-effacing manner and method. Although Eastwood's persona has
played a crucial role in the development of his *oeuvre*, his aesthetic presence
is as prominent and significant as his six-foot, four-inch frame. In all of his
films as a starteur and director—*Play Misty for Me* (1971); *High Plains Drifter*
(1973); *Breezy* (1973); *The Eiger Sanction* (1975); *The Outlaw Josey Wales*
(1976); *The Gauntlet* (1977); *Bronco Billy* (1980); *Firefox* (1981); *Honkytonk
Man* (1982); *Sudden Impact* (1983); *Pale Rider* (1985); *Heartbreak Ridge*
(1986); *Bird* (1988); *White Hunter, Black Heart* (1990); *The Rookie* (1990);
Unforgiven (1992); *A Perfect World* (1993) and *The Bridges of Madison County*
(1995)— not to mention the Malpaso films he has supervised and started
in—*Hang 'Em High* (1967, Ted Post); *Coogan's Bluff* (1968, Don Siegel); *Two
Mules for Sister Sara* (1970, Siegel); *The Beguiled* (1971, Siegel); *Dirty Harry*
(1971, Siegel); *Joe Kidd* (1972, John Sturges); *Magnum Force* (1973, Ted Post);
Thunderbolt and Lightfoot (1974, Michael Cimino); *The Enforcer* (1976, James
Fargo); *Every Which Way But Loose* (1978, Fargo); *Escape from Alcatraz* (1979,
Siegel); *Any Which Way You Can* (1980, Buddy Van Horn); *Tightrope* (1984,
Richard Tuggle); *City Heat* (1984, Richard Benjamin); *The Dead Pool* (1988,
Van Horn) and *Pink Cadillac* (1989, Van Horn)— Eastwood mediates

between his boundless cinematic presence and his rigorous directorial presence. His prolific body of work is built upon — yet oddly removed from — the persona it ostensibly serves.

Because of his formidable record at the box office, Eastwood has had to contend with the mixed blessings of being a starteur. Eastwood has had to rely on his persona — which is as culturally ingrained as Budweiser or McDonalds — to remain independent and marketable. In spite of the fact that his films have made more than $2 billion, Eastwood makes commercial films out of necessity, rather than by choice:

> Hopefully, I've made enough money for financiers in the business that I can afford myself a change of pace now and then. If you do a few small films you love and they're not commercial, they're sometimes better for you than doing a massive commercial thing that people take lightly [Thompson, 1992, p. 172].

> Some people don't want you to take that big swing. It's just not what they expect or want from you. But I can't let that stop me. If you think about that, you're going to make decisions for all the wrong reasons. If you don't take some chances, why do it? [Thompson, pp. 183–4].

By defying the expectations of his audience and taking on personal projects with little or no commercial value (*Breezy*; *Bronco Billy*; *Honkytonk Man*; *Bird*; *White Hunter, Black Heart*; *A Perfect World*) and genres outside of his iconic range (sexual thriller [*Play Misty for Me*], espionage [*The Eiger Sanction, Firefox*], screwball comedy [*Every Which Way But Loose, Bronco Billy*] and tearjerker [*The Bridges of Madison County*]), Eastwood has been able to age gracefully on screen, assume roles that would have been inconceivable two decades ago, and remain in the director's chair. Eastwood's whole directorial career has been a successful attempt to balance the demands and realities of commercial filmmaking with his desire to test the boundaries of his style and persona. Through four distinct phases, Eastwood has freed himself from the constraints of his persona without losing his status as a bankable filmmaker. In his first phase (1970–75), Eastwood weaned himself from the technical and aesthetic influence of his two mentors, Sergio Leone and Don Siegel, and claimed his persona as his own. During his second phase as a starteur (1976–85), Eastwood tried to heal his persona by ridding it of its spiritual wounds, but discovered in vain that audiences did not want the Man with No Name or Dirty Harry exorcised of their demons. Eastwood dealt with this dilemma in his third phase (1986–93) by retiring and making his persona more ambiguous in *The Rookie* and *Unforgiven*. With *A Perfect World* and *The Bridges of Madison County*, the flagship of his fourth phase, Eastwood made it be known in no uncertain terms that his on-screen presence would no longer be determined by his persona — Eastwood the director finally surpassed Eastwood the actor-icon.

Eastwood belongs to two periods of American cinema: the Warner Bros. studio era and the New Hollywood of the 1970s. Eastwood has the same instinct for genre that Warner Bros. and its house directors had in the 1930s and 1940s. His ability to revamp his persona to fit a variety of genres is reminiscent of Warner Bros.' canny evolution of the gangster film from the dawn of sound (*Public Enemy* [William Wellman, 1931]) to the twilight of the studio era (*White Heat* [Raoul Walsh, 1949]) and the studio's ability to adapt to changing audience tastes (musicals in the early 1930s; costume dramas starring Errol Flynn in the mid- to late 1930s; film noir in the early to late 1940s). Eastwood's style, however, is more reminiscent of the 1970s — the elliptical narratives, the revisionist analysis of genre, the parade of embattled anti-heroes menaced by malaise and institutional corruption, and the convoy of blue-collar drifters drinking, loving, and driving themselves senseless. As the codes of the 1970s succumbed to the hermetic conventions of the post-modern 1980s, Eastwood retained his style but shifted his focus. He concluded his overview of American society and concentrated instead on his core concern: the individual, particularly individuals of artistic temperament (in *Play Misty for Me*; *Bronco Billy*; *Honkytonk Man*; *Bird*; *White Hunter, Black Heart*; *The Bridges of Madison County*).

Eastwood's films are undeniably American, but his aesthetic sensibilities are frequently at odds with modern, mainstream filmmaking. Eastwood refuses to march in step with a metronomical narrative. In contrast to the MTV school of filmmaking, which has turned American cinema into a rampant, remote-controlled assault on the senses, Eastwood remains faithful to Howard Hawks' character studies and John Ford's majestic use of composition and landscape to convey mood and feeling. Eastwood likes to wander and appreciate the moment. Narrative does not govern Eastwood — it serves as a vehicle, a chassis for Eastwood's genuine love of phenomenology and characterization. To understand Eastwood is to recognize and relish his love of balance and aesthetic restraint. As Eastwood himself has proclaimed, "sometimes you can tell more with economy than you can with excess gyration" (Cahill, p. 22).

Like Ford's melancholy and wistful westerns, Eastwood's films question the codes that constitute American cinema and society without degenerating into impassioned, dogmatic critiques of the system or human nature. Eastwood investigates, but does not indict masculinity or American culture. Men are frequently upstaged and put to shame by intelligent, outspoken women who refuse to accept the status quo. In Eastwood's cinema, "if a character doesn't grow in each film, if he doesn't learn something about life as he goes along, there isn't any sense in doing the film" (Thompson, p. 180). Allegedly conservative, Eastwood straddles the fence politically and socially—he critiques *and* celebrates America, the American dream, the rule of law, the sanctity of the individual and, to an even greater extent, the essence of his own persona. Eastwood does not subscribe to the myths of the frontier, nor does he believe that America will become a dystopia in the 21st century. He has faith in the American spirit and landscape, even if it seems to be in decline.

For Eastwood, "sometimes the imperfection of things is what makes them real. Many times I've seen movies that are beautifully composed, beautifully laid out, but there's something dead there and the deadness comes out of its having been overworked" (Hentoff, 1988, p. 27). This dynamic quality of Eastwood's work—a commingling of deliberateness and spontaneity—comes out of Eastwood's time-honored shooting style, a complementary mixture of speed and precision:

> I'm rather quick. I try to get on without losing the emotion, the intensity, the interest ... it's difficult to give energy to a film, and that energy can be lost if shooting takes too long.... I'll talk to the actors about the film but I don't rehearse. I'd be afraid to leave a good take out of the camera [Plaza, 1991, p. 222].

> I shoot fast. It's not just a matter of money, I like to have momentum, to keep the spirit and energy going. To me, directing is knowing the concept you want and getting it [Thompson, p. 180].

Eastwood moves swiftly but decisively. He edits in-camera and frequently shoots first or second rehearsals after blocking the shots with his cinematographer. Eastwood rarely exceeds two or three takes. He strives toward bringing his films in ahead of schedule and under budget: "If a picture cost five million, I hope it looks like ten million on the screen. If it cost five million and it looks like three million on the screen, then that's a failure to me" (Thomson, 1984, p. 68). Eastwood's mania for a tight, well-planned shoot comes from his long apprenticeship in the film and television industry. His exact, but impromptu shooting style makes his style seem extemporaneous even though it is pre-planned.

Eastwood has been able to stay lean and pragmatic thanks to the loyalty of the Malpaso unit, a cadre of technicians who have helped him sustain his cinematic style and vision. Unlike some directors who insist on being benevolent despots, Eastwood has no need or desire to rule his company by fiat. He relishes the fellowship and ingenuity of his crew, to which he grants a great deal of autonomy. Eastwood's crew knows what he wants, allowing him to concentrate on the essentials:

> I think of making a movie as an ensemble. It's the work of a lot of people and it's presumptuous to credit it all to one person. A director is merely the person who keeps waving the flag and encouraging everyone to charge the hill. You can shape the direction or shape the tone, but by and large, you're only as strong as the support you surround yourself with [Keough, 1992, p. 15].

A thorough examination of Eastwood's films cannot be done without recognizing the enormous contributions of the Malpaso company. The consistent look and spirit of Eastwood's films for the past 25 years can be credited to the overlapping members of the Malpaso crew who stay for long stretches of time, guaranteeing a seamless transition from film to film. Except for *Play Misty for Me* and *Breezy*, which suffer from an excess of early seventies chic, Eastwood's cinema has resisted the trends and conventions of the last quarter century. The long-term contributions of key Malpaso personnel (particularly cinematographers Bruce Surtees and Jack N. Green) have helped to preserve Eastwood's style and to keep it consistent: *High Plains Drifter* and *The Outlaw Josey Wales* bear a striking resemblance to *Unforgiven* and *A Perfect World*. (See the appendix for a detailed filmography of the Malpaso unit, showing how much of a continuum has existed since the late 1960s.)

Asked to describe his style, Eastwood has replied:

> Most of my films have a different look, depending upon what the film calls for. It's a combination of pace, and an eye for composition. I can't explain exactly what it is, because there isn't as much a style to my films — an individualistic style — as there is to Don Siegel. Mine vary [Thomson, p. 69].

Irrespective of his own opinion, Eastwood has as many stylistic mileposts as Don Siegel or Sergio Leone. Eastwood's 17 films yield a treasure-trove of common elements. His style can be divided into nine major categories: (1) Backlighting; 2) 180° reverse masters; (3) Secondary colors; (4) Extensive location shooting; (5) A balance of formal, accelerated, invisible, and elliptical montage; (6) Fixed and fluid mise-en-scène; (7) A circular construction of narrative; (8) A latent, informal acting style; and (9) A mythic (the Man with No Name) and modern (Dirty Harry) persona.

1. Backlighting. Eastwood has testified, "I hate the flatness of TV lighting" (Rayns, 1985, p. 83). Key, or front, lighting bathes a subject with light. Back, or side-cross lighting, comes from behind, veiling the subject in shadow or darkness. To avoid the soft, diffuse properties of high-key lighting, Eastwood makes ample use of low-key backlighting. He prefers a high-contrast lighting scheme in which hard, unpolarized light produces strong illumination and sharp outlines, brings out detail and texture, and separates light from shadow. Eastwood is the auteur of eventide and postmeridian lighting. His films are marked by an expressive, understated equilibrium of shadow and sunlight, pitch black darkness and penetrating spot lighting. Light and darkness, and sunlight and shadow form an arabesque: a person's face can be animated by the restless reflection of a swinging tree branch (*Unforgiven*) or quietly revealed by the slow tilt of a hat (*High Plains Drifter*). Whenever Eastwood delves in darkness, he usually keeps away from diffusion or middle grays. In *The Gauntlet*'s sepulchral cave sequence and *Bird*'s many nightclub scenes there are no medium grays — only a sharp contrast between isolated sources of light and expressive shrouds of darkness. Eastwood's lighting schematic can be misconstrued as realistic because it makes use of natural, available light, but his reliance on a crepuscular melange of light and shadow works against a true representation of reality or nature. His dusk-driven cinematography captures an autumnal mood and texture, not a faithful window on the world.

Eastwood's aversion to high-key lighting extends to his coverage of performers, most notably himself. Eastwood feels no need to bathe himself or his cast in light: "I'm not that enamored of my face that I think it should be absolutely plastered in front of the camera every minute…I feel that if the presence is there, when you want to you can pump the light in, but it's got to be at the right moment" (Combs, 1992, p. 13). Eastwood has known since *A Fistful of Dollars* that the surest way to be cinematic is to pull back, to reveal only a select or shadowy part of his face or character. Backlighting allows Eastwood to meld with — rather than melt into— the image. Backlighting mythologizes Eastwood and maximizes his cinematic effectiveness by minimizing his on-screen presence. Eastwood stays in perpetual shadow in *Pale Rider* to suggest the supernatural essence of the Preacher and his peripheral, spiritual relationship to the community he protects.

2. **180° Reverse Masters.** Eastwood creates the illusion of a composite 360 degree space by crossing the action axis and alternating between two shot and reverse shots that share a 180 degree axis. This yields a shot set up that preserves the flow of time as it splinters space. By using reverse masters, Eastwood achieves a temporal continuity and a circular, yet elliptical sense of place. Space becomes dynamic and expressive. In *Bronco Billy*, Eastwood uses reverse masters to suggest the unity of Billy's Wild West Show and Ms. Antoinette Lily's estrangement from it. When Billy learns that two of his employees, Chief Big Eagle and Running Water, are expecting a child, he congratulates them with a two-gun salute, drawing the rest of his troupe into the tent. A reverse master embraces Billy and his adopted family, holding

them in a 360 degree hug. Eastwood then pivots the camera back, revealing the forlorn figure of Ms. Lily in the rear, backgrounded by a shallow focus and a short lens. Antoinette is left out of Billy's circle and universe. She is an outsider, an intruder who is outside the parameters of the reverse master. Reverse masters give Eastwood the opportunity to manipulate space and time and achieve a compound sense of place and mood.

3. **Secondary Colors.** In keeping with his low-key cinematography, Eastwood abstains from a saturation of color. Eastwood prefers "muted colors and earth tones" (Plaza, p. 102). He has capitalized on primary colors in key sequences of his films — the apocalyptic red of *High Plains Drifter*, the patriotic red, white, and blue of *Bronco Billy*—but he mostly relies on cool colors, such as green or brown. Too much saturation of color would undermine Eastwood's postmeridian palette, which relies on a subtle, unassuming expressionism that is stylish but does not draw too much attention to itself.

4. **Extensive Location Shooting.** Eastwood thrives on location: "I love exteriors. I feel more at ease there than in some studio or other. There's nothing like an atmosphere of an authentic place to inspire oneself and one's crew" (Plaza, p. 161). Eastwood's films have a robust alfresco flavor and a warm affinity for the rural vistas and open highways of America (*Bronco Billy, Honkytonk Man, A Perfect World, The Bridges of Madison County*). Landscape in an Eastwood film never degenerates into incidental, postcard-like scenery. The African exteriors of *White Hunter, Black Heart* never detract from Eastwood's disciplined character study. Eastwood rarely fixates on a landscape or vista to admire its formal beauty. When he does, it is to accentuate a theme or a mood. The peaceful, timeless shots of the Congo that end *White Hunter, Black Heart* underscore John Wilson's catharsis and the primacy of nature. The Eiger in *The Eiger Sanction* is not just a surrogate for CII, the amoral intelligence organization Jonathon Hemlock serves, but a projection of Hemlock's own inner fears and doubts — the mountain is as inaccessible as his conscience. In Eastwood's westerns, where nature has an anthropomorphic mystique, landscape and location shooting add an allegorical depth to the images. The lake and blue sky that accompany the town of Lago in *High Plains Drifter*, the valley that brings *The Outlaw Josey Wales* to a close, and the mountains that stand watch over *Pale Rider* and *Unforgiven*'s Big Whiskey have an indirect omniscience that forms a mythical firmament over Eastwood's westerns. Landscape does not exist in Eastwood's films to be glorified; it is there to create a mood and atmosphere.

5. **A Balance of Formal, Accelerated, Invisible and Elliptical Montage.** To Eastwood, "the easiest thing is to shoot long shots and close-ups, the hard part is in between, the connective tissue" (Thompson and Hunter, 1978, p. 31). Eastwood does not adhere to the accordion rule of progressive

montage, the traditional A-B-C of establishing shot, medium shot, close-up. He prefers to leap into a scene, to cut directly to a close medium shot or pan into the action. Eastwood is interested in creating an impression of time and space, not a condensation of it. He uses a lion's share of establishing shots and two-shots, but tends to shift to a low-angle or reverse master shot before the establishing shot or two-shot asserts itself over the scene. According to Eastwood:

> A director should change camera angles a lot. My theory is when you're looking at a film, you're looking at a flat piece projected onto a flat surface. The only way you can approach a 3-D feeling is to cross over and get that camera right in there so the audience can feel a part of a group rather than just observers of a group [Thompson, p. 180].

To make the audience 'part of the group', Eastwood combines both formal montage (shots of near-equal length) and accelerated montage (abrupt cutting, usually achieved by assembling random point-of-view shots) and fuses it together with invisible montage, the American convention of making films appear seamless and natural. Eastwood also makes use of elliptical montage in several of his films (including *Bird* and *A Perfect World*) to condense, extend, or distort time. Although he willingly subscribes to the American school of unobtrusive and invisible montage, Eastwood makes elastic and effective use of formal, accelerated, and elliptical montage. He belongs to the Jean Renoir school of montage (loose) more than the Hitchcock school of story boarding (tight). Eastwood loves to extend his shots for several extra seconds to prevent the narrative from overtaking the overall mood of a film. His shots tend to dovetail into one another without telegraphing what the next shot will be. In compliance with his shooting style, Eastwood does not like to fixate on one shot unless it plays a crucial part in the film (the forward tracking shot that creeps toward John Wilson in *White Hunter, Black Heart*; the slow-motion shot of Francesca's ashes falling out of an urn in *The Bridges of Madison County*). He reaches for an overall, not immediate effect. Invisible, formal, accelerated, and elliptical montage are used not to distract, but to lure the viewer in.

Eastwood's dynamic use of cutting corresponds to his attitudes toward, and treatment of, violence. He sees violence as an unfortunate but natural part of existence, as well as a potent source of dramatic conflict:

> Violence is a fact of life. It's what people are most curious about — like slowing down to see car crashes on the highway. It's unusual. It goes on the front pages of newspapers, not the back

page. That's what people want to know about. What about people who don't accept that? I tell them to fuck off [Thompson, p. 44].

I am not an advocate of violence, but on the other hand if it is one of the narrative elements in the story, I am not as upset by it as other people are. The world is a violent place — no one can escape that. In films, when it is justified, violence acts as a sort of release [Thompson, p. 38].

Violence in an Eastwood film can take two forms: instantaneous or ritualistic. It can occur unexpectedly or be the teleological resolution of an entire narrative. When violence occurs unexpectedly, Eastwood shifts to a series of low-angle, point of view, hand-held shots that disorient the viewer and de-emphasize time and space, inducing us to identify with the stress and fear of being assaulted or attacked. Vivid examples abound: Evelyn Draper's two frenzies in *Play Misty for Me*, the nerve-wracking sanctions of *The Eiger Sanction*, the opening massacre of *The Outlaw Josey Wales*, the numerous brushes with death in *The Gauntlet*, Harry's ambush-crucifixion in *Sudden Impact*, David Ackerman's roadhouse rampage in *The Rookie*, and the elephant attack in *White Hunter, Black Heart*.

When violence is expected or anticipated in a film, Eastwood stages it with a formal detachment. He uses the rectangular expanse of the anamorphic frame and the serenity of formal and elliptical montage to prompt us to observe the action rather than identify with the interior feelings of the combatants. Distance is kept. Time and space are emphasized. By abstaining from intimate montage, Eastwood ritualizes the cycles of violence and retribution that distinguish his mythic westerns. The denouements of *High Plains Drifter* and *Pale Rider* are as distant and preordained as the wedding sequence in Sergei Eisenstein's *Ivan the Terrible, Part One* (1943). Instead of being hectic and personal, the gunfights proceed like stately funerals. Their slow pace and lack of anxiety seem almost liturgical.

In all of his films, Eastwood combines both montage styles (accelerated montage+point of view+hand-held shots= instantaneous violence and audience identification; formal montage+long distance shots= ritualistic violence and passive observation) to elicit an ambiguous reaction to violence and its effects. *High Plains Drifter, The Outlaw Josey Wales, The Gauntlet, Sudden Impact, Pale Rider, The Rookie,* and *Unforgiven* ask us to both identify with and observe violence. Eastwood never shoots violence in slow motion, à la Arthur Penn's *Bonnie and Clyde* (1967), Sam Peckinpah's *The Wild Bunch* (1969) or Martin Scorsese's *Taxi Driver* (1976). He has no desire to poeticize or celebrate bloodshed. When violence does occur, it happens instantly, without repetition or optical illusion. To make things even more complex, Eastwood never fails to acknowledge the absurdity of violence and to parody and complicate the viewer's reaction to it. *The Gauntlet* encourages us to identify with, then observe with bemused amusement, the desperate and ludicrous plight of Ben Shockley and Gus Mally. The violence in the film is so random, savage, and excessive that it becomes slapstick — violence so gratuitous and unprovoked it cannot be watched with a straight face. Violence is an incorrigible phenomenon in Eastwood's work; a phenomenon that strips people of their humanity and robs them of their capacity to feel or to love. Eastwood's characters rarely initiate or salivate over violence; they respond to it with a weary, stoic stare. None of his characters walk away from a violent encounter unscathed. Exposure to violence can compel an Eastwoodian character to go into spiritual, emotional, and psychological paralysis (*The Eiger Sanction, The Outlaw Josey Wales, Firefox, Unforgiven, A Perfect World*) or experience a spiritual, emotional, and psychological rebirth (*Play Misty for Me; The Outlaw Josey Wales; The Gauntlet; White Hunter, Black Heart; The Rookie; Unforgiven*). On the whole, violence can be a source of redemption and/or damnation. In *Unforgiven*, the alternating point of view shots of Munny drawing a bead on the supine Little Bill visually buttress Eastwood's ambivalence toward violence, and the audience's insatiable hunger for it.

Not all of Eastwood's films have violent themes or content. In his films about artists (*Play Misty for Me; Bronco Billy; Honkytonk Man; Bird; White Hunter, Black Heart; The Bridges of Madison County*) or lovers (*Breezy, The Bridges of Madison County*), Eastwood focuses on character and emphasizes phenomenology over action. He brings us into the interior space of his characters by reducing the aspect ratio to 1:1.85, de-emphasizing the importance of space or location. In *The Bridges of Madison County*, Eastwood scales down his montage until the film seems to be one impressionistic moment after another — the mystery of human existence, behavior, and desire take precedence over action or conflict.

6. **Fixed and Fluid Mise-en-Scène.** Whether working in aspect ratios of 1:2.35 or 1:1.85, Eastwood maintains a geometric focal plane, positioning performers and objects in symmetrical, asymmetrical, parabolic, triangular, and/or diagonal clusters. His compositions are formal but not fixed in time or space; they place us in the midst of a scene without being too intrusive or remote. Eastwood blocks shots or shifts the camera so that the vectors formed by his performers or decor can be transgressed or transformed. Characters frequently cross the visual plane, causing the composition of a shot to alternate from symmetrical to asymmetrical or vice versa. When Eastwood blocks himself, he uses tracking shots or camera angle and placement to assert his dominance over space or location: in *Sudden Impact* he highlights Dirty Harry's defiant entrance by having the camera track several feet ahead of him. Eastwood visually positions his camera slightly below

the horizontal diameter of the frame, angling his shots so that a transverse sense of depth prevails. He prefers his visual fields to be somewhat askew and does not like one-point perspectives. When Eastwood does employ linear perspective, he uses split-field diopters and wide lenses to make space grandiose and expressive. In *A Perfect World*, Eastwood eliminates the middle ground between Red Garnett and his retinue with a split-field diopter to suggest Red's apprehension, his guilty conscience, and his misgivings with having to pursue Butch Haynes.

Eastwood strives for a harmonization of identification and observation, a subdued push and pull of montage and mise-en-scène that keeps space and perspective linear, but also fluid and elliptical. Although he leans toward formal montage, Eastwood does not allow the deliberate pace of his shots to impair the narrative. In *Bird*, Eastwood uses both long, episodic dialogue sequences and short, transitive montage to manipulate time and space. Eastwood keeps moving, even as he shoots protracted scenes or shots that seem to be fixed in time and space. He strives for a cumulative, rather than an immediate effect. Rarely will he favor an individual shot or a camera position unless it has vital importance to the film. Instead of singling out an individual shot or camera set-up, Eastwood will cut around a pivotal shot or perspective, embellishing it with a variety of cutaways, angle-reverse angle, and reaction shots. Eastwood will track slowly toward the pivotal subject or shot, intensifying the scene as the ancillary shots lessen in number. In *Honkytonk Man*, Red Stovall realizes, as the studio musicians finish 'Honkytonk Man' and the tracking shot has become a still medium close-up, that tuberculosis has finally won and his career is over; in *White Hunter, Black Heart*, John Wilson, weighed down by Kivu's death, can only whisper, "action" when the drums and cutaways have finally stopped. Of all of Eastwood's films, only *The Gauntlet* has a continuous long take, a close two-minute shot of Ben and Gus in their fortified bus, sharing their hopes and dreams as they head toward Phoenix and their self-appointed destiny.

7. **A Circular Construction of Narrative.** Eastwood has no patience for exposition: "I don't like expository scenes, unless they have an important pay off. As a rule, I always shy away from exposition" (Thompson and Hunter, p. 32). Eastwood's films move into the narrative without an excess of introductory flourishes or passages. Eastwood will either de-emphasize his front credits (*Firefox, Honkytonk Man, The Rookie*), preempt them until the close of the film (*White Hunter, Black Heart; Unforgiven; A Perfect World*) or use them as a transitional device (*The Outlaw Josey Wales, Bird*) so that he can leap into the narrative. Eastwood's best films revolve around a central image or impression that functions as a nexus, a matrix from which the film emerges from and returns to: the aerial shots of the Monterey coast in *Play Misty for Me*; the telephoto long shot of the Stranger materializing from and

returning to nothingness in *High Plains Drifter*; the Las Vegas dawn and dusk that frame *The Gauntlet*; the Bird's eye view of *Bronco Billy*'s pre- and post-Antoinette tents; the dust marking Red's homecoming and death in *Honkytonk Man*; the airborne cymbal that eventually crashes to the ground in *Bird*; the silhouetted prologue and epilogue of *Unforgiven*; and the surreal shots of Butch Haynes in his death throes as the helicopter hovers overhead in *A Perfect World*.

Eastwood's films can be antipodal as well as circular. The introduction will quickly set up a dilemma or a conflict that will be resolved not by returning to the matrix, but by inverting it. To resolve a conflict or dilemma, Eastwood will use a diametrical shot rather than return to the opening image or setup: a peaceful valley replaces Wales' war-torn homestead in *The Outlaw Josey Wales*; Mitchell Gant ascends from the earth to the stratosphere in *Firefox*; a resplendent hero's welcome supplants the stark black and white stock footage of the Korean War in *Heartbreak Ridge*; and a tranquil, stationary climax-epilogue refutes the anxious, motive opening of *White Hunter, Black Heart*. Circular construction enables Eastwood to sustain a balanced narrative without sacrificing his love of phenomenology and character. When Eastwood founders and allows his films to proceed without a balanced or inversive image, the results can seem labored and stolid (*Pale Rider* never feels whole despite the centrality of mood and milieu) or careless and slipshod (*The Rookie* suffers from overkill and a lack of palpable construction).

8. A Latent Acting Style. Eastwood belongs to "the small but unique band of actors who can dominate the screen simply by being on it, most perfectly exemplified by Gary Cooper" (Frank, 1982, p. 7). Like Cooper, Eastwood has an easygoing intensity and a naturalness that comes from deft and disciplined underplaying. Eastwood relies on presence over presentation. He minimizes his acting to maximize his presence:

> Because I'm not an extroverted, extremely mobile type, I play things in reserve a lot of times. But if you look back through history, the people who have been the strongest in film were people who could express a lot by holding certain things in reserve so that the audience is curious to find what the reserve is [Plaza, p. 222].

Eastwood is no grandstander. He is more of a re-actor than an actor, relying on other performers to complement his acting and bring out the humorous and subtle shades of his personality and persona. As Eastwood himself has observed, "a lot of the humor is not in what you say, but in how you react" (Plaza, p. 134). Eastwood is not a neurotic Method actor, straining to achieve a *trompe l'oeil* and become another person. His method is straight-forward:

> If I sat there and thought, 'what do I look like?' then I'm thinking about the wrong things. I've got to think of the character. You've got to donate yourself to the character [Plaza, p. 222].

> Acting is more than ranting and raving and rolling around on the floor. I've always felt that a full barrel makes a lot less noise than an empty one. Still waters run deep [Thompson, p. 183].

Although he can deliver lines with the insouciance or assurance of Cary Grant or Sean Connery, Eastwood is primarily a taciturn, physical actor who understands the importance of mise-en-scène and montage. The most effective cinematic performers comprehend the primacy of the gait and pause and the geometry and formal architecture of body language and decor. Like Buster Keaton, Eastwood's true costars are space and depth of field. For him, acting is an intermixture of blocking and emotion. Movement, gesture, and expression supersede dialogue and histrionics.

Eastwood's reactive acting style — his ability to interact with the lens, the frame, and other performers — does more than buttress his presence: it provides a key to what goes on inside the mind and soul of his protagonists. Eastwood's characters accept the vicissitudes of life with a weary persever-ance and a knowing sense of humor. The Eastwoodian antihero "is a deeply damaged guy who has been profoundly hurt and is aching out of that hurt" (Breskin, 1992, p. 68). He hurts, but refuses to show it. He is either celes-tial and implacable (*High Plains Drifter, Pale Rider*) or irredeemably mor-tal, plagued by guilt, rage and/or a broken idealism that has deteriorated into bitter cynicism. Eastwood has an athletic, yet wayworn style of movement that suggests a lode of inner pain and conflicting emotions. His body lan-guage has traces of wariness and hesitation, suggesting the repressed, angst-ridden nature of a majority of his characters. Eastwood's on-screen intimacy with space and composition rather than people is a by-product of his char-acter's alienation from others. Spatially and temperamentally, the East-woodian antihero craves isolation and independence. He exercises a rigor-ous self-restraint to keep from losing his self-control — as Eastwood has succinctly put it, "I play a guy always on the edge of violence" (Frank, p. 51). If possible, he tries to remain distant, silent, and self-possessed, for when he resorts to violence it is with a lethal grace that threatens his tenu-ous self-control. Very few of Eastwood's characters initiate violence. None of them mete it out with abandon or glee. The fortunate Eastwoodian characters are allowed to relax, romance, or retire (*Breezy, The Outlaw Josey Wales, The Gauntlet, Bronco Billy, Firefox, Heartbreak Ridge, The Rookie*), return to a mythic or legendary world (*High Plains Drifter, Sudden Impact, Pale Rider*), or die (*Honkytonk Man, Bird, A Perfect World*). The others have to go through purgatory and acknowledge their crimes and shortcomings (*Play Misty for Me; The Eiger Sanction; White Hunter, Black Heart; Unforgiven*).

Eastwood's latent style of acting accentuates a major theme that runs throughout his work — the motif of the individual and the difficulty of being one:

> Maybe the thing that makes me work in the type of roles I'm
> more famous for, like the lone Westerner or the rebel police
> officer, is that I'm an individual in real life...I think there's a
> dream in every man's mind of being an individual, but it's harder
> every year to be one [Guerif, 1986, p. 9].

> To some people I represent a dying individuality within our sys-
> tem. I feel there is a crying out for individuality. I feel that
> because of the intellect, the human race, we've bogged ourselves
> down in such bureaucratic nonsense, that it seems like we have
> made life much more complicated than it should be [Thompson,
> p. 178].

All of Eastwood's protagonists — from *Play Misty for Me*'s Dave Garver to *The Bridges of Madison County*'s Robert Kincaid — are loners who, whether they want to or not, have to contend with themselves and the world they are detached or estranged from. Although Eastwood's loners are self-sufficient, the price of solitude can be selfishness (*Play Misty for Me*), complacency (*Breezy*), moral decay (*The Eiger Sanction*), alcoholic self-pity (*The Gauntlet*, Antoinette Lily in *Bronco Billy*), psychosis (*Firefox*), or a rootless, migratory existence (*Honkytonk Man, Heartbreak Ridge, Bird*, Butch Haynes in *A Perfect World, The Bridges of Madison County*). Either the loner relinquishes his or her independence or accepts it with a plaintive resignation and a shrewd and knowing laugh. The choice is one of community or alienation, change or regression, romance or narcissism, versatility or inflexibility.

Eastwood's low-key approach to acting extends to his co-performers. Jessica Walter's performance in *Play Misty for Me* is a good example of Eastwood's method — she suggests hysteria without acting too hysterical. Eastwood abhors overacting. He reserves 'excess gyration' for villains (Paul Drake and Audrie J. Neenan in *Sudden Impact*) or unsavory characters (Thayer David and Gregory Walcott in *The Eiger Sanction*). His insistence on low-key acting is part of his overall aesthetic and gestalt. Eastwood's films prosper when the performances are both casual and precise. The rapport William Holden and Kay Lenz achieve in *Breezy* comes from a gentle sincerity that is never pushed to emotional extremes. When Eastwood fails to temper his performers, the results can be forced or distracting — Mario Van Peebles' loose performance in *Heartbreak Ridge* contributes to the film's overall sloppiness.

9. **A Mythic (the Man with No Name) and Modern (Dirty Harry) Persona.** Eastwood's persona — the seal that marks Eastwood's work as his own — consists of two primary archetypes: the Man with No Name and Dirty Harry. The Man with No Name dwells in a Biblical land full of anointed (mythic, immortal) and legendary (human, yet Herculean) warriors; Dirty Harry lives in the modern demythologized city. Eastwood, along with other directors who came of cinematic age in the early 1970s (Robert Altman, Francis Ford Coppola, Sam Peckinpah, Arthur Penn, Martin Scorsese) felt that the cultural climate no longer dictated nor required the sort of unvarnished heroism that satisfied Joseph Breen and the defunct Production Code:

> John Wayne played, and he did it quite well, probably as good as anybody, that kind of very moral and very strict ideals-type person, who won't bend too much one way or the other.... Nowadays I think that people want other dimensions. They like to see somebody with flaws and other desires.... People don't believe in heroes. Everybody knows that nobody else stood in the street and let the heavy draw first. It's me or him. To me that's the stuff Wayne would never do — I play bigger-than-life characters, but I'd shoot the guy in the back [Johnston, p. 51].

Eastwood's antiheroes behave in ruthless and calculated ways that nullify the romantic traditions associated with or ascribed to heroism. His archetypes "may avenge, punish or merely survive, but without the assurance that his triumph is socially meaningful" (Leniham, 1980, p. 173). They are heroes by default more than deed.

Eastwood's mythic Westerners are either extraterrestrial archangels who are apocalyptic messengers and executors of God's divine judgment (*High Plains Drifter, Pale Rider*) or legendary gunslingers who have exiled themselves from the rest of mankind (*The Outlaw Josey Wales, Unforgiven*). The more mythic Eastwood's persona is, the more inhuman, invulnerable, and abstract he becomes. The Stranger and the Preacher are archangels anointed by God to punish the wicked and/or shepherd a chosen flock or group of people. They emerge from and fade into oblivion, descending from and returning to God's mountain court. Although they are the cynosures of *High Plains Drifter* and *Pale Rider*, the archangels seem curiously indistinct. Their omniscience makes them invisible. Shrouded in darkness and full of wrath, their lack of emotion or humanity makes them iconic, and thus, ephemeral. They are not men, but horsemen of the apocalypse.

Unlike the mythic heroes, who are intangible, Eastwood's legendary heroes are mortal men who have attained a level of expertise or notoriety that has marked or marred them for life (Josey Wales is marked like Cain, his scar a gruesome reminder of his blood feud; William Munny is haunted by the dark specters of his past). The legendary heroes-antiheroes form a bridge between Eastwood's mythic and contemporary personae. They represent the puzzle of Eastwood's persona: the contradictory elements of myth and modernity, immortality and human frailty. While the mythic archangels do the direct bidding of God, the legendary heroes are unwittingly torn from their lives to do the Lord's work. In *The Outlaw Josey Wales*, *Sudden Impact*, and *Unforgiven*, Wales, Dirty Harry, and William Munny go through a transformation, a mutation from one form of consciousness and corporeality to another. Dirty Harry and William Munny are mortal men who, after being humbled and symbolically crucified, are resurrected into invincible, untouchable executioners. Wales goes into a trance and becomes a legendary force of justice and vengeance.

In the contemporary world, Eastwood's antiheroes stand apart from mankind not because they are mythical or legendary, but because they are alienated from themselves and society. Isolated and besieged by the complexities of modern existence, the mid- to late 20th-century antiheroes show little virtue: they are rude, selfish, self-destructive, rebellious, and stubborn. Each of them has a conspicuous character defect, a weakness or shortcoming that prevents them from being full-fledged heroes or healthy members of society. Invariably, they come into contact with people or events that force them to come to terms with their lack of conscience or ideals: Jonathon Hemlock's last sanction forces him to accept the poisons within; the Firefox offers Mitchell Gant the opportunity to overcome his fears; Highway's Marine landing at Grenada frees him from the disappointments of Korea and Vietnam. Women frequently provide the catalyst for an antihero's redemption: Gus Mally inspires Ben Shockley and reawakens his buried idealism in *The Gauntlet*; Aggie forces Tom Highway to take responsibility for his adolescent behavior and to behave like a man in *Heartbreak Ridge*.

Half of Eastwood's modern heroes are policemen, spies, or warriors. The other half are artists: jazz enthusiast and disc jockey Dave Garver in *Play Misty for Me*, showman "Bronco" Billy McCoy in *Bronco Billy*, itinerant songwriter-singer Red Stovall in *Honkytonk Man*, jazz saxophonist Charlie Parker in *Bird*, malcontent film director John Wilson in *White Hunter, Black Heart*, and the peregrine photographer Robert Kincaid in *The Bridges of Madison County*. All six of these artists learn that their fervent devotion to art, music, and showmanship means a devaluation of something in return, whether it be relationships, sanity, sobriety, or human decency. They have the difficult choice of accepting the world as it is, with no illusions (*Bronco Billy, Honkytonk Man, Bird, The Bridges of Madison County*) or ignoring it, thus risking their livelihood and well-being (*Play Misty for Me; White Hunter, Black Heart*). Both Dave Garver and John Wilson realize that their obsessions have allowed them to stay in suspended animation — when they are confronted by something they cannot evade, they quietly and painfully look within.

The more Eastwood strays from the mythic or legendary aspects of his persona, the more personal the project becomes. Eastwood's personal projects — *Play Misty for Me; Breezy; Bronco Billy; Honkytonk Man; Bird; White Hunter, Black Heart; A Perfect World;* and *The Bridges of Madison County* — all take mortality and fallibility as a given. Eastwood has had to reanimate the Man with No Name and Dirty Harry in cycles (*The Outlaw Josey Wales* and *The Gauntlet; Sudden Impact* and *Pale Rider; The Rookie* and *Unforgiven*) to appease his audience, which seems to have an endless appetite for violence and mayhem. This back and forth relationship with the public has engendered the love-hate relationship between Eastwood and his persona. His struggle to pique rather than pacify his audience has resulted in a fascinating body of work, an *oeuvre* that is unmistakably "Eastwoodian."

2

Formative Years, 1931–1971

> Really, you're taking an art form that is not an intellectual art
> form, it's more of an emotional art form, so you approach it on
> more of a gut level, and you're bound to have better luck with it
> [Breskin, p. 68].

Eastwood's *oeuvre* did not originate in a vacuum. All of the elements
that distinguish Eastwood's work — his levelheaded shooting style, subdued
aesthetic, mythic-contemporary persona, and thematic interest in the individual — can be traced to his working-class background, his extensive experience in the film industry, and his successful collaborations with directors
Sergio Leone and Don Siegel.

Leone helped Eastwood create the Man with No Name, a mythical role
that gave Eastwood a ready-made persona and jettisoned him into international stardom. In Leone's world of desolate Mediterranean villas and operatic gunfights, Eastwood grew to epic proportions and became as mesmer-
izing as Leone's ground-breaking style.

Siegel helped Eastwood make the transition back to Hollywood, initi-
ate Malpaso Productions, and create Eastwood's modern alter ego, Dirty
Harry. He demystified and Americanized Eastwood by taking him out of
Leone's larger than life world and putting him into the urban backdrop of
New York City and San Francisco.

Eastwood would eventually appropriate Leone and Siegel's style and
take possession of both the Man with No Name and Dirty Harry, making
them a part of his own vision and a cinema distinct from that of Leone or
Siegel.

Origins

> A guy sits alone in a theater. He is young and he's scared. He
> doesn't know what he's going to do with his life. He wishes he
> could be self-sufficient, like the man he sees up there on the
> screen, somebody who can look out for himself, solve his own
> problems. I do the kind of roles I'd like to see if I were still dig-
> ging swimming pools and wanted to escape my problems [Frank,
> p. 7].

> Moving has always been sort of a lifestyle for me. Basically, I've
> been a drifter [Zmijewsky, 1993, p. 9].

Born on May 30, 1931, Eastwood had to cope with the Great Depression and the stress of rootlessness and economic uncertainty from birth
through adolescence. Clinton and Ruth Eastwood, his parents, were forced
to move up and down the Pacific Coast in search of work until the war years,
when Clinton found a permanent job in Oakland, California. Forced to
endure a migratory existence, Eastwood developed a loner temperament
and a congenital strain of rugged individualism that would fuel his mete-
oric rise to "starteurdom":

> I can't remember us being poor or suffering as children. Maybe
> my father did have his worries but neither Jean (his sister) nor I
> ever knew about them. When I look back I know dad had to
> think pretty fast at times because there were a lot of people out of
> work in America around the time I was born. He often moved
> from one stocks and bonds company to another to try and better
> himself. That's why although I was born in San Francisco, my
> earliest memories are of living in Oakland. But it seems to me
> now we didn't live much in houses at all — we lived in cars. I can
> remember only a few of the places like Oakland and San Fran-
> cisco and Sacramento — twice — and Seattle. The frustrating thing
> about moving around like this as a kid is that you're constantly
> having to make adjustments. Just as soon as I'd get to make
> friends in a place and start making progress at my studies, we'd
> be on the move again [Thompson, p. 10].

Eastwood's films are dominated by individuals who are on an endless exo-
dus to nowhere. The protagonists of *Breezy* (Kay Lenz); *The Outlaw Josey
Wales*; *Bronco Billy*; *Honkytonk Man*; *Heartbreak Ridge*; *Bird*; *White Hunter,
Black Heart*; *A Perfect World*; and *The Bridges of Madison County* are

peripatetic beings with no fixed home or residence. The road is their sanctuary. In *A Perfect World*, Butch Haynes has a set destination in mind, but that destination is an illusion, a projection of his lost innocence and childhood. The road offers Butch the only solace he will find before his untimely end. The protagonists who do have fixed residences, whether it be a home (*Play Misty for Me*, *Breezy* [William Holden], *The Eiger Sanction*) or a city (*The Gauntlet* [Phoenix], *Sudden Impact* [San Francisco]), are forced by circumstances beyond their control (*The Eiger Sanction*, *The Gauntlet*, and *Sudden Impact*) or a woman trespassing through their property (*Play Misty for Me*, *Breezy*) to embark on a journey and a search for a new self. For many of Eastwood's characters, romance, marriage, and family are inconceivable and/or unattainable (*High Plains Drifter*; *The Eiger Sanction*; *Firefox*; *Honky-tonk Man*; *Bird*; *White Hunter, Black Heart*; *A Perfect World*; *The Bridges of Madison County*). Several of Eastwood's characters are able to fall in love and settle down (*Play Misty for Me*, *The Gauntlet*, *Bronco Billy*, *Heartbreak Ridge*), but the ones who already support a family have a difficult time keeping it together: in *The Outlaw Josey Wales*, Wales cannot prevent his family from being butchered and raped; in *Unforgiven*, William Munny shows little concern for his two children when he departs for Big Whiskey — he leaves them unsupervised, with a pen full of feverish pigs. *Bronco Billy* features the ideal arrangement for an Eastwoodian character: Billy enjoys the company of a woman he loves and respects, a surrogate family of like-minded misfits, a career in show business, and a nomadic existence that keeps him far away from the dreary, dreaded city.

Eastwood has always believed in the virtues of the protestant work ethic:

> I've worked ever since I was thirteen years old. My parents had a hard life when they were raising us. My father drilled into me that nobody does anything for you but yourself. Today we live in a welfare-oriented society and people expect more from Big Daddy government, more from Big Daddy charity. In my young days, that kind of society never existed. That philosophy never got you anywhere [Thompson, p. 13].

As a young man, Eastwood labored tirelessly, becoming, among other things, a truck driver, a lumberjack, an amateur drag racer, an athlete (swimmer), and an aspiring musician. His faith in hard work and his wanderlust enabled him to become a working-class jack of all trades. Eastwood was roughing it, à la Mark Twain, peregrinating from Oregon to Texas to California and gaining valuable insight into the American experience and character. Eastwood's casual manner and Rabelaisian sense of humor surely came from his youthful travels and travails. His westerns, *The Gauntlet*, *Every Which*

Way But Loose, Bronco Billy, Honkytonk Man, Heartbreak Ridge, and *A Perfect World* all have a rural, relaxed blue-collar feel. In all of Eastwood's films, the most flawed characters are those who have lost their dignity and faith in their profession. Either they sober up and regain their self-respect (*The Gauntlet, Heartbreak Ridge*) or they succumb to substance abuse and despair (*Honkytonk Man, Bird*). In *White Hunter, Black Heart,* Eastwood stresses the importance of taking one's life and work seriously by playing his polar opposite: John Wilson, a flamboyant, self-indulgent film director who refuses to take his career seriously. Wilson's lack of professionalism eventually leads to a senseless death and a profound moral crisis. In Eastwood's world, there is nothing worse than being irresponsible and unaccountable. Redemption comes not only from a change of heart, but a change of work habits (when Wilson finally starts shooting the film, we know he has experienced a catharsis).

Eastwood had planned on studying and pursuing music as a career (a sign that he always has been an artist at heart), but was drafted into the army instead. Korea beckoned, but Eastwood did not go overseas. Relying on his resourcefulness and aquatic expertise, Eastwood managed to become a swimming instructor at Fort Ord near Monterey, California (the site for his future home and *Play Misty for Me*). He never saw combat. What Eastwood did experience was an ad hoc introduction to the motion picture industry. While stationed at Fort Ord, Eastwood met David Janssen (later the star of the television series "The Fugitive") and several other enlisted actors who thought Eastwood should take a screen test and pursue an acting career. Around the same time, Eastwood hung out with an assistant director supervising second-unit shooting for Universal on the base. The seed was planted. After being discharged from the army, Eastwood went to Universal studios to network with the assistant director. Unfortunately, he was no longer affiliated with the studio. Assuming his future as an actor was star-crossed, Eastwood took advantage of the GI Bill and enrolled at Los Angeles City College to learn business management. He married Maggie Johnson in 1953. His interest in a film career, however, never waned. Encouraged by his wife and his old army buddies, Eastwood visited Universal once again and did a screen test for director Arthur Lubin. Three weeks later, Eastwood was offered a 40-week contract as a stock actor.

Eastwood had excellent instincts. Universal was one of the few lots still operating as a full-fledged studio. The climate of the early to mid-1950s had severely hampered the film industry. The consent decrees of 1948 had stripped the major studios of their theaters, eliminating the economic security of block booking. Inflation and television had reduced box office receipts by nearly one half. To reduce costs and remain solvent, the studios gravitated toward financing and distribution instead of in-house production.

They reduced their output and allowed long-term contracts to expire, forcing many enterprising actors and directors to form their own production companies and market their own projects. What allowed Universal to still operate as a traditional studio was its niggardliness, television production, and independent percentage deals with such freelance stars and directors as James Stewart and Alfred Hitchcock:

> If any Hollywood studio was prepared for the coming media age, it was Universal. With its long-standing dual agenda of low-cost formula pictures and A-class productions via outside independents, Universal had been gearing up all along for TV and the New Hollywood. No one at Universal quite realized this at the time, of course, and certainly not when the new age was first upon them. Universal was simply another company struggling to survive in a rapidly changing industry, with no better sense than any other studio of what the postwar conditions and the emergence of commercial television might bring [Shatz, 1988, p. 463].

Universal could still afford to hire and retain contract players and directors (Don Siegel would eventually sign with Universal in 1964) as well as maintain a talent school, a luxury few actors received in 1955. Eastwood took full advantage of the facilities, learning the fundamentals of screen acting, all stages of film production, western-style horse riding (something he was already proficient at), and such fineries as ballroom dancing and dinner etiquette.

Eastwood made an inauspicious debut as a lab assistant in Jack Arnold's *Revenge of the Creature* (1955). Other minor films followed, in which Eastwood made cursory, peripheral appearances: *Francis in the Navy* (1955, Arthur Lubin), *Lady Godiva* (1955, Lubin), *Tarantula* (1955, Jack Arnold), and *Never Say Goodbye* (1956, Jerry Hopper). After *Never Say Goodbye*, Universal allowed Eastwood's contract to lapse. Having to fend for himself, Eastwood landed a contract with RKO as a bit player, appearing in *The First Traveling Saleslady* (1956, Lubin) and *Escapade in Japan* (1957, Lubin). Because of Howard Hughes' poor management, however, RKO went bankrupt in 1957, leaving Eastwood unemployed once again.

Catapulted from the security of a contract, Eastwood became a freelance stock player, going from picture to picture. He secured a supporting role in William Wellman's *Lafayette Escadrille* (1958), but found himself submerged in a substandard Tab Hunter vehicle. *Ambush at Cimarron Pass* (1958, Jodie Copeland), a bottom of the bill western, did even less for Eastwood's career or confidence. Eastwood was witnessing firsthand the decentralization of the American studio system; he was enduring a gauntlet of sorts, an initiation into the madness of film production that would provide the inspiration for Malpaso Productions. Eastwood knew, as he trudged from studio to studio, that being independent and in control of one's career was the only way to resist the continual shifts of the industry, a business that was falling behind both financially and culturally. While Hollywood churned out one bloated spectacular after another, notable only for their cost and technical innovations, European filmmakers such as Ingmar Bergman, Jean-Luc Godard and Michelangelo Antonioni were rewriting the stylistic and narrative rules of commercial filmmaking.

Television, the arch-enemy of the motion picture industry, became Eastwood's passage to the Shangri-La of stardom and starteurdom. Eastwood had already appeared in several television shows when his film prospects looked bleak, but, like most Hollywood insiders, Eastwood viewed the work with some distaste. While lunching with Sonia Chernus, an old friend of his who happened to be a script assistant at CBS, Eastwood met Robert Sparks, a network producer. Soon after, Eastwood won the second lead role in the CBS western "Rawhide" and quickly lost his disdain for the new medium. Based on the Howard Hawks film *Red River* (1948), "Rawhide" featured an endless cattle drive led by Eric Fleming and his surrogate son, Rowdy Yates (Eastwood).

In the late 1950s, as big screen westerns were losing their vitality and profitability, television westerns were growing inversely popular. Eastwood finally tapped into a medium that could guarantee years of exposure and employment. It was also a genre he was comfortable with: "I have to admit that I'm drawn to the style and spirit of the western. I'm identified as a man from the west and that's no accident. I've always lived out west. I've always liked the way of life, the code" (Guerif, p. 3).

"Rawhide" began its six-year run on January 9, 1959. The role of Rowdy Yates allowed Eastwood the welcome opportunity to hone and perfect his acting skills: "That's one big advantage of doing a series. You get to looking at yourself on film so much that you can almost step away with a third eye, or as a second person" (Plaza, p. 222). By the early 1960s, Eastwood had watched and taken stock of everything he wanted or needed to know about film production. He requested the chance to direct an episode, but was prevented from doing so because of CBS policy. Eastwood wanted to tinker with the equipment and experiment, but could not exploit the vast resources surrounding him. He yearned for a persona, a character that would separate him from the well-scrubbed and well-mannered Rowdy Yates: "I was tired of playing the nice clean-cut cowboy in 'Rawhide.' I wanted something earthier, something different from the old-fashioned western" (Guerif, p. 43). Enter Sergio Leone.

Sergio Leone and the Man with No Name

Eastwood moves like a sleepwalker between explosions and hails of bullets, and he is always the same — a block of marble...Clint first of all, is a star [Hamill, 1984, p. 24].— Sergio Leone

Like Eastwood, Sergio Leone toiled in the bottom of the film industry pyramid for a decade before achieving a degree of independence. Leone endured a decade-long apprenticeship at Italy's Cinecitta Studios, serving as a second-unit and assistant director for the numerous American film crews taking advantage of the government-subsidized film industry. After directing the Italian version of Robert Aldrich's *Sodom and Gomorrah* (1963), Leone was prepared to personalize the techniques he had so patiently adhered to:

> I made 58 films as an assistant. I was at the side of directors who applied all the rules; make it, for example, a close-up to show that the character is about to say something important. I reacted against all that and so the close-ups in my films are always the expression of an emotion [Frayling, 1981, p. 100].

Leone's vision of film was that of a poetic Bayeux Tapestry, an iconic realm of representative visuals, sounds, and feelings. For Leone, film was a ritualistic undertaking and experience, a celluloid Eucharist in which we share in the chemicals and composition of cinema: "I'm more a director of gestures and silences and an orator of images (Hamill, p. 25) ... I go to the dubbing room as if I'm going to Mass, and mixage for me, is the most sacred rite" (Hamill, p. 23). Leone tapped into his Roman Catholic heritage and crafted a grandiloquent, orchestrated style that turned the western into an ornate landscape of greed and vengeance. His primary influence was Homer and the epic world of the Illiad: "For me, and I say this with a smile, the greatest screenwriter of western films was Homer, because Achilles, Ajax, Hector, and the others are the archetypes of western characters" (Frayling, p.74). Homer used lyrical poetry to make his heroes so full of strength, valor, or desire that they attract the attention of the Gods; Leone used cinema to give his characters the same resonance and simplicity. His heroes exhibit characteristics much like Achilles' vaunting pride or Helen's matchless beauty. All of Leone's leads have a singular trait that bestows upon them

A Fistful of Dollars— Clint Eastwood as the Man with No Name, the cornerstone of his mythic Western persona and directorial career.

a mystery or an aura, whether it be the trance-like state of the Man with No Name or the vivid memories that haunt the protagonists of *For a Few Dollars More* (1965), *Once Upon a Time in the West* (1969), *Duck You Sucker* (1972) and *Once Upon a Time in America* (1984). Leone's world is one steeped in myth, memory, and a hard-bitten, displaced heroism. As Robert C. Cumbow has described in *Once Upon a Time: The Films of Sergio Leone*, Leone's lead characters are "a kind of wandering clergy, ministering confessions, giving penance and absolution, and offering what sacraments they and the situations deem appropriate" (Cumbow, 1987, p. 172). This wandering anti-clergy administers to a wasteland where money means more than morality; marksmanship more than mortality.

What truly isolated Leone from his contemporaries and elevated Eastwood to international stardom was his revolutionary approach to cinema. Taking full advantage of the non-anamorphic properties of Techniscope — a widescreen process that preserves the depth and focus of a standard lens — Leone took inordinate delight in testing the limits of cinematic grammar. He dropped the coverage of medium shots and reinvigorated the dynamics of foreground and background. Space and time became malleable. The smallest gesture or shift in scenery or perspective became totemic, like the mosaics of a Greek Orthodox church or the figures inscribed into an Egyptian obelisk. Leone mythologized the very elements of cinema, making them so overt and graphic that they took on a spirit and meaning of their own: "It's a terrible pity you can't make time stand still," Leone has mused, "There are moments that you want to relive over and over, very slowly, moments that you never want to end" (Cumbow, p. 171). Those moments inspire the surreal, *Cabinet of Dr. Caligari*-like rapture of Leone's films. His gunfights, set in the diameter of a mock corrida, are studies in infinity: what matters is not the resolution, but the increasing crinkling of the eyes, the rising crescendo of the score and the narrower scope of the image as the hands slowly reach for the holster. Once the shots are fired, the spell is broken. Time resumes its course and the film comes to a reluctant close. Leone took cinema and carried it to a plane where it became an animated Elgin Marble, a 24 frieze per second relief.

Leone "froze" Eastwood too: "What I saw simply, was a block of marble" (Hamill, p. 24). Leone sculpted Eastwood's mannerisms into a cogent set of codes: "what struck me was his indolent way of moving about. Clint, to my mind, closely resembles a cat. Cats are indolent, they are apparently lazy. More than laziness, it is a style of nonchalance, apparent fatigue, drowsiness" (Johnstone, p. 35). He took Eastwood's laconism and natural reticence and broadened it into a stellar silence: "The early Eastwood image is based entirely on holding back: a rigid control of words, gestures, actions and emotions ... these almost supernatural powers coupled with his frequent associations with death give him a mystical otherworldly stature. Not just an outsider, he is somehow beyond" (Kehr, 1985, p. 64).

Leone was able to sculpt Eastwood into the Man with No Name because Eastwood was ready to turn Rowdy Yates inside out and transform him into a self-centered, ill-tempered antihero without surface virtues or feelings; a man who maintained his independence and control over a chaotic wasteland of avarice and duplicity. To do this, Eastwood tested how impassive he could be without losing any presence or intensity. Surrounded by Italian performers, Eastwood took full advantage of being the only American by playing against them: "Italian actors come from the Helzapoppin' school of drama. To get my effect I stayed impassive and I guess they thought I wasn't acting. All except Leone, who knew what I was doing" (Cumbow, p. 146). By pulling back, Eastwood jutted out of the screen and into the imagination of the audience:

> The original screenplay (for *A Fistful of Dollars* [1964]) had endless pages of dialogue all explaining the character's background but I wanted to play it with an economy of words and create this

whole feeling through attitude and movement. It was just the
kind of character I had envisioned for a long time — keep to the
mystery and allude to what happened in the past. It came about
after the frustration of doing "Rawhide" for so long. I felt the less
he said the stronger he became and the more he grew in the imagination of the audience. You never knew who he was, where he
came from and what he was going to do next [Thompson, p.34].

Leone originally wanted Henry Fonda to be the Man with No Name.
He then considered James Coburn and Charles Bronson (two of *The
Magnificent Seven* [1960, John Sturges]) and even Steve "Hercules" Reeves
before settling for Eastwood. Despite a language barrier, Eastwood and
Leone became willing collaborators, each having a keen grasp of who the
Man With No Name should be. Eastwood brought his wardrobe from
'Rawhide' and a collection of cigarillos that kept him in "a sour frame of
mind" (Guerif, p. 44). Leone added props to the ones Eastwood introduced:
"I placed that poncho on his shoulders to give a veil of mystery. The cigar
acted as a sort of pendant to those ice-cold eyes" (Johnstone, p. 37). Eastwood reciprocated by cutting his dialogue to a minimum, ridding No Name
of any biographical material save for a cryptic remark about not being able
to help someone in the past. Weary of "Rawhide," Eastwood did not want
to be part of an extended family with a past. He wanted to play a scavenger,
a lone individual whose past was dead and not worth revisiting.

Sergio shot the film in a whitewashed town, giving the western a
Mediterranean look foreign to John Ford's Monument Valley (Leone had to
shoot it in Spain for budgetary reasons; as soon as he had the capacity to do
so, he rushed to Monument Valley for *Once Upon a Time in the West*).
Because Leone was not restricted by the American Production Code, he
ignored tie-ups — the censure that one person could not be shot by another
in the same frame or shot. This gave *A Fistful of Dollars* a bloodthirstiness
unseen in American westerns. Ennio Morricone's operatic music and the
Italian practice of post-synchronization gave the film an additional eeriness
that enriched and enchanted the visuals.

What made the film an overnight phenomenon, however, was Eastwood's performance as The Man with No Name. Leone saw No Name as,
"an incarnation of the angel Gabriel" (Frayling, p. 183). Eastwood saw him
as the antithesis of Rowdy Yates and John Wayne. Leone's mythic and cinematic and Eastwood's minimalistic and antiheroic conception met at a fer-
tile crossroads and forged a persona that was moral and amoral, greedy and
gracious, human and Herculean. Riding into the town of San Miguel on a
mule, No Name can be seen as a messiah with a mean streak; a contradictory
Christ figure who fleeces the town in order to cleanse it of its irredeemable

sinfulness. San Miguel is controlled by two warring families, the Rojos (gun-runners) and the Baxters (bootleggers). No Name's method is surreptitious and Machiavellian — he forces the Rojos and the Baxters to end their feud by alternating his services as a hired gun, gathering valuable information and selling it to the other side for profit. As the two ruling families badger and butcher one another, No Name relaxes in a tavern, sipping whiskey, and sharing his winnings with the proprietor, Silvanito (José Calvo). No Name's policy of divide and conquer goes awry, however, when he takes pity on a captive family and liberates them. His moral act undermines his subterfuge and causes him to be beaten and figuratively crucified by Ramon Rojo (Gian Maria Volonte). No Name leaves San Miguel in a coffin as Ramon merci-lessly kills the last remnants of the Baxters. After convalescing in a cave for several days, No Name is resurrected from a disinterested confidence man and mercenary into a bruised and angry savior. He returns to San Miguel as an avenging knight (he wears a steel plate underneath his poncho) and teaches Ramon that his pistol is indeed much faster and more lethal than Ramon's rifle. No Name leaves San Miguel a rich man, a man content to wander and stumble into, but not search for, another lucrative adventure. Eastwood, immortalized by Leone's dynamic framing and composition, became the crux and dominant interest of *A Fistful of Dollars*. His reserved performance and precise movements made No Name a stoic exercise in complex simplicity; a Christ figure without any of the descriptions found in the New Testament.

Eastwood returned for the second and third installments of the Dol-lars Trilogy, *For a Few Dollars More* and *The Good, the Bad and the Ugly* (1966), but No Name diminished in importance as Leone broadened the scope of his films and appropriated more of the emblems and established stars of the Hollywood western. In *For a Few Dollars More*, Eastwood had to surrender the screen to Lee Van Cleef. By *The Good, the Bad and the Ugly*, Eastwood felt eclipsed not only by the returning Van Cleef, but by Eli Wal-lach, another veteran of *The Magnificent Seven*: "In the beginning, I was just about alone; then there were two. And now there are three of us. I'm going to wind up in a detachment of cavalry" (Guerif, p. 50). Eastwood felt restive and constrained. His visage was becoming one of too many; his persona was losing its potency. Eastwood refused to make a cameo appearance in Leone's western to end all westerns *Once Upon a Time in the West* for rather shrewd reasons. Leone planned on symbolically killing the three leads of *The Good, the Bad and the Ugly* to make way for the new Trinity of Charles Bronson, Henry Fonda, and Jason Robards. By killing the Man with No Name, Leone could have done irreversible damage to Eastwood's persona. Leone wanted to sacrifice and retire No Name; Eastwood wanted to develop his persona further:

He offered me other films, since *The Good, the Bad and the Ugly* but at that point I felt like he was looking for a different thing in film than I was. I was looking for more character development and maybe a smaller film, and he was looking for more panorama, a David Leanesque kind of thing. So we just drifted, though it was very amicable [Thomson, p. 69].

The collaboration had come to an end.

Leone parleyed his commercial success into creative independence. Eastwood strove for the same. He was ready to export his persona to America. The Dollars films, released in the United States in 1966, fostered a new climate of mayhem that filmmakers like Arthur Penn and Sam Peckinpah avidly exploited to redefine the gangster and western genres. The antihero, personified by *Bonnie and Clyde* was catching on as an American institution. Eastwood wanted to join the cavalcade. The first major phase of his career — apprenticeship and the rise to stardom — had peaked. Eastwood needed an American director who could assist him in setting up an organization that would enable him to be autonomous. He found that ideal partner in Don Siegel, an auteur whose technical expertise provided Eastwood with his next two major inspirations: Malpaso Productions and the quintessential antihero, Dirty Harry.

Eastwood owes an immense debt to Leone. Leone helped him realize the Man with No Name, the role that enabled Eastwood to become a star-cum-starteur. *A Fistful of Dollars* did what few films do: it transformed a television actor into a full-fledged cinematic icon. In *High Plains Drifter, The Outlaw Josey Wales, Pale Rider*, and *Unforgiven*, Eastwood evolved the Man with No Name and made use of the religious and spatial iconography of Leone's films, but he never copied Leone's style. Eastwood makes ample use of the widescreen and composition in depth, but unlike Leone's style, which screams for attention, Eastwood's style is much more invisible and subdued. While Leone concentrated on abstract form and the trinity of profile, space, and music, Eastwood prefers to be more concrete and character driven. Leone's films aspire to be Renaissance operas; Eastwood's films are closer in spirit to a jazz composition or a rough and tumble country song. Leone, if he could have, would have devised a way to fit all the dreams and desires of mankind in one shot. Eastwood had to struggle with his persona and the rigors of the film industry before he could attempt to do the same.

Don Siegel and Dirty Harry

I think if there is one thing I learned from Don Siegel, it's to know what you want to shoot and to know what you're seeing when you see it — and that's something I haven't seen a lot of over the years [Siegel, 1993, p. x].

Whenever Clint comes up with a better idea, I call it a 'Clintus Shot.' If his ideas spark me to a better one, I call it a Siegelini shot [Siegel, p. 326].—Don Siegel

Leone's plans for the opening sequence of *Once Upon a Time in the West* threatened to be a *coup de grâce*, a premature and most unwelcome coda to the Man with No Name and Eastwood's burgeoning career. Eastwood had seen the writing on the wall. He wasted no time in returning to the Hollywood back lot, forming Malpaso Productions, and negotiating with United Artists to produce *Hang 'Em High* (1967). Malpaso gave Eastwood total control over his acting career. He became an independent agent, able to influence the content and character of his films. What he lacked was a director like Leone who understood his instincts and ideas, a director who could assist him in his growth from star to starteur.

Directed by Ted Post, a "Rawhide" veteran, *Hang 'Em High* failed to amplify the persona Eastwood had so carefully constructed with Leone. More akin to a "Bonanza" episode than a studio western, *Hang 'Em High* attempted to merge Rowdy Yates with the Man with No Name with awkward results. Eastwood's antiheroic mannerisms jostled with the plot-heavy, moral sentiments of the film. No Name required a newer, rawer cinescape, the sort of revisionist frontier Sam Peckinpah was about to discover with the epochal *The Wild Bunch*.

Hang 'Em High proved that Eastwood's persona was not *a priori* outside of Leone's lens. Eastwood needed a filmmaker who could help him shape and Americanize his persona into different forms without robbing it of its initial inspiration and impact. He needed a maverick with sound judgment and instincts, a director who would collaborate with him as an equal and assist him in securing the creative and technical independence he craved since "Rawhide." Eastwood's involvement with Leone and *A Fistful of Dollars* was unexpected and unforeseeable. That same fortuity occurred when Universal suggested that Eastwood consider Don Siegel for *Coogan's Bluff*.

Leone was an unabashed auteur, a filmmaker whose grandiloquent vision permeated every frame and edit; Siegel was a craftsman who loved the day-to-day logistics and challenges of screenwriting, shooting, and editing.

Siegel, like Leone and Eastwood, had a long and varied apprenticeship in the film industry. From 1934 — 46, Siegel worked for Warner Bros. as an editing assistant, assistant director, second-unit director, and supervisor of the montage unit. He provided the linking montage for such Warner Brothers classics as *The Roaring Twenties* (1939, Raoul Walsh), *They Died With Their Boots On* (1941, Walsh), *Yankee Doodle Dandy* (1942, Michael Curtiz), and *Casablanca* (1942, Curtiz). With the upheaval of the Paramount Decree, postwar inflation, and declining industry profits, Siegel pursued a directing career, drifting from studio to independent producer, directing a string of compact, cost-effective B movies (*The Big Steal* [1946], *Riot in Cell Block 11* [1954], *Invasion of the Body Snatchers* [1956], *Baby Face Nelson* [1957], *The Line-Up* [1958], *Flaming Star* [1960], *Hell is for Heroes* [1962]). Siegel earned a reputation as a trustworthy director who could shoot a quality picture in a minuscule amount of time. His output remained in flux until the mid-1960s, when he signed on as a contract director with Universal and directed *The Killers* (1964) and *Madigan* (1968), a remarkable police thriller that anticipated *Coogan's Bluff* (1968) and *Dirty Harry* (1971).

Siegel's aesthetic is a by-product of his unsparing shooting style. Siegel shot on location, edited in-camera, and kept his takes to a minimum whenever possible to save time and money. He visualized his shots before principal shooting: "It seems to me it's expensive and time-consuming for a director to go on the set each day unprepared, not knowing how he is going to do things" (Kaminsky, 1974, p. 293). Because of Siegel's frugal methods, his films have a taut, athletic structure and tone. If Siegel deplored anything, it was inertia. His cutting — lean yet seemingly random — gives his films a visceral urgency, a kineticism lacking in most action thrillers of the 1960s and 1970s.

Siegel's heroes have "the doomed peculiarity of the antisocial outcast" (Kaminsky, p. 198). They are resourceful men who struggle against a conformist America (*Invasion of the Body Snatchers*), criminals who reach for the elusive American Dream (*The Killers*, *Charley Varrick* [1973]), or policemen who struggle against lawlessness and bureaucracy (*Madigan*, *Dirty Harry*). Except for *Coogan's Bluff* or *Charley Varrick*, the Siegelini "antisocial outcast" either perishes or gives in to disillusionment and despair. In *Escape from Alcatraz* we do not know if Frank Norris has drowned or escaped — what matters is that he devises and successfully executes a plan that does not go awry, a plan that proves Alcatraz wrong. Whether he survives or not is incidental to the film.

While Leone allegorized Eastwood and devoured him with style, making him as intangible as the director's surreal camera work, Siegel's matter-of-fact temperament and aesthetic complemented Eastwood and brought him back to earth. Thanks to Siegel's terse and functional approach to filmmaking, Eastwood was able to diminish the titanic proportions of No Name and to humanize, Americanize, and sexualize his persona: the indestructible, Christ-like Man with No Name resurfaced as Dirty Harry, a mortal man beset by social disarray, bureaucratic interference, and personal turmoil. By transporting Eastwood to the present, Siegel stripped him of his shell and revealed the passions and emotions underneath — No Name's celestial detachment gave way to Harry's seething resentment. In Siegel's films, Eastwood must grapple with some kind of confinement, whether it be sexual (*Two Mules for Sister Sara*, *The Beguiled*), urban (*Coogan's Bluff*, *Dirty Harry*), or actual imprisonment (*Escape from Alcatraz*). Eastwood either adapts to and surmounts his new surroundings (*Coogan's Bluff*, *Escape from Alcatraz*) or suffers a defeat or a rebuke that kills or debilitates him (*Two Mules for Sister Sara*, *The Beguiled*, *Dirty Harry*). In *Coogan's Bluff*, Eastwood learns to be more compassionate and tolerant; in *Dirty Harry*, Harry embarks on a desperate crusade to rid San Francisco of a mad killer, only to discover that he is alienated from himself and the people he has ostensibly sworn to protect. In *Two Mules for Sister Sara* and *The Beguiled*, Eastwood meets women of commensurate strength and intelligence who challenge and subvert his masculinity. Eastwood loses his machismo and independence in *Two Mules for Sister Sara*. In *The Beguiled* he fares much worse — he loses his penis, and finally, his life. As with his other antiheroes, Siegel places Eastwood's characters into difficult situations that cannot be negotiated without some loss of pride, humanity, or blood. Even Frank Norris' victory in *Escape from Alcatraz* is hollow: we do not know if he is alive or dead.

Although Siegel did not initiate *Coogan's Bluff* (eight scripts had been written to no avail), he quickly made the film his own and established a solid working relationship with Eastwood:

> We started out on that picture with a cautious mutual admiration. He started to come up with ideas for camera set ups. I started to call these Clintus shots and even if I decided not to use them they invariably gave me another idea, threw me into a Siegelini shot [Kaminsky, p. 220].

Siegel knew that Eastwood needed to be reintegrated into American cinema gradually, without a precipitous change of identity or milieu that would jeopardize his Leonesque origins. To accomplish this, Siegel cast Eastwood as a contemporary western lawman, thus bridging the gap between the mythic (the western, Arizona) and the modern (film noir, the police thriller, New York City). *Coogan's Bluff* is essentially Eastwood's cinematic introduction to the metropolis, the counter culture (a phenomenon Eastwood would later explore with *Play Misty for Me*, *Breezy* and the "society in flux" *Dirty Harry* sequels *Magnum Force* and *The Enforcer*), bureaucracy, and the modern liberated woman. Eastwood, in the guise of Coogan, is literally forced to leave the frontier and come to terms with the social and urban dynamics of the late 1960s. In Siegel's words:

> In Arizona, when hunting his two-legged prey by means of scent, 10/10 vision — and that includes girls as well as malefactors — Coogan used Western lore and knowledge. But in New York City he can only see across the street, his vision is blocked by huge skyscrapers. He is assailed by a thousand scents. He is indeed a fish out of water [Siegel, p. 306].

Siegel's staccato camera work and montage and his expert use of locations bring Eastwood down to human scale. As Coogan, Eastwood is no longer an invincible; he is no longer lord and master over all he surveys. Coogan has no trouble tracking and arresting a fugitive Indian in Arizona, but when he is flown to New York City to escort Ringerman (Don Stroud), a prisoner awaiting trial in his home state, Coogan finds himself in a hostile and alienating environment. The local authorities prohibit Coogan from taking direct action. The city disorients him. Events spin out of control. People deceive and distract him. Coogan's attempts to seduce Julie (Susan Clark), a self-reliant social worker, are in vain. To get to Ringerman, Coogan has to familiarize himself with the counter culture and the city streets. *Coogan's Bluff* spearheads the Americanization, humanization, and urbanization of Eastwood. The film allowed him to be a modern antihero, a man defined by his weaknesses rather than by his strengths.

After *Coogan's Bluff*, Eastwood tried the star route with a trio of huge studio pictures — *Where Eagles Dare* (1968, Brian Hutton), *Paint Your Wagon* (1969, Joshua Logan), and *Kelly's Heroes* (1970, Brian Hutton) — none of which enriched his persona. In all three films, Eastwood found himself relegated to a two-dimensional prop. *Where Eagles Dare* and *Kelly's Heroes*, both World War II pictures — the first heavily influenced by James Bond films of the mid 1960s and the second by Robert Aldrich's *The Dirty Dozen* (1967) — stifled Eastwood. He had little to do but scowl and shoot. *Paint Your Wagon* ignored Eastwood's formidable persona altogether, casting Eastwood as a modern-day Gene Autry, a soft-spoken and sweet-natured troubadour who sings ballads alone in the woods. In all three films, Eastwood found himself curiously marginalized despite his star billing. The meatier roles went to his costars: Richard Burton in *Where Eagles Dare*, Lee Marvin in

Paint Your Wagon and Telly Savalas in *Kelly's Heroes*. Yoked to pedestrian directors and woebegone, bloated studio fare, Eastwood could not develop his persona or establish a cinematic foothold. *Paint Your Wagon*, with its infamous cost overruns and horrible mismanagement, inspired Eastwood to upgrade Malpaso from a tax shelter to a full-fledged production unit managed and owned by him and a select number of associates: "the reason I started Malpaso in the first place was I saw a lot of inefficiencies, and I thought I can screw up as good as the next person. I'd rather be the cause of my own demise" (Thomson, p. 70). Malpaso became Eastwood's stronghold, a fortress from which he could protect himself from the irritating experiences of *Paint Your Wagon* and *Kelly's Heroes* (which was substantially rewritten and re-edited, eluding many of the anti-war sentiments that had attracted Eastwood to the project in the first place):

> *Paint Your Wagon* took six months to make — it should have been
> three. It made me crazy, all that hanging around. *Where Eagles*
> *Dare* took five months. A monumental bore. I hated seeing
> money flung away like that. So I decided it was time to make my
> own pictures. If studios want to chuck their money away that's up
> to them. I want no part of it [Thompson, p. 39].

Not until *In the Line of Fire* (1993, Wolfgang Peterson) would Eastwood leave the auspices of Malpaso and star in a film without the company's oversight.

Having established Malpaso as his base of operations, Eastwood needed a house director, a mentor and kindred spirit who could guide him to the promised land of starteurdom. He naturally turned to Don Siegel, who resumed the task of rehabilitating the Eastwoodian persona. In *Two Mules for Sister Sara* (1970) and *The Beguiled* (1970), Eastwood is paired with women who deprive him of his pride and freedom, a theme that would eventually give rise to *Play Misty for Me*, Eastwood's directorial debut. Eastwood has always believed that for most films to work, there must be a strong female lead:

> I grew up on pictures in which the women always played very
> important roles. Barbara Stanwyck, Bette Davis. And Clark
> Gable's role in *It Happened One Night* (1934, Frank Capra) was
> only as good because he had Claudette Colbert to play off of.
> Those movies are more true to life than many films now where
> you have the guys sort of motivating most of the stories and the
> women in secondary positions [Hentoff, p. 28].

Coogan's Bluff introduced No Name to the modern world. *Two Mules for Sister Sara*— a screwball western-action comedy that anticipated *The Gauntlet* and *Bronco Billy*— exposed No Name once again to the opposite sex and the dynamics of gender in a supposedly male universe. A sly, playful reduction of the whole No Name ethos and mentality, *Two Mules for Sister Sara* gleefully fuses the rugged topography of the Mexican Revolution western (typified by Richard Brooks' *The Professionals* (1966) and Sam Peckinpah's *The Wild Bunch*) with the wacky repartees and hijinks of a 1930s screwball comedy. Siegel and Eastwood give No Name a nomen — Hogan — then pair him with the willful and resourceful Sister Sara (Shirley Maclaine), a Marxist revolutionary prostitute disguised as a nun. Sarah is the motivator: Hogan reacts, responds, and finally recapitulates to a power greater than he (Don Siegel on the hapless Hogan: "He thinks he's leading her around, but she is leading him" [Kaminsky, p. 229]). The climax is a wry reversal of the *Dollars* persona and aesthetic. No Name no longer towers over the hostile landscape, his eyes majestically panning across the horizon. Hogan is seen in long shot as part of Sara's entourage. He is now part of the landscape, a subsidiary figure answerable to Sister Sara, master of the frame and Hogan's destiny.

The Beguiled stretched Eastwood's persona to the near-breaking point. Set during the turmoil of the Civil War, *The Beguiled* is a Gothic allegory about the equality of the sexes: their equal proclivity for perversity, lust, duplicity, and evil. Eastwood is Corporal John McBierney, a Union soldier wounded in Confederate territory who takes refuge in a Louisiana all-girls school. McBierney is confident that he can trick the headmistress, Martha (Geraldine Page), schoolmarm, Edwina (Elizabeth Hartman), and their seven teenage charges into keeping his presence secret until he is well enough to rendezvous with his regiment. McBierney's presence, however, unleashes pent-up desires that have been festering for years at the school. McBierney woos one woman too many, and when he is found seducing Carol Ann (Jo Ann Harris), a coquettish sixteen year old, he is thrown down a spiral staircase by Edwina, who is livid with rage and jealousy. His leg twisted and torn, McBierney is at the mercy of Martha, who decides to amputate his left leg, a clear metaphor for castration. After going on a drunken spree of venom, the corporal is deemed to be a threat to Martha's dominion, the Confederacy, and the school's carefully maintained veneer of Southern gentility. He is poisoned, carried outside, and disposed of.

Siegel and Eastwood went out on a limb with *The Beguiled*. McBierney is nothing more than a Lothario who takes women for granted and betrays their trust and intimacy. He pays dearly for his chauvinistic impertinence. *The Beguiled* marked Eastwood's first on-screen demise (for Eastwood, box office poison: *The Beguiled, Honkytonk Man, Bird,* and *A Perfect World* all failed because of the loss of omniscience and the death of the protagonist; only *The Bridges of Madison County* has been a certifiable success). It is apt that *The Beguiled* died at the box office: the public could not fathom such a disturbing reworking of Eastwood's masculine persona. Jokingly called 'Pussyfooting on the Ole Plantation' by the crew, *The Beguiled* had the nerve to pit the sexes against each other with the male as the victim. Eastwood would resume this battle royal of the sexes with *Play Misty for Me*, a chilling exercise in emasculation.

Having deconstructed his persona to the near-breaking point, Eastwood rebuilt it with *Dirty Harry*. *Dirty Harry* would establish Eastwood's modern persona as definitively as *A Fistful of Dollars* established his mythic persona. It provided Siegel with a property that enhanced his talent for location shooting, muscular editing, and action-driven narrative. The character was wholly Eastwood's; the film wholly Siegel's. *Dirty Harry*, like *A Fistful of Dollars* was not written for Eastwood — it was slated to be a Frank Sinatra vehicle then a possible vessel for Paul Newman before Malpaso took it over. Siegel recommended that the standard New York City locale — the setting for such benchmark cop dramas as Siegel's own *Madigan* and Gordon Douglas' *The Detective* (1968) — should be moved to San Francisco. A native of the Bay Area, Eastwood has set a majority of his films on the West Coast (*Play Misty for Me*, *Breezy*, *Sudden Impact*, *The Rookie*) or the Southwest (*The Eiger Sanction*, *The Outlaw Josey Wales*, *The Gauntlet*, *Bronco Billy*, *Honkytonk Man*, *A Perfect World*). In *Bronco Billy*, the East Coast is associated with decadence and the end of the American dream and frontier. *Bird*, the only Eastwood film to be set predominately in New York City, turns the Big Apple into a subterranean nightclub. Eastwood made a figurative return to contemporary cinema via New York City (*Coogan's Bluff*), but *Dirty Harry* establishes the West Coast as Eastwood's cinematic homeland. Eastwood, ready to take Coogan to the next level, envisioned Harry as the ultimate antihero — an idealistic cop with a cruel streak:

> In *Dirty Harry*, after shooting the guy (Scorpio), actually torturing the confession out of him — that was my idea — and his (Siegel) feeling was that most actors conscious of a certain image would be afraid to do that. But I felt it as the immediacy of the character. At this point, I didn't care about his motivation [Thomson, p. 67].

Siegel's conception was no less sanguine:

> Dirty Harry is a bigot. He's a bitter man. He doesn't like people. Harry thinks that when a guy is bad you get him. You don't worry about his rights. You don't play with him [Lowell, 1975, p. 60].

Harry can be seen as the successor to the antihero pioneered by Humphrey Bogart in the 1940s. In his genre pieces (*High Sierra* [1941, Raoul Walsh],

While Sergio Leone helped Clint Eastwood originate the Man with No Name, Don Siegel played a major role in the creation of Eastwood's modern persona, Inspector "Dirty Harry" Callahan.

The Maltese Falcon [1941, John Huston], *The Big Sleep* [1946, Howard Hawks]), and film noirs (*Dark Passage* [1947, Delmer Daves], *Dead Reckoning* [1948, John Cromwell], Bogart played the cynical romantic, the shrewd but secretly sentimental private eye who forages for truth in the rubble of the post-World War II Naked City. Bogart retains his idealism, even as femme fatales, hoodlums, and feckless socialites guide him through an endless and maddening maze of greed, corruption, and murder. Ambushed and double-crossed at every turn, Bogart doggedly pursues the truth, even if it means the downfall of his client, love interest, or best friend. If he has to resort to violence to survive or break the case he will, but as a rule Bogart prefers to be cool and detached. When his characters do lose their temper or self-control, it mushrooms into a fatal character flaw that cannot be reversed or repressed (*The Roaring Twenties, The Treasure of the Sierra Madre* [1948, John Huston], *In a Lonely Place* [1950, Nicholas Ray]) resulting in death or psychosis.

Harry shares many of the characteristics associated with the Bogartian antihero, but while Bogart has only the subconscious underworld to contend with, Eastwood must stand his ground against a collective Id that has gone wild. In *The Big Sleep*, all Bogart has to do is decode the subtextual evil (pornography and drug dealing) to deprive it of its menace and mystery. What is the value of Eastwood uncovering the truth, when Pandora's Box has already been open and civil unrest and cowardice have become the order of the day? Compared with Bogart, what the Eastwoodian antihero must do is quixotic: restore order to society and subdue the collective unconscious (*Dirty Harry* and *Sudden Impact*), supersede the CIA (*The Eiger Sanction*), and expose a conspiracy and end police corruption (*The Gauntlet*).

Armed with his .44 Magnum and consumed with a righteous fury that frequently explodes into violence, Harry refuses to stand aside and watch America deteriorate into chaos. In his efforts to become a one-man superego, Harry becomes obsessive and deranged. Harry cannot afford to be as composed and nonchalant as Sam Spade or Philip Marlowe. He strives to maintain his self control, but finds it impossible not to disobey his superiors and replace civic law with his own code of frontier justice. Harry cannot be witty or charming. His pursuit of Scorpio is too urgent and desperate. He does not have time to hang out in nightclubs and romance socialites; times have changed. The splendid nightspots of the 1940s have been replaced by strip clubs and urban decay. Harry's crusade to end Scorpio's reign of terror is symptomatic of a society and a soul in crisis. As society breaks down, Harry refuses to let go of his immanent belief in justice. To him, Scorpio is a disease, a synecdoche of everything that is wrong with post-Vietnam America. His pursuit of Scorpio is so intense, it becomes an aberration in itself, a sickness as profound as Scorpio's. Scorpio is Harry's Doppelgänger.

Both are violent creatures on the fringes of society — Scorpio uses violence to disrupt society; Harry uses violence to preserve it. Despite his prowess and persistence (Eastwood on Harry: "who believes there's some guy out there with that kind of tenacity?"[Gentry, 1989, p. 22]), Harry is woefully human. He is too sensitive and idealistic for his own good. Harry claims that he doesn't know why he carries a badge, but we know why every time Harry visits a crime scene with a heavy heart and questions the mediocrity and idiocy that emanates from City Hall. Harry is a misanthrope, but he is also a public servant who believes in law enough to risk his life to preserve it.

Harry's struggle is not only with Scorpio and the SFPD; he is also in conflict with the very city he has sworn to protect and serve. The first major image in *Dirty Harry* is a crane shot of Harry surveying the San Francisco coastline. The shot stresses the spatial and physical struggle between the two: Harry, by walking alongside the crane shot, seeks to gain mastery over the skyline, but San Francisco — immense and picturesque — prevents him from doing so. Harry is constrained by the streets and buildings of San Francisco — he spends a great deal of time on rooftops, discouraging jumpers from committing suicide and waiting for Scorpio to appear. During the long sequence when Scorpio leads Harry to Golden Gate Park, the city becomes a nocturnal labyrinth, an obstacle course that stands between Harry and his quarry. Harry must breathlessly negotiate hills, stairs, tunnels, and subway cars to reach Scorpio. As long as Harry has to pursue Scorpio in the dark city, he is as much the hunted as the hunter. When he finally corners Scorpio in a football stadium, Harry moves in for the kill, but because of the city and its institutions, Harry's efforts are in vain. Scorpio is released from custody; the teenage girl he kidnapped and raped dies. While he is in the city, Scorpio is safe. The law protects him from Harry's wrath. To get to Scorpio, Harry must harass and make him so paranoid that he will leave the city. Scorpio does so, hijacking a bus full of elementary school children. Harry waits for Scorpio on top of a train trestle, his figure the dominant interest of the frame. Disconnected from the city, from his constitutional rights, from the vantage point of a rooftop and the easy trigger pull of a telescopic rifle, Scorpio becomes a slobbering, slathering idiot, a pathetic id-creature who must be slain and submerged. By going outside the city, and consequently outside of the law, Harry becomes an anomaly, a person who has no role in society. He throws his badge into a river, knowing full well that it has lost its meaning. Harry finds himself estranged from the very institutions he has sworn to uphold and the city he calls his home.

Dirty Harry set the mold for the Eastwoodian modern antihero: the troubled individual with an enormous cross to bear, whether it be of his own or other people's making; a man uneasy with himself, his job and his place in society; a man who coexists uneasily with the city; a man, who, in his search for justice, finds himself outside of and inimical to the law he is supposed to represent. Harry walks away angry and alone, but intact. Faced with an amoral universe, Harry uses immoral means to bring about a moral end. His tenacity is a substitute for traditional heroism; his perseverance, his salvation and redemption. Self-doubt is his *bête noire*, for in a demythologized world, Harry plays God, demanding that some sort of morality — even if it is arbitrary and primitive — prevails.

The success of *Dirty Harry* marked a watershed for both Siegel and Eastwood. Earlier that year, Eastwood had already directed his first film, *Play Misty for Me*. With *Dirty Harry*, Eastwood solidified the modern persona he had been developing since *Coogan's Bluff*. Now a filmmaker in his own right with his archetypes in tow, Eastwood no longer needed Siegel to be his mentor. In *Dirty Harry*, during the "I Know What You're Thinking" bank robbery scene, Harry walks in front of a theater showing *Play Misty for Me*. The star and director were becoming one. Siegel encouraged Eastwood's metamorphosis from icon to filmmaker. To mark Eastwood's coming of age as a director, Siegel gladly sponsored Eastwood's Director's Guild membership and appeared for the first time on-screen as Murphy the bartender in *Play Misty for Me*. As a symbolic gesture, Siegel switched places with Eastwood, taking direction from the star he once assisted. Siegel's role as Eastwood's mentor and coach is acknowledged and then gracefully phased out. The old master's last scene is a coy benediction — Murphy (i.e., Siegel) flashes a middle finger and then quickly substitutes it for a peace sign.

The conclusion of the Eastwood-Siegel partnership did not mean the conclusion of Siegel's career. The 1970s would be the decade when Siegel finally secured the independent status that had long eluded him. The hard working metteur grew into an acknowledged auteur. From *Charley Varrick* on, all of his films were graced with the introductory title "A Siegel Film". Siegel returned to his favorite themes and collaborated with the leading stars and legends of the era: Walter Matthau (*Charley Varrick*), Michael Caine (*The Black Windmill*, [1974]), John Wayne (*The Shootist* [1976]), Charles Bronson (*Telefon*, [1977]), Burt Reynolds (*Rough Cut* [1980]) and, of course, Clint Eastwood (*Escape from Alcatraz*). With *Alcatraz*, Siegel directed a film that was defined by his aesthetic and ethos, not Eastwood's. As Frank Morris, the shrewd and observant convict who uses his intelligence and ingenuity to escape from prison, Eastwood is the heir to Lee Marvin in *The Killers*. He is the quintessential grim and resourceful Siegelini antihero; a stern and private man who focuses entirely on being the first inmate to escape from Alcatraz. Morris is not an Eastwoodian antihero. He is not an archangel or a flawed human being in need of love and redemption. He is a block of stone, an implacable force of will that cannot be broken. Morris is a man with a mission — once he chisels his way out of his cell and leaps into the Pacific Ocean, the film is over. It is fitting that *Escape from Alcatraz* would be the creative and commercial climax of Siegel's career: the director finally succeeded in crafting Eastwood into his own image, separate from that of the Dirty Harry persona he helped Eastwood discover and develop. The collaboration had come full circle.

Siegel's legacy to Eastwood can be summed up with one quote from Eastwood: "I'm always trying to get it on the first take — a Don Siegel technique"(Thompson and Hunter, p. 33). Siegel taught Eastwood how to be lean and economic without being sloppy or prosaic. He helped him conceptualize his persona in an American and antiheroic format and formulate the themes that would play a major part in Eastwood's work. Eastwood kept Siegel's no-nonsense shooting style, but moved in a direction closer to Leone's in terms of style. The first phase of Eastwood's work would be a conscious effort to forge a personal style out of the shadow of both Leone and Siegel.

3

First Phase, 1971–1975

My theory was that I could foul up my career just as well as anyone else could foul it up for me, so why not try it [Zmijewsky, p. 23]?

Although the elements that comprise Eastwood's style are evident in *Play Misty for Me*, it took three more films (*High Plains Drifter, Breezy, The Eiger Sanction*) for Eastwood to shake off the diegetic and aesthetic influence of Sergio Leone and Don Siegel and forge his own style. Eastwood's first four films cover a wide variety of genres and themes: *Play Misty for Me* initiates the artistic cycle (*Bronco Billy; Honkytonk Man; Bird; White Hunter, Black Heart*) and examines the pitfalls of promiscuity and the intricacies of male-female relationships; *High Plains Drifter* appropriates the Man with No Name and casts him into a mythical world unlike Leone's, a world ruled by God and a wrathful cavalry of archangels; *Breezy* is a low-key, cross-cultural love story that gives Eastwood an opportunity to be behind the camera exclusively; *The Eiger Sanction* features Eastwood's first contemporary anti-hero, a spy without conscience or compassion. Eastwood's first two films establish his penchant for circular construction, location shooting, and an abbreviation of exposition. With its savvy use of Eastwood's persona and its compact construction (not to mention its expressive use of the wide screen), *High Plains Drifter* anticipates Eastwood's cinema of the mid-1970s and beyond, particularly his interest in morality and complimentary use of montage and mise-en-scène. *Breezy* lacks the visual and thematic unity of *Play Misty for Me* and *High Plains Drifter*, as does *The Eiger Sanction*, a travelogue that collapses under the weight of too much location shooting. Eastwood strives for a more casual, incidental style in *Breezy* and *The Eiger Sanction*, a style counter to the loose — tight-systematic — spontaneous dichotomy of *Play Misty for Me* and *High Plains Drifter*. With *The Outlaw*

Josey Wales, Eastwood would harmonize style and content and perfect a casual, yet carefully constructed style that has sustained him for over 20 years.

Play Misty for Me, 1971

> I think the secret to a well-defined male character is a strong
> female complement. She could even be the antagonist in some
> cases. But I think it's important for dramatic reasons alone that
> there's a balance there [Gentry, p. 18].

For his first film, Eastwood selected a morality play similar to *The Beguiled,* a film that warns that he who lives by the sword shall die by the sword. That sword is the phallus of the one-night stand, of taking the soul and sexuality of another for granted. A Hitchcockian thriller in the tradition of *Shadow of a Doubt* (1943) and *Strangers on a Train* (1951), *Play Misty for Me* is a riveting battle of the sexes in which Dave Garver (Clint Eastwood) is confronted with his Doppelgänger, Evelyn Draper (Jessica Walter), a psychotic Id-Woman who sees their one-night stand as an all-encompassing love affair. *Play Misty for Me* is a film about miscommunication and sick jealousy, of a man not being able to comprehend or withstand the emotional and psychological demands of a woman. In Eastwood's words:

> It looked at that problem of commitment, that misinterpretation
> of commitment between a man and a woman [Guerif, p. 85].

> This was an opportunity to do a film that had that kind of ele-
> ment and at the same time a story which everyone knows — it's
> not polarized one sexual way or another; it could be man against
> woman or woman against man — about suffocation, that misin-
> terpretation of commitment, one person's casually dating the
> other, who's saying 'forever and ever'. The guy is the victim, he is
> the subject certainly. I think it's maybe more conflicting to have a
> man who handles himself in a more physical situation stuck in a
> situation where he can't handle it physically, a frustrating situa-
> tion [Plaza, p. 30].

Dave, the victim and subject of *Play Misty for Me,* is Eastwood's first artist and man of non-action, a jazz DJ who enjoys the uncomplicated pleasures of bachelorhood. Dave's world is a self-enclosed mellow groove, a pastel canvas of sports cars, jazz LPs, and cold imported beer. His life revolves around his exclusive beach-side bungalow, KRML, where he hosts an evening jazz show, and the Sardine Factory, a cocktail lounge where he hobnobs with Murphy the bartender (Don Siegel) and picks up an occasional one-night stand.

All is not well with Dave, however. *Play Misty for Me* opens gracefully, with an aerial shot that swoops down over the Monterey coastline and glides down toward Dave, who stands outside of his ex-lover Tobie Williams' (Donna Mills) house, pining for her return. The entire film revolves around Tobie's home and the need for Dave to overcome his fears and go inside. He wants to cross the threshold and become part of her life, but resists doing so out of fear of losing his cherished space and freedom. Tobie's residence is the nexus of *Play Misty for Me*, the source of the film's conflict and narrative.

As the opening credits continue to roll, Eastwood cuts to Dave leaving Tobie's home. The contemplative reverie of waves softly breaking against the shore is rudely broken by jazz music blaring out of Dave's car stereo as he drives along the coastline. Dave gets more comfortable as he gets farther away from Tobie's home. He leaves her pictorial, sunlit home and heads toward the dark, nocturnal interior of KRML. Secluded in the basement studio, Dave indulges in jazz and pillow talk as he keeps the outside world at a safe distance. The microphone allows Dave to be charming without being sincere — an extension of his singles lifestyle and flippant attitude toward women and relationships. The whole conflict of *Play Misty for Me* is Dave's unwillingness to reverse his route to KRML and let go of his hermetic lifestyle. The dichotomy of light and dark permeates the film, suggesting the different natures of Tobie and Evelyn, of love and obsessional madness. Evelyn is associated with darkness and confinement, Tobie with daylight and the open space of the Monterey coast. *Play Misty for Me* moves toward dawn: the meeting of light and dark, of commitment and casual sex, of adult and infantile behavior. For the first 10 minutes of the film, Dave remains the focus of *Play Misty for Me*. That changes as soon as Evelyn — a creature from Dave's subconscious, a force of guilt, penitence and feminine fury — calls KRML and requests 'Play Misty for Me'. Evelyn seduces Dave with her voice, then her body. She waits for Dave in the Sardine Factory and moves slowly and stealthily from the rear of the frame into the foreground, supplanting Dave's space, a space that will be mercilessly violated and disrupted for the rest of the film.

Cut to Dave and Evelyn in her apartment: she is chopping ice with an ice pick, a portent for what is to come. Evelyn is a parody of what Dave wants in a woman. She says all of the things he wants to hear and offers her body unconditionally. Dave does not seem to question Evelyn's advances or her overly complimentary behavior. To Dave, Evelyn is the ultimate one-night stand, a whore without any cost or complications. What he does not know is that she is a vampire waiting to bare her fangs and suck the very lifeblood out of him. Lacking self-worth and a coherent personality, Evelyn embodies the popular cult of love for love's sake, of teenage games, possessiveness, and melodramatic excess. Evelyn is a neurotic pastiche of *Cosmopolitan* and come-ons, a pretty face with all the trappings of an attractive woman but none of the deep emotions or levelheadedness that a healthy person should have. She is a projection of the negative side of the singles scene, of obsessive unfounded love, and of Dave's own mistreatment of women in the past. Evelyn serves as "his (Dave's) alter-ego, a projection of his suppressed furies and fear of love — a pull toward death and self-destruction that he must battle and exorcise within himself" (Thompson and Hunter, p. 32). According to James F. Calhoun's *Abnormal Psychology, Current Perspectives*, Evelyn meets all the criteria for an antisocial, psychotic personality. She is exactly what Dave does not need: a hysterical pit of hurt that would quickly wear out the most compassionate or selfless therapist. Dave falls for her passive-aggressive advances, unable to see that Evelyn is a terribly disturbed woman without an identity, a compulsive psychotic and emotional and psychological leech who smothers him with her voracious need for love, affection, and approval. Throughout *Play Misty for Me*, Evelyn is the dominant figure, a force of vengeance and irrationality that puts Dave on the defensive. Dave's one-night stand with Evelyn sets up Tobie's return, and the central conflict of the film: which pole will Dave be attracted to: Tobie (love, life) or Evelyn (lust, death)?

Dave and Evelyn's love scene is in sharp contrast to Dave's lovemaking with Tobie in the woods later in the film. Dave and Tobie share an intimate interlude amongst nature; Dave and Evelyn fuck in the dark. Evelyn's orgasm is too forced, as if she is acting and wants it to be more than it actually is. The next morning Dave slips out of Evelyn's apartment but is photographed through a window, a sign of confinement. He is no longer free. To enforce this, Eastwood has Evelyn move into the foreground of the shot, watching Dave leave. A shrewd manipulator of Dave's accommodating personality and sex drive, Evelyn commandeers Dave's space and foils his attempts to reunite with Tobie.

In a reverse zoom, we are introduced to Tobie, who is blowtorching a piece of modern sculpture. Tobie is the antithesis of Evelyn: she is an incandescent flame, not a raging conflagration. Like Dave, Tobie is a bohemian, but she is an artist with promise (Dave is more of a dilettante). While Evelyn has no apparent occupation or friends, Tobie has a career and a wide assortment of roommates and colleagues. Tobie does not want to devour

Dave, but to form a lasting relationship with him. Evelyn wants to possess Dave and absorb him so that she can be whole. Tobie does not need Dave to validate herself; she has pride and a strong sense of self. Because she has no positive identity, Evelyn has no shame, and will go to any lengths to possess Dave. If she cannot have him, no one will.

As Evelyn lashes out, begging for limitless attention, Dave and Tobie share quiet walks along the seashore peacefully contemplating their past relationship and the possibility of a future one. Dave's scenes with Tobie are tender. The scenes he shares with Evelyn are cacophonous, tense, tightly edited, and darkly lit. Dave and Tobie can communicate. Dave's exchanges with Evelyn are exercises in miscommunication. Evelyn — as one-way as Dave's microphone — can only drown Dave out with her childish screams of denial. Having a "total lack of conscience and a lack of insight and an inability to learn from experience" (Calhoun, 1977, p. 190). Evelyn cannot listen. Until he is forced to take action, Dave foolishly sleeps with Evelyn, hoping that she will listen to reason and release her hold over his life.

The closer Dave gets to Tobie, the more desperate and pervasive Evelyn becomes (her tenacity is similar to Robert DeNiro's in *The King of Comedy* [Martin Scorsese, 1983]). Back at KRML, Dave seems uncomfortable and cramped for space: even in his basement retreat Dave cannot evade Evelyn. All she has to do to contaminate his space is call and say "Play Misty for Me". Evelyn's mania for "Misty" is a sign of her psychosis: she never tires of the song because she is not capable of changing or growing. She is stuck like Dave, but in a much more frightening way. Dave has a life; Evelyn does not. Weary of Evelyn's claustrophobic presence, Dave thinks he can reason with an Id-woman who is completely irrational. Evelyn believes that if she prepares Dave some corned beef sandwiches and dons a gaudy pair of lounge pajamas, he will fall under her spell. Instead, he tells Evelyn to get off his back, to which she replies, "Isn't that where you have been keeping me?" Dave has finally met a woman who will not passively accept being discarded, who boils with righteous anger when he turns his back to her. Just because Dave has decided to end their sexual trysts does not mean their mock relationship is over. Through the use of a sound dissolve, Eastwood shows us that Evelyn is still in control of the film and Dave's space. While Dave drives home after an ugly confrontation with Evelyn, she calls his bungalow repeatedly. Dave's private drive from KRML is violated by the constant ringing of the telephone. The ringing dominates the soundtrack, up to the time that Dave returns home and picks up the receiver, hanging it up immediately when he hears Evelyn begging for forgiveness. Evelyn cannot control her impulses and feelings — one minute she is remorseful, the next vindictive. By dissolving the ring of the phone over the images of Dave driving home, Eastwood shows us that Dave's lifestyle is compromised by Evelyn's suffusive presence. Dave takes the receiver off the hook and sits back against a wall, a look of fear and entrapment on his face.

After being rejected by Dave, Evelyn never rests until his personal space is hers. We never see Evelyn in her claustrophobic apartment again; instead, we see her spying on Dave and Tobie at the beach, her cold stare revealed by a forward zoom. Later that evening, Evelyn storms into Dave's home, expecting to see Tobie in 'her' bed. The only thing she encounters is a very sleepy and irritated Dave. Evelyn resorts to tears, but cries artificially as if she applied drops to her eyes. Tears being ineffective, Evelyn locks herself in Dave's bathroom and cuts her wrists. She attempts suicide not to harm herself, but to inflict so much guilt on Dave that he will not desert her. When Dave pries the bathroom door open, we see Evelyn's bloody wrists and an eerie, frozen face of despair, made even more ghoulish by an out-of-focus dissolve.

With Evelyn's suicide attempt comes the threat of a police investigation, something Dave, who cherishes his privacy and considers his space to be inviolable, cannot accept. Instead of calling an ambulance or the police, Dave calls Frank (Jack Ging), a friend who happens to be a doctor. He is warned by Frank that Evelyn should not be moved and should be monitored carefully. Evelyn takes full advantage of Dave's guilt — he has no choice but to feed and comfort her, just as Tobie calls, ready to forgive Dave and resume their relationship. Dave cannot renounce his lifestyle and embrace Tobie without confronting Evelyn, the Id-woman who represents his deep-seated fears of love and commitment. Realizing that Dave and Tobie are growing closer together, Evelyn prevents him from returning to her coastal home by emitting a bloodcurdling scream, breathlessly telling Dave that "I had a dream. I was drowning in the ocean, but you just stood there watching, watching. Oh god, I'm so alone. Oh Dave, hold me please." Evelyn's hysterical but calculated outburst has some validity to it: Dave will punch her in self-defense, causing her to fall to her death and drown in the sea.

Evelyn's grip grows tighter as Dave grows closer to Tobie. She violates his personal space and ruins his chances of hosting a syndicated radio program. By desecrating Dave's cult of self, Evelyn unwittingly pushes him toward Tobie. When Dave goes to her, seeking solace and forgiveness, she is sunbathing. (To emphasize that Dave has not renounced his lifestyle, Eastwood has him meet Tobie at the beach rather than her home). Tobie is associated with nature and the soothing sound of the surf hitting the coastline. Evelyn, the woman of artifice and enclosure, prevents Dave and Tobie from becoming too intimate by reaching out and crushing a branch in the foreground. She 'grabs' the shot from Dave and Tobie, and heads back to his bungalow, where she goes on an Id-like rampage, destroying his property and assaulting his beloved housekeeper, Birdie (Clarice Taylor). Only

First-time director Clint Eastwood demonstrates to co star Jessica Walter how to wield a knife against his character, Dave Garver, a jazz DJ who grapples with the dark side of the sexual revolution.

when Evelyn lashes out can she find any personal or sexual fulfillment. She tries to demolish Dave's world, but is unsuccessful. The authorities (in Hitchcockian fashion, the police are either meddlesome or symptomatic of an absent or ineffectual superego) arrest and take her away for treatment, but do not incarcerate her — until Dave confronts his own fears and doubts and suffers for his own sins, Evelyn will hold sway over the film. Temporarily free of Evelyn's machinations, Dave is able to reunite with Tobie and share a romantic interlude in the coastal woods, a delicate (and somewhat hackneyed) montage orchestrated by the song "The First Time Ever I Saw Your Face."

The next scene, the Monterey Jazz Festival, gives Dave a chance to be outdoors with his other love — jazz — and for Eastwood to put the narrative on hold and allow his camera to capture — in cinema-verité style — the mood and texture of an actual jazz festival. The scene is the first instance of a phenomenological bent in Eastwood's work, of mood making mincemeat out of narrative. For most of the shots, Eastwood is not in the frame, and when he is, we see him primarily in long shot, lolling around with thousands of other spectators, enjoying the warm weather and music. For the viewer, the festival scene is an intermission, a recess from Dave and Evelyn's psychological conflict. For Eastwood, the scene is a chance to minimize his physical presence, experiment with form, and find the balance between phenomenology and narrative. For Dave, the scene is a second interlude and a false reprieve. The festival dissolves into a record being played on the air at KRML: despite Evelyn's rampage and Dave's reconciliation with Tobie, he remains sequestered in the basement of the radio station, unwilling to make the symbolic journey back to Tobie's house, a journey he is incapable of making until Evelyn forces him. To underscore this and to remind us that Dave has not reclaimed his space or privacy, Eastwood has Evelyn call and request "Misty" as if nothing has changed. She, and the forces associated with her, can no longer be repressed. The look of horror returns to Dave's face. Evelyn appears in the middle of the night and plunges a knife next to his sleeping head. Repressed for too long, the Id returns to reclaim its psychic space and force Dave into leaving his precious KRML and taking responsibility for his actions and desires.

Like Birdie, Tobie suffers for Dave's sins. Evelyn is no longer satisfied with violating Dave's personal and psychic space; she must have Tobie's as well. Evelyn poses as Tobie's new roommate and terrorizes her at knife point, forcing Dave to leave KRML and reverse the route he took at the beginning of the film. When Dave enters Tobie's home, it is dark and foreboding. To lift the darkness and ensure Tobie's survival, Dave must struggle with Evelyn and send her to a watery grave. Evelyn falls to her death, landing on the same rocks Dave gazed upon earlier in the film. As " Misty" wafts through the radio, we pull away from Dave and Tobie limping out of the darkness and into the sunlight, returning to the bird's eye view used in the beginning shot. We see Evelyn dashed among the rocks, a necessary sacrifice so that Dave and Tobie may nurture each other. Tobie's home no longer has the significance it had in the opening — the conflict has been resolved. Dusk becomes dawn.

Play Misty for Me does not demonize sex. Compare it with *Carnal Knowledge* (1970, Mike Nichols), *Klute* (1971, Alan J. Pakula) or *Looking for Mr. Goodbar* (1977, Richard Brooks) or such later films as *Fatal Attraction* (1987, Adrian Lynne) or *Basic Instinct* (1992, Paul Verhoeven), films that associate sexual freedom with death or impotence. In *Carnal Knowledge* and *Looking for Mr. Goodbar*, sex is a dead end. The main characters pursue it with a single-minded zeal, only to discover death or disillusionment. Both films fixate on sexual intercourse, not love. The protagonists of both films are lost souls who cannot see beyond their next orgasm. *Play Misty for Me* argues that sex without love, communication, or commitment can be as lethal as the AIDS virus. Eastwood does not like to subject the act of intercourse or the naked body to voyeurism. His camera does not objectify the female body. Eastwood strives for intimacy, not titillation or voyeurism.

The love scenes of *Play Misty for Me*, *Breezy*, *The Eiger Sanction*, *The Outlaw Josey Wales*, *Every Which Way But Loose*, and *The Bridges of Madison County* are shot in an ethereal way to suggest that sexuality is a mystery that should be treated with respect and restraint. Without Evelyn's cathartic presence, Dave would degenerate into Jack Nicholson in *Carnal Knowledge*, alone, impotent, and emotionally eviscerated. *Play Misty for Me* treats the Doppelgänger with sympathy. Evelyn is a monster but she is also a tragic figure to be identified with or pitied. She is the catalyst that drives the film to its redemptive climax.

Shot in four and one half weeks for a mere $750,000, *Play Misty for Me* was intended to be a personal project, an opportunity for Eastwood to make a smooth transition from star to star-director: "Anybody could have done it, with a lot of different concepts. It was a small enough picture, small cast, not overly difficult — not like starting out with a massive thing" (Thompson and Hunter, p. 27). The film was shot on location in the Monterey area near Eastwood's home in Carmel. Although it was shot in a short period of time, *Play Misty for Me* lacks some of the earmarks that characterize Eastwood's later work as his own. Bruce Surtees' cinematography does not have the sharp outlines and shadows of *High Plains Drifter* or *The Outlaw Josey Wales*. There are an abundance of cuts and zoom shots, rather than long takes or reverse masters. 'The First Time Ever I Saw Your Face' montage dates badly and is too derivative of *Love Story* (Arthur Hiller, 1970), in contrast to the Monterey Jazz Festival sequence, which establishes Eastwood's dedication to phenomenology and a style that would link formal and invisible montage into a cohesive whole. Eastwood's passage from star to director to starteur would not come about until he perfected his style and confronted his own Doppelgänger: the Man with No Name.

High Plains Drifter, 1973

It's just an allegory, and it wasn't intended to be the West that's been told hundreds of times over. *High Plains Drifter* was a speculation on what happens when they go ahead and kill the sheriff and somebody comes back and calls the town conscience to bear [Plaza, p. 48].

Then I heard another voice from heaven saying,
Come out of her my people,
lest you take part in her sins,

> lest you share in her plagues,
> for her sins are heaped high as heaven,
> and God has remembered her iniquities.
> Render to her as she herself has rendered,
> and repay her double for her deeds;
> mix a double draught for her in the cup she mixed.
> As she glorified herself and played the wanton,
> so give her a like measure of torment and mourning.
> Since in her heart she says, 'A queen I sit,
> I am no widow, mourning shall never see,
> so shall her plagues come in a single day,
> pestilence and mourning and famine,
> and she shall be burned with fire;
> for mighty is the Lord God who judges her.
> Revelation, 18: 4-8

An audacious mixture of Revelation, *High Noon* (Fred Zinneman, 1952) and *A Fistful of Dollars*, *High Plains Drifter* is Eastwood's first successful blend of style and self-analysis, a western allegory of sin and deliverance that transforms the Man with No Name into the Stranger (Clint Eastwood), an archangel sent by the Lord to punish the wicked town of Lago. A Petri dish for the Seven Deadly Sins, Lago is an abomination and an aberration, an unholy Potemkin Village that collapses mercilessly to the ground when the Stranger rides into town. Eastwood had the town built on location next to Lake Mono in the California Sierras to stress Lago's moral and topographical isolation: "I wanted to get an off-look to it rather than a conventional western look ... Mono Lake has a weird look to it, a lot of strange colors — never looks the same way twice during the day" (Thompson and Hunter, p. 28) Although prosperous, Lago is poor in spirit and community. No western town has looked so new, yet seemed so threadbare and desolate. It is isolated from the outside world, a town without children or a future. There is no railroad, newspaper, or telegraph office. Visitors are unwelcome. Sheriff Sam Shaw (Walter Barnes) is a cowardly glutton, the preacher (Robert Donner) a hypocritical weakling, and Mayor Jason Hobart (Stefan Gierasch) a tool of Dave Drake (Mitchell Ryan) and Morgan Allen (Jack Ging), the beneficiaries of the mining company and the architects of Lago's growth and prosperity. The church is located in the rear of the town, eclipsed by the Lago Mining Company and the Belding Hotel, the site of Marshall Jim Duncan's fatal bullwhipping. Lago owes its existence and prosperity to the murder of Duncan, who was the moral and ethical nucleus of the town. In response to Marshall Duncan's dying curse and Lago's sinfulness, the Lord sends the Stranger to town to do His handiwork.

The first and last shot of *High Plains Drifter* reveal the Stranger's supernatural origins and Eastwood's love of circular construction and anti-exposition. The Stranger materializes out of (and into) nothingness, his form compressed by a long lens and warped by the heat of the sun. The telephoto establishing shot suggests a netherworld, a threshold the Stranger must cross to reach (and leave) the earth. Red credits are superimposed as the Stranger descends from a series of hilltops (in religion and mythology, mountain tops are frequently the home of God and his celestial court), pre-signifying the crimson paint and bloodshed that will transform Lago into a hell on earth. Eastwood cuts to a wide vista of Lago in the distance as the credits and the Stranger's descent ends. Lago is nestled in an elemental realm where air, water, and earth converge; a realm soon to be consumed by God's fury and the fourth element: fire. Bruce Surtees' cinematography emphasizes the azure sky, blue lake, and brown soil, eclipsing Lago, which is an intrusion on the otherwise natural landscape, an artificial assemblage of wood and glass erected on the unmarked grave of an honest man. Surtees stresses the polarity between the natural space of the elements and the man-made space of Lago by shooting the interiors with available light. Lago's guilt is so pervasive that the sun cannot warm the conscience of its inhabitants or illuminate the interiors of its structures, despite the preponderance of clear skies and picture windows. Surtees uses backlighting to give Lago a sinister and suspicious aura. He contrasts the blue sky that permeates each shot with the dark interiors of the buildings. Instead of being outside, the citizens of Lago prefer to hide in the shadows — they do not want their secret exposed. In addition to available light and backlighting, Surtees uses foreshortening and anamorphic lenses to reduce space and emphasize the flat character of Lago and its people. Except for Mordecai (Billy Curtis) and Sarah Belding (Verna Bloom), the citizens of Lago are a humorless, two-dimensional collection of buffoons and cowards. They have no charm or character.

If it can be pared down to essentials, *High Plains Drifter* is about motion and stasis; moral forcefulness and paralysis. The Stranger, the catalyst and prime mover of the film, is active and mobile; the citizens of Lago, passive and immobile. When the Stranger arrives in Lago, Eastwood alternates between compound tracking shots of the Stranger and passing shots of the citizens to associate the Stranger with motion and the citizens of Lago with stasis. The Stranger is the center of *High Plains Drifter*. He remains the dominant interest even when he is not in the frame. Eastwood uses tracking shots, cross-in shots, and angle-reverse angles to make the Stranger the adhesive that holds the mise-en-scène and montage together. During the Stranger's opening ride into Lago, Eastwood varies the perspective of the camera and cuts across several axes to make the Stranger the center of attention. By alternating between compound tracking shots and passing shots and

An archangel with an attitude. The Stranger (Clint Eastwood) inspects the town of Lago with his wrathful blue eyes.

varying the angle or position of the camera, Eastwood stresses not only the centrality of the Stranger, but he gives us a comprehensive visual introduction to the town of Lago and its inhabitants in less than five minutes, forgoing the need for a cumbersome exposition. Eastwood also claims the Man with No Name as his own by restaging No Name's opening ride into San Miguel in *A Fistful of Dollars*. Because No Name was the brainchild of both Leone and Eastwood, it is unclear in the Dollars trilogy whether or not No Name is a Christian figure of justice and retribution (Leone never resolves this question — in *The Good, the Bad, and the Ugly*, No Name has angelic qualities, but he is still a fortune hunter driven by greed and self-interest). In *High Plains Drifter*, Eastwood redefines No Name as an eschatological force, a spiritual entity who has much more command over the frame and the narrative. Unlike No Name, who, in *A Fistful of Dollars*, must wear a piece of armor to survive a gunfight, the Stranger is truly invincible.

As the Lago Mining Company looms in the rear of the frame, the Stranger hears a whip crack and is reminded of Duncan's murder, a crime that cannot be repressed or hidden by the townspeople. Before he reacts to the noise and turns to the camera, the Stranger's features are immobile and obscured by shadow. Upon hearing the whip crack, the Stranger's face "lightens up" and his elemental blue eyes burn with a wrathful, smoldering fury. It does not take long for the Stranger to lay the foundation for the Lord's judgment. As soon as he enters a saloon and orders a drink, the Stranger is accosted and threatened by three of the Lago Mining Company's hired guns. The Stranger never goads these men. He has no zeal for gunfights and bloodshed. It is his appointed task to engage in violence, a duty he performs perfunctorily without emotion or enthusiasm. Whenever possible, the Stranger gives his adversaries an opportunity to relent or repent. Very few of the inhabitants of Lago take that opportunity. That includes the three hired guns who follow the Stranger into a barbershop and accost him further, until the Stranger has no choice but to open the first of many seals and shoot them dead.

With three dead men in his wake, the Stranger inserts a cigarillo in his mouth (a coy reference to the Man with No Name) and strides down Main Street, his spurs jingling with menacing authority. As the Stranger passes in front of the offices of the Lago Mining Company for the second time (its presence an unspoken reminder of the town's mortal sin), he encounters the town strumpet, Callie Travers (Marianna Hill), a 19th-century whore of Babylon. Callie collides with the Stranger intentionally, but when he shows little interest in flirting with her, she questions his manhood and berates him in public. The Stranger makes a valiant effort to ignore Callie's taunts and challenges until she smacks his precious cigarillo out of his mouth — the worst action anyone can take against the Man with No Name. The Stranger drags Callie into a nearby barn and rapes her. Because Callie enjoys the sexual assault several seconds after being violated, Eastwood encourages us to question her character. Instead of being terrified, Callie responds to the Stranger's advances and achieves an orgasm soon after the Stranger is inside her. After being mounted, Callie averts her eyes as if she were committing a sin, rather than vice versa. *High Plains Drifter*'s code of divine justice resembles that of the Pentateuch or the Book of Job. Neither the corrupt men nor women of Lago deserve clemency: while the men are shot and beaten for their sins, the wicked women of Lago are raped and assaulted. The Stranger does not consider women to be the weaker sex — he holds them up to the same standards as men, and punishes them with equal severity.

The people of Lago make no effort to intervene as the Stranger commits three murders and one rape. Their passivity harks back to the evening of Duncan's murder, when he pleaded for help as Stacey Bridges (Geoffrey Lewis), Dan Carlin (Dan Vadis), and Cole Carlin (Anthony James) bullwhipped him to death. By not responding nor reacting to the Stranger's crime spree, the people of Lago tacitly condone it. The Stranger's antisocial and criminal behavior becomes excusable; rape and murder become an everyday occurrence. Only the dwarf Mordecai and Sarah Belding, the two people who identified with Duncan and mourned his passing, take an active interest in the Stranger. The victim of abuse and ridicule, Mordecai has no affinity for the people of Lago. He accompanies the Stranger and eagerly helps him pass judgment on those who have belittled him for years. Sarah, the estranged wife of hotelier Lewis Belding (Ted Hartley), who tried to stop Duncan's murder, is outraged by the Stranger's conduct and views him with contempt until she senses his true purpose and identity. The Stranger graces Mordecai and Sarah with his presence and inspires them to defy the moral vacuum of Lago. The rest of the citizenry of Lago can be divided into two groups: the weak and the wicked. The weak include the sheriff, the mayor, the preacher, and all of men who have opened small businesses in Lago. The weak do the bidding of the wicked (namely Dave Drake, Morgan Allen, and Lewis Belding), who are much more intelligent and devious — the ones who hired Stacey Bridges and his gang to kill Duncan, and then framed Bridges so they could hoard Lago's gold for themselves. The weak are forced to bear witness to the Lord's wrath and to atone for their sins; the wicked are butchered and sent straight to hell.

Although the Stranger shows little enthusiasm for his divine assignment, he does relish being in human form and enjoys the sentient pleasures of eating, drinking, smoking, bathing, and lovemaking. He even lies down and rests for awhile. While resting, the Stranger taps into Lago's collective memory-guilt and watches Duncan's murder via a dream-flashback vision that gives us a composite impression of the event as witnessed by Mordecai, the people of Lago, and Marshall Duncan. During Duncan's bullwhipping, the weak show shame; the wicked nothing but self-interest. Everyone is draped by darkness and framed by static, symmetrically composed shots — a sign of their passivity and moral paralysis. Duncan pleads for help repeatedly as the Bridges gang whips him to death. No one reacts. They merely recede further into the shadows of their stores and offices, too ashamed or avaricious to act. As his life ebbs away, Duncan eyes the people of Lago with malice and whispers, "damn you all to hell." With that malediction, Duncan dies and the Stranger's dream-flashback vision comes to an end. Later in the film, Mordecai dreams about the same event, augmenting the Stranger's dream-flashback. Again, we see the people of Lago frozen in place, framed in static, symmetrical compositions, unwilling or unable to move or respond to Duncan's suffering. Sarah Belding tries to break the static mise-en-scène and move out of the frame, but is restrained by her husband. The second memory-flashback associates the people of Lago with their storefronts: commerce triumphs over conscience. Silhouetted in darkness, the weak and the wicked merge with the wood and the glass of their businesses; they become one with their property, inanimate objects without any human conscientiousness whatsoever.

The fact that Mordecai has the same dream as the Stranger indicates that the past is present in Lago: the dream is a collective memory-curse that will hover over the town until morality is restored and Duncan's grave is properly marked. Because the Stranger dreams of Duncan's death, it can be argued that the Stranger is Duncan's spirit, haunting Lago until it can be released from limbo (the Stranger rides through a graveyard before he enters the town). Eastwood himself has downplayed that interpretation: "As for me justifying the role, he (the Stranger) was the brother (of Duncan) but as far as the audience is concerned, if they want to draw him as something a little more than that, that's fine" (Thompson and Hunter, p. 32). To make the Stranger's identity less concrete, Eastwood had his stunt coordinator, Buddy Van Horn, trade shots with him during the flashback. Duncan's physiognomy is not defined — it is hinted at. Who Duncan was and what he looked like is unimportant; it is his death and the moral crisis which caused it that is the central focus of the film. The Stranger comes to Lago in a form similar to Duncan's so that the town can recognize its sins; that no one except Mordecai and Sarah senses a resemblance is evidence of Lago's moral blindness and ignorance. By sharing shots with Van Horn, Eastwood wants us to concentrate on the Stranger, not Duncan. The convergence of events (the Stranger's arrival coincides with Stacey Bridges' release) and the moral foundation of *High Plains Drifter* encourage an eschatological reading of the film. The Stranger is an archangel; God uses a dead man's curse to pass judgment on a weak and wicked town. In Christian folklore, the archangel is God's agent of punishment, a "created being with no special relation to God, and thus no part in divine theophany" (Myers, 1987, p. 56). The Stranger is a messenger, an emissary who takes on human form and the spirit of Duncan to render God's judgment. He is a western version of Michael the messenger and Gabriel the warrior, an archangel associated with apocalyptic images of fire and blood.

The citizens of Lago do not see the Stranger as a threat. They are terrified of the Bridges gang, and their fear causes them to turn to the Stranger as their protector and leader. The Bridges' release from prison coincides with the Stranger's arrival: God's design involves both archangels and locusts. The Stranger is the architect of Lago's downfall; the Bridges gang are the horsemen of the apocalypse, the beasts that burn and pillage Lago. When they are released from prison, the Bridges gang seems to be emerging from a dark, sulfurous pit. They have an instinctual need to rob, pillage, and kill. A passage from Revelation alludes to the role the Bridges gang plays in *High Plains Drifter*:

> Then from the smoke came locusts from the earth, and they were
> given power like the power of Scorpions of the earth; they were

told not to harm the grass of the earth; or any green growth or
any tree, but only those of mankind who have not the seal of God
upon their foreheads [*Revelation*, 9:1-16].

The Stranger paves the way for the locusts' arrival by usurping the town
of Lago and throwing it into chaos. Lago is so craven, it actually invites this
archangel of death and retribution to be its guardian. To coerce the Stranger
into being a hired gun, the sheriff and the mayor promise him "unlimited
credit" and a "free hand in this town", giving him license to paint the town
red and prepare it for the Bridges' arrival. The Stranger does not encourage
this Faustian bargain. In fact he rejects it until it is thrust upon him. The
Stranger insists that Lago does not need him to stop the Bridges gang and
tells the sheriff that, "all you have is a short supply of guts." Indeed, the people of Lago have the manpower and the wherewithal to defeat Bridges, but
are too timorous to act. The Stranger provides the town with the tools and
the strategy to vanquish the locusts, but exclaims "Shit" when he realizes
Lago is full not only of cowards and turncoats, but also some of the worst
marksmen in screen history.

Having been appointed the de facto warrior-king of Lago, the Stranger
makes a mockery of capitalism and usurps the Invisible Hand of avarice and
duplicity. He enjoys watching the merchants laugh at each other's misfortune as he strips each store of its prized goods and commandeers the Belding Hotel. The Stranger disrupts not only the financial but the political institutions of Lago as well, installing Mordecai as the new sheriff and mayor.
Morgan Allen, with the assistance of Callie, tries to ambush the Stranger but
fails, destroying a portion of the hotel instead. The Stranger tests Belding's
character by taking over the remainder of the hotel and abducting his wife.
Again, as he did on the evening of Duncan's murder, Belding remains frozen
and refuses to take a moral stand. He allows the Stranger to go upstairs with
his wife without any show of resistance or outrage. If Belding had shown
any concern or made a token effort to stop the Stranger from ravishing his
wife, he and Lago would be spared, but he, like the preacher who offers
sanctuary to the hotel's patrons for an un-Christian-like fee, dooms Lago
with his lack of morality. The Stranger sleeps with Sarah and liberates her
from her husband, giving her the resolve to end her marriage and leave
Lago. The good woman, a female of conscience and principle, is made love
to and redeemed; Callie, the whore who uses her body to cajole and manipulate men, is raped and demeaned.

Using Mordecai as his proxy, the Stranger orders Lago to paint the
entire town red, "especially the church." The red paint is a sign that Duncan's blood still drips on every square inch of Lago, that the town will soon
be consumed by flames and overrun with locusts. The men killed during

Morgan Allen's abortive ambush (the Stranger shoots Allen, but allows him to escape so that he can rendezvous with the Bridges gang and aggravate their blood lust) are buried near Duncan's unmarked grave without any regret or sorrow. The people of Lago fail to respect or pay homage to the dead — they repeat the sin that has brought forth the Stranger. Sheriff Shaw says, without pity or compassion, "Don't mark the grave, ain't likely anyone's going to cry over them anyway." No one is loved, missed, or respected in Lago. The Stranger responds to this chilling lack of humanity and community by painting the word hell over Lago's sign with bright red paint. As the camera pans toward the foregrounded sign, the short-lived funeral party makes its way back to the town limits. We see them in the far distance, walking behind the sign — a sign that their ultimate destination, if they do not repent, is hell. Only Mordecai, contemplating Duncan's unmarked grave in the distance, is spared the foregrounded fate.

His preparatory work done, the Stranger rides into the hills to ensure that the Bridges gang is full of sufficient blood lust. He then returns to town to inspect his handiwork and organize the so-called Lago volunteer militia. Covered with splotches of red paint (a symbol for the blood they have collectively shed), the men of Lago climb to their rooftops, load their weapons, and timidly await the arrival of the Bridges gang. To their utter dismay, the Stranger mounts his horse and rides off into the distance, leaving Lago alone to meet its fate. The Stranger has no stomach for gratuitous torture and bloodshed; he lets Stacey and his two cohorts burn Lago and terrorize the population into submission. Night takes over. The locusts run wild, setting fire to the town, killing the wicked, and scourging the weak. After a sufficient amount of time, the Stranger returns to subdue the locusts and avenge Duncan's murder. Backlit by flames, the Stranger wields the same bullwhip that killed Duncan and uses it to torture and execute the two Carlin brothers. As the Stranger whips Cole to death, Eastwood cuts to the reactions of the townspeople, who slowly realize who the Stranger is (or at least what he represents) and the enormity of their sins. By executing the Bridges gang, the Stranger makes it known that no one is exempt, that evil is punished whether it be innate or chosen. As Stacey cries out for his clandestine adversary to come out into the open, we see the Stranger stride into the rear of the frame, the long lens rendering his form transparent and indistinct. Backlit again by flames, the Stranger assumes a supernatural aura — truly he is a creature of the elements and God's fury, a fiery presence in human form. He outdraws Stacey and ends his reign of terror. The curse is lifted. Lago is decimated, the wicked are killed (Mordecai shoots Belding) and the weak are reminded of their mortality and impending damnation if they do not rediscover faith and mercy.

The next morning, the Stranger rides out of Lago, reversing the route he took when he arrived. Again, the Stranger is the nexus of a cross-axis series of compound and passing tracking shots. He gives Sarah his blessing but glares at the other bruised and bleeding survivors of the previous night's Armageddon with a hard, cautionary stare. Everyone is wrapped up in bandages — no one is without a mark of some kind to remind them of the Lord's judgment and their tentative deliverance. Exiting through the graveyard, the Stranger pauses as Mordecai finishes Duncan's headstone. Mordecai peers into the Stranger's eyes and asks, "I never did know your name." With a celestial smile, the Stranger replies, "Yes you do." Is the Stranger Jim Duncan? Or is he Gabriel? Or is he Eastwood himself, bravely reshaping a persona into a moral force of divine proportions? The question remains unanswered as the Stranger returns to the void, vanishing the same way he appeared: a telephoto enigma, an archangel without a name.

Breezy, 1973

There's nothing in it to overshadow the people [Thompson and Hunter, p. 29].

Having directed himself in two films, Eastwood decided to stay behind the lens and direct a film that concentrated on character, rather than on mood or style. *Breezy*, Eastwood's second personal film, is a positive response to the sexual and emotional terrorism of *Play Misty for Me*. In *Breezy*, Eastwood plays with the generation gap of the early 1970s by pairing Frank Harmon (William Holden), a member of the establishment, with Breezy (Kay Lenz), a member of the counterculture. Frank is a divorced real estate salesman who lives alone; he tells Bob Henderson (Roger C. Carmel), his one close friend, "I don't think I know what loneliness is. If I ever did, I've forgotten it." Breezy is a cheerful teenage waif-drifter who loves humanity and lives a transient and guilt-free existence. Eastwood saw *Breezy* as "the story of a rejuvenation of a cynic, (Guerif, p. 98) and just as Dave is saved by Evelyn, Breezy frees Frank from his glum, self-imposed exile. Frank discovers, much to his surprise and consternation, that he has much more in common with Breezy than with his middle-aged peers. Eastwood felt he was too young to play Frank. He makes only two brief appearances in the film: as Eastwood the man and Eastwood the myth-icon. His first appearance is during a scene when Frank and Breezy are eating ice cream and strolling down a wharf. Leaning indolently against a wooden balustrade is Eastwood, idly watching the two go by. Eastwood makes his second cameo when Frank and Breezy enter a movie theater playing *High Plains Drifter*— we see a lobby poster of the Stranger glowering into the lens. By inserting a lobby poster for *High Plains Drifter* into the film, Eastwood pokes fun at his own persona for what it is: a fictional construction, an image to lure moviegoers into the theater. The real Eastwood is the unglamorous man in the crowd, not the fictional Eastwood Frank and Breezy go out of their way to see. Eastwood gives us the man and the myth.

Of all of Eastwood's films, *Breezy* is the most invisible and *dégagé*. Style is subordinate to dialogue and performance. The tight construction of *Play Misty for Me* and the widescreen visuals of *High Plains Drifter* are absent. *Breezy* has an immediate charm, but lacks a circular construction of narrative and *High Plains Drifter*'s balance of mise-en-scène and montage. *Breezy* is just that: a gentle, unassuming character study and love story that degenerates into melodrama, even as it tries to be as low-key as possible.

Breezy has much in common with *Play Misty for Me*. Both are about relationships and how tenuous and difficult they are to establish and maintain. Both films are set in California (*Breezy* takes place in Los Angeles) and have beach scenes that are photographed with telescopic lenses. Both feature male protagonists who prefer to be aloof and single, but give up their privacy and philandering when they encounter a woman whose will and personality is stronger than their own. Breezy disrupts Frank's private life and violates his home, but she does so playfully, with none of the menace or misunderstanding that characterizes Dave and Evelyn's relationship. Breezy's invasion of Frank's residence and consciousness is a welcome intrusion: she does not force herself on Frank and does not need to be sacrificed so that he can overcome his fear of love and commitment. Both Frank and Breezy have grown tired of their social and cultural circles: Breezy, an orphan, seeks love, kindness, and honesty, something the counterculture devalues. She sees nothing wrong in spending the night with a stranger for food and shelter, but underneath the surface we sense her growing disenchantment with being a hippie. Breezy is not a synecdoche for the counterculture. She is merely a participant, and a skeptical one at that. Frank is the same way. He is dissatisfied with his own bourgeoisie social set: the cocktail lounges and dinner parties populated by lawyers, businessmen, and on the make divorcees. Worn out by a rancorous divorce, Frank, as with his peers, has lost his passion for life. As he sees it, "nobody matures, they just grow tired." Frank has allowed himself to grow very drowsy.

Frank and Breezy's initial meeting has none of the predatory elements of *Play Misty for Me*. Frank's consciousness does not conjure Evelyn out of the dark; Breezy appears in broad daylight, wondering if Frank can give her a ride to the valley, a favor he begrudgingly grants. Right from the start,

Free from the pressures of having to be the star of *Breezy*, Eastwood stays behind the camera and chats with his leading lady, Kay Lenz.

Breezy exhibits a remarkable talent for discerning what goes on inside Frank's head. Frank's conversations with his peers lack any honesty or inspiration; they seem rehearsed, as if everyone is following a script. Breezy is unaffected. She turns everyday conversations into heartfelt philosophical discussions. Breezy disorients Frank with ingenious rejoinders and perceptive replies. For a woman her age, she has remarkable wit and wisdom. It takes a while for Breezy to persuade Frank that she actually enjoys his company. When Breezy says with obvious sincerity, "I really like talking with you," Frank replies, "You certainly know how to shovel it, don't you?" to which Breezy responds, "Wow, if you don't have the most suspicious, rancid mind." Breezy knows she has met a kindred spirit. It takes Frank a lot longer to realize that he has no ordinary hippie in his car. He has a woman who is wiser and more accepting than females twice her age.

As Breezy begins to visit Frank on a regular basis, Frank's resistance to her and his need for privacy diminishes. Frank's home is the nexus of his existence. Like Dave Garver, Frank prefers to be alone and isolated. The glass picture windows and sliding doors that constitute Frank's home allow him to separate himself from the outside world. When Breezy visits his home, forcing him to change his monastic lifestyle, the windows seem transparent and confining — the home suddenly becomes a glass prison, a box that anyone can see through, but that Frank cannot see out of. He offers Breezy an apple, a sign that he courts temptation and the end of his anti-Eden. Breezy moves her body around the living room, chewing contentedly on the apple, turning on the stereo, and wondering aloud why Frank doesn't take advantage of his elegant fireplace (Frank will eventually light a fire, a sign that Breezy has brought warmth and comfort to his life and home). Frank does not mind her interruptions. He sits behind his desk and feigns interest in his work, unsure of his feelings or desires. Breezy asks to use the shower and without any embarrassment or concern takes off her clothes. Eastwood does not objectify Kay Lenz's body. Her breasts and behind do not have an exclusive, objective life of their own. Even when Eastwood photographs Lenz's entire body, he draws us toward her face, the source of many an infectious smile. *Breezy* stresses the private over the pornographic: as with *Play Misty for Me*, Eastwood does not segment the female body; he opts for intimacy instead. *Breezy* also shows us that people from different cultural backgrounds can have the same adult attitudes toward sex and nudity. Frank is not offended or surprised by Breezy's willingness to strip in front of him. He takes it in stride as much as she does.

What Breezy cannot take in stride is Frank's separation of love and sex. For her, they are interdependent, but for Frank sex has become a routine, a pattern much like Dave's in *Play Misty for Me*. Breezy has had many lovers, but she can still look at Frank and say, "I never woke up in the morning and had to look at someone who made me sorry I was there. But I bet you have." Frank has indeed: Breezy reminds us of our first glimpse of Frank in the film, sheepishly escorting an embarrassed one-night stand out of his home. Breezy continues to visit Frank, convinced that he is her soul mate, regardless of his age or misgivings. Even after he takes Breezy to the ocean and admits he is falling in love with her, Frank does not have the courage to sleep with her until she gently seduces him after he returns from a party. Eastwood sees their lovemaking as private; the camera does not intrude. Breezy encourages Frank to go out into public and to frolic in the park, but he still worries about the social stigma of being with a 19 year old. When he muses, "Maybe sometimes it's better to be alone," Breezy responds, "Sure, just like if you have something incurable, it's better to be dead." Frank eventually comes to his senses and realizes that his time with Breezy is precious, even if it may be limited.

The main strength of *Breezy* is its two lead characters and how they interact. William Holden and Kay Lenz achieve a warm and infectious chemistry without being mawkish or heavy-handed. Their relationship is poignant, but the plot contrivances that bring it into fruition are not. The injured dog, Sir Love-a-Lot, that Breezy begs Frank to help, is a conventional sop to the audience, as is a hackneyed hospital confession. Unlike *High Plains Drifter*, *Breezy* lacks a balanced narrative and a quid pro quo of mise-en-scène and montage — its acting and themes are not complemented by the visuals or the music. Michael LeGrand's score and title song push the film into melodramatic excess, even as the naturalistic acting and the location shooting pull it in the opposite direction. *Breezy* proved that Eastwood could make a credible film without being its star, but it also proved that he would continue to make passable films until he developed a tighter aesthetic style that straddled naturalism and expressionism. This struggle would continue with *The Eiger Sanction*, a film with an entirely different set of problems.

The Eiger Sanction, 1975

I will never do anything like that again — just too damn dangerous. Even though I had practiced for weeks, it was still terrifying. I don't see how you can ever get used to dangling on the end of a rope, thousands of feet above nothing, held up by a man you hardly know. And when a glacier moves with that terrible groan, that's terrifying. One of the British guys said I'd get used to it. I never did [Thompson, p. 48].

The Eiger Sanction is Eastwood's ode to location work. From Monument Valley to Switzerland, the film is an outdoor odyssey, a test of Eastwood's physical endurance and dexterity. Obsessed with shooting a feature film on an actual mountainside, Eastwood approached the film not as an aesthetic, but a technical challenge:

> I didn't totally visualize *The Eiger Sanction*. It was difficult to place the way the story should be told — whether to go completely outlandish like James Bond, or to go for the middle line ... I got wrapped up in wanting to be the first guy to shoot totally on the side of a mountain, not papier-mâché rocks — outside of the documentaries, that is. We did everything, dangling 2,000 feet over the first splatter [Thompson and Hunter, p. 29].

Eastwood spent months rehearsing in Yosemite National Park so that a double would not be required for the rigorous climbing sequences. David Knowles, a British stunt man and alpinist, was killed right in front of Eastwood during the shoot. By taking a film crew up the face of the Eiger, Eastwood came too close to the location. The hand-held shots that make up most of the climbing footage do not mesh into a visually coherent climax and detract from the rest of the film. Eastwood creates the same phenomenological illusion of time and space that he achieves during the Monterey Jazz Festival scene in *Play Misty for Me*, but the climbing sequence interrupts the film's narrative, neutralizes the role of the protagonist, Jonathon Hemlock (Clint Eastwood), and compromises the grim resolution of the film. Eastwood's reduced coverage of Dave Garver during the Monterey Jazz Festival sequence in *Play Misty for Me* serves as a narrative break and a refreshing experiment in style and phenomenology. The same reduction of Hemlock in *The Eiger Sanction* diminishes our identification with him and the anxiety of his climb. The Eiger footage is too realistic. Eastwood's laudable desire to shoot everything on location is a testament to his creative prowess and courage, but it derails *The Eiger Sanction* and brings it to an unsatisfying climax. We identify too closely with Eastwood the actor persevering against the elements, not with Eastwood's character, Jonathon Hemlock. It is as if *The Eiger Sanction* turned into a documentary about mountain climbing. The last 20 minutes are breathtaking, but incidental to the film's narrative. As with *Breezy*, Eastwood let his enthusiasm for one element overwhelm the others. If a myopic focus on character prevented *Breezy* from being more than an offbeat *Love Story*, a mania for location shooting keeps *The Eiger Sanction* from being more than a revisionist James Bond film. Without a balance of form and a circular narrative structure, Eastwood does not give his persona and themes the coverage they deserve. His second phase would rectify — and complicate — this problem.

Although it is handicapped by over-extensive location work, *The Eiger Sanction* is still a worthwhile reduction of the James Bond myth. During the 1960s, Bond and the Man with No Name had much in common — both were macho icons who killed without compunction. Having confronted No Name with the apocalyptic *High Plains Drifter*, Eastwood confronted Bond by taking on the guise of Hemlock. Eastwood subverts Bond's cool demeanor by introducing his own kind of cool to the spy genre: a tenuous cool that hides a seething discontent. As portrayed in Trevanian's source novel, Hemlock is an emotionless husk, a man who cannot find emotional or erotic fulfillment (unlike the literary character, Eastwood's Hemlock is not sexually dysfunctional). Eastwood's Hemlock is more flexible and forgiving. He does not reject Jemima Brown (Vonetta McGee), despite the fact that she is a CII operative who has been assigned to seduce him into taking another assignment (the fact that Jemima is black should dispel any complaints that Eastwood is not fond of diversity — Hemlock and Brown's sensual and adult relationship is one of the chief pleasures of the film). However charming and understanding he may be with Jemima, Hemlock is still a ruthless antihero who personifies the amorality of the Cold War and the people who perpetuate it for their own selfish ends.

The Eiger Sanction owes more to *The Spy Who Came in from the Cold* (Martin Ritt, 1965) than the chic James Bond, Matt Helm, and Our Man Flint films churned out in the mid to late 1960s. Hemlock is no Bond. He may be suave and sophisticated, but his temperament is closer to Richard Burton's in *The Spy Who Came in from the Cold* than Sean Connery's in *From Russia with Love* (1963, Terence Young) or *Goldfinger* (1964, Guy Hamilton): both are burned out, double-crossed, and spiritually desiccated. When Jemima asks Hemlock why he retired from CII, a clandestine intelligence agency run by Dragon (Thayer David), a melanin-impoverished ex-Nazi, Hemlock responds: "You know what purposes these sanctions (assassinations) serve? Absolutely none at all ... I quit because of mathematics. Assassins who stay around get assassinated." Hemlock has only three things in life he holds dear: art, climbing, and his former relationship with CII agents Ben Bowman (George Kennedy) and Miles Mellough (Jack Cassidy). CII takes advantage of all three to pressure Hemlock into accepting one last sanction, an assignment that forces him to see how monstrous he has truly become.

Throughout the first three-quarters of *The Eiger Sanction*, we are presented with a somewhat sympathetic Hemlock. He is blackmailed by CII, deceived by Jemima, threatened by Miles (who has become Hemlock's archfoe), and betrayed by Ben, his climbing coach and trainer. When he arrives in Switzerland to climb the Eiger, Hemlock has no way of knowing who the enemy spy is among his three climbing partners, Freytag (Reiner Schoene),

Clint Eastwood's determination to shoot the climax of *The Eiger Sanction* on an actual mountain side yielded an impressive array of shots, but compromised the film as a whole.

Meyer (Michael Grimm), and Montaigne (Jean-Pierre Bernard). He can only bide his time and hope that his unknown adversary does not fray his lines or kill him in his sleep. Once on the mountain, however, we begin to wonder: is Hemlock a victim of circumstance or a cold-blooded killer with no scruples? All of the climbers lose their footing and die, except for Hemlock, who, ironically enough, is saved by Ben, his actual quarry. Does Hemlock watch helplessly as his team plummets to their death, or does he intentionally kill all three, making it look like a tragic accident? Fraught with fear and paranoia, does Hemlock overreact and kill everyone to ensure his own survival and the completion of his assignment? Jemima gives voice to our doubts when she asks Hemlock, "You didn't really sanction all three of them, did you?" Hemlock does not answer. He is either disgusted by the mere introduction of the idea or he is astonished by his own lack of humanity. The myth of James Bond is deconstructed as we look into Hemlock's blue eyes and see nothing but an ambivalent void.

With *The Eiger Sanction*, Eastwood uncovers the moral decrepitude of international espionage, exposing it as a meaningless crap game that taints all of its participants (*Firefox*, Eastwood's second espionage film, has the same critical view of the Cold War). He also introduces us to his vision of the modern world — a world poisoned by duplicity, institutional corruption, and amoral one-upmanship. Hemlock is Eastwood's least sympathetic antihero, an irredeemable man who cannot fathom how evil he truly is. If Eastwood had concentrated on Hemlock and foregrounded him instead of the Eiger, *The Eiger Sanction* could have been a stinging indictment of the Bond myth and mentality. Instead, *The Eiger Sanction* is a curiosity, a demonstration of Eastwood's skill at shooting on location and modifying his persona to suit other genres. With *The Outlaw Josey Wales*, Eastwood would be much more fortunate.

4

Second Phase, 1976–1985

When you reach out and try something different, and the audience doesn't go for it, it makes you wonder what the hell is the matter. You've got to be philosophical about that. You can't think: "Well, I'll just do genre flicks now. If they want killing, I'll just kill. If they want mayhem, I'll out-mayhem myself." If you succumb to that, you become a self-parody. And I'm not interested in that [Breskin, p. 68].

I can't just do — regardless of some fans — the mysterious kind of character who has everything under control. That's fine to play, but I've done it a lot. I'll do it again, probably, but I have to broaden the scope [Thomson, p. 66].

After experimenting with form (*Play Misty for Me* and *High Plains Drifter*: harmony of character, milieu and theme; visuals=theme; *Breezy*: character over milieu, visuals incidental to theme; *The Eiger Sanction*: milieu over character, visuals overwhelm theme), establishing a mythic (*High Plains Drifter*) and modern (*The Eiger Sanction*) universe, and investigating the beauty and madness of male-female relationships (*Play Misty for Me*, *Breezy*), Eastwood launched into his second phase, one underscored but also undermined by the iconic presence of Dirty Harry and the Man with No Name.

With his second phase, Eastwood was ready to redeem his persona and to alleviate the hostility of *High Plains Drifter* and *The Eiger Sanction*. *The Outlaw Josey Wales* heals the Man with No Name by giving him a family, a traumatic past, and a higher purpose; *The Gauntlet* heals Dirty Harry (in the guise of Ben Shockley) and allows him to outmaneuver the city and its corrupt institutions and officials; *Bronco Billy* heals the cloistered artist and helps him to coexist with modern America; *Firefox*— the only mediocre film of the lot — heals the most egregious of Eastwood's antiheroes — the spy — by merging him with technology and lifting him into the heavens. *The Outlaw Josey Wales, The Gauntlet, Bronco Billy*, and *Firefox* form a redemption cycle, a clever and heartfelt reappraisal of the Dollars trilogy and *Dirty Harry*. In all four films, Eastwood gives his persona more nuance and meaning by pairing it with women of superior intelligence (*The Gauntlet, Bronco Billy*) and/or a small community or surrogate family that forces him to be selfless and magnanimous (*The Outlaw Josey Wales, Bronco Billy*). Except for *Firefox*, which redeems Mitchell Gant by stripping him of his conscience, the redemption cycle rejects the isolation and alienation of *High Plains Drifter* and *The Eiger Sanction*, revealing instead the human within the myth, the man inside the icon. *The Outlaw Josey Wales, The Gauntlet, Bronco Billy*, and *Firefox* serve as archetypal therapy: Eastwood forces his persona to drop his guard, admit his faults, and to let go of the seething anger and resentment that keeps him from being a well-adjusted member of society.

After the redemption cycle, Eastwood found himself in a difficult position: retain his persona as the sole signifier of his work or create a cinema independent of the Man with No Name and Dirty Harry. Eastwood tried the latter with *Honkytonk Man*, the first of his films to confront mortality and the inevitability of death, but it failed to attract moviegoers — his audience could not accept him as a comic and tragic artist coming to terms with the realities and disappointments of existence. Unlike Eastwood, the American public did not want the Man with No Name and Dirty Harry to be healed of their psychic wounds. To placate the public, Eastwood directed *Sudden Impact* and *Pale Rider*, an anticlimactic postscript to *High Plains Drifter* and the redemption cycle. In both, Eastwood tries to distance himself from his persona by reducing it to an iconic shell. Unlike *High Plains Drifter*, which makes the Stranger so ubiquitous that he seems invisible, *Sudden Impact* and *Pale Rider* make Dirty Harry and No Name so indistinct and vague, they seem to be abstractions without substance. There is no redemption, no sense of release or catharsis in *Sudden Impact* and *Pale Rider*— only weariness and emptiness.

Eastwood's second phase demonstrates the advantages and disadvantages of making his persona the focal point of his cinema. Increasingly, Eastwood needed to go beyond the Man with No Name and Dirty Harry and formalize a cinema in which his presence could be expected, but not essential. Not till *Bird*; *White Hunter, Black Heart*; *A Perfect World*; and *The Bridges of Madison County* (notwithstanding *Breezy*) would Eastwood be able to make a film without having to be its *raison d'être*; only then could he go beyond his persona and revolutionize his cinema.

The Outlaw
Josey Wales, 1976

> You can only do so much with the solitary hero. When you give
> him family ties, you give him a new dimension, and this creates
> conflicts that enrich the story [Plaza, p. 76].

During his first phase as a filmmaker, Eastwood proved that he had a
catholic understanding of his persona and the intricacies of film form.
High Plains Drifter, with its purity of vision and form, was a harbinger of
Eastwood's emerging style. With *The Outlaw Josey Wales*, Eastwood stan-
dardizes his aesthetic into a definitive style. A picaresque and classical
response to *High Plains Drifter*, *The Outlaw Josey Wales* is more inspired by
John Ford (*Stagecoach* [1939], *My Darling Clementine* [1946], *The Searchers*
[1956]) and Howard Hawks (*Red River*, *Rio Bravo* [1959]), than by Sergio
Leone. *The Outlaw Josey Wales* is not a Western allegory of sin and salvation. It is a Western epic of rage and redemption. The film displays Eastwood's love of location shooting and backlighting, which is integrated
seamlessly into the narrative to suggest Josey Wales' (Clint Eastwood) psychological state:

> I wanted to backlight the whole movie ... It's very easy to do if
> you shoot in the fall. It's the best time to shoot a western: the sun
> stays low and you've got cross-light, it's not overhead and flat all
> the time. I love that cross-lighting ... Especially for the opening
> montage of the war, I didn't want any sunlight. It gives a much
> more somber effect. The first part of the film showed a kind of
> idyllic light; then all of a sudden it gets to a much more somber
> tone. Then it gradually gets to a nicer tone as his life gets better,
> when he gets to the ranch and starts winning — going from a loser
> to a winner. That was the way it was planned, and fortunately the
> head gaffer up above stayed with us [Plaza, p. 79].

The Outlaw Josey Wales has the right blend of mise-en-scène and montage,
character and milieu, space and expression, and spontaneity and structure.
It has a distinct rhythm and tone that stays constant, even as the mood of
each scene changes. Eastwood pairs Wales with a wide assortment of supporting characters and vignettes to give the film a Dickensian flair and his
performance added depth and resonance.

As with *The Eiger Sanction*, Eastwood did not originally intend to direct

The Outlaw Josey Wales. Philip Kaufman (*The Right Stuff* [1983], *The Unbearable Lightness of Being* [1988]) was hired to direct the film, but his conception of Wales contrasted too much with Eastwood's. Kaufman wanted to demystify the Man with No Name, something Eastwood could not tolerate. After the extreme iconography of *High Plains Drifter*, Eastwood knew it was time to play the middle of the spectrum: the legendary western hero, a man who takes on mythic proportions against his will. In *High Plains Drifter*, Eastwood takes the surreal qualities of No Name and magnifies them to gargantuan proportions. With *The Outlaw Josey Wales*, Eastwood brings No Name back to earth by giving him a past, a name, and a pretext for his nomadic, solitary existence. Instead of intensifying No Name's enigmatic nature, Eastwood asks us to relate to and sympathize with Wales, a simple homesteader who is torn from his Edenic home and hurtled into the maelstrom of the Civil War. Stripped of everything but his two pistols and his unrequited rage, Wales becomes a unwitting Messiah who leads a family of misfits and undesirables into the frontier to create a new Jerusalem. Like the Stranger, Wales is a servant of the Lord, but he does his work unwillingly and involuntarily. *The Outlaw Josey Wales* begins with a woodland and ends with a valley: in between is the great divide, a landscape of trial and tribulation through which Wales rides without hope of peace or forgiveness. Wales and the film cannot stop moving and changing location until Wales re-experiences the horrible images that open the film. When he does, his pistols lose their fire and a smile graces his face. As in *High Plains Drifter*, the past must be dealt with directly and penitentially before the present can be free of guilt or misery.

The opening of *The Outlaw Josey Wales* is a textbook example of an Eastwood exposition: it is lean, economical, and ruthlessly effective. Eastwood gives us a brief glimpse of Wales' home life and then mercilessly whisks it away. Tilling the soil, Wales is in sync with the earth and the verdant world around him. He looks at his son (played by Eastwood's own son, Kyle) with fraternal love and pride as his wife (Cissy Wellman) calls them for dinner. Bruce Surtees' cinematography captures the warm illumination of the sun and the promise of spring. That promise is broken by the arrival of Capt. Terrill (Bill McKinney) and his Red Legs, a bloodthirsty Union calvary regiment that murders Wales' family and burns his property to the ground. All that is dear to Wales is raped and butchered. His identity as a father, husband, farmer, and homesteader disappears. We see the massacre from Josey's perspective as he writhes on the ground — a succession of low-angle, hand-held, point of view shots that suggest panic and chaos. Wales hears his family cry out to him, but he cannot see them through the legs of horses and the burning remains of his household. Terrill strikes Wales in the eye with a sword, branding him with a Cain-like scar that serves as a permanent reminder of the massacre and his traumatic loss. Wales' wound is both physical and psychological; it is a mark that will curse and hound him. Wales collapses, the point of view shots of men shouting and pillaging overwhelming him and the montage. The disorientation, panic, and helplessness are too much — Wales loses consciousness and everything he holds dear.

Eastwood uses two dissolves to bring Wales (and the viewer) back to consciousness: an optical dissolve of the smoking ruins of Wales' property and a sound dissolve of Wales plaintively swinging an axe into the ground. Eastwood tastefully communicates to us that the Wales family is no more by cutting to a shot of Wales dragging a sack that opens and reveals the singed arm of his son. Wales pauses and tenderly places the arm back into the sack. Eastwood lets the axe and the gesture of placing the arm into the sack express Wales' shock and sorrow. We then hear another expressive sound as Wales hammers a makeshift cross into the ground, his features growing increasingly strained as the shovel forces the cross deeper into the soil. While reciting "ashes to ashes, dust to dust, the Lord gives and the Lord takes away," Wales lets go of his emotions and sobs uncontrollably, the weight of his body forcing the cross to the ground. Wales tries to accept the loss of his family and livelihood as the Lord's will, but he finds no solace in prayer. The only object to emerge unscathed from the wreckage of Wales' home is a pair of pistols. Wales builds his new identity from the ashes of the past. Consumed by rage, he loses his faith and grabs hold of a gun rather than the cross. The sound of the cross being hammered into the ground is replaced with the angry thunder of gunfire. As Wales empties chamber after chamber, his grip tightening and his aim improving, we see, contrapuntally, images of his charred household, unattended plow, and the graves of his wife and son. With each round he fires, Wales moves farther away from the cross that could not bear the weight of his sorrow — literally, the cross offers him no support. In *The Outlaw Josey Wales* and *Unforgiven* — the two films in which the Man with No Name is not an archangel — Eastwood relies on a central paradox: Wales and William Munny must lose or renounce their faith to become an agent of the Lord's will. The scene then cuts to Wales crouched beside the graves of his loved ones, rooted to the spot, unsure of what to do next. Wales' calling as a farmer comes to an end; his new life as a warrior and protector of the innocent is heralded by the entrance of Bloody Billy Anderson (John Russell) and his Confederate guerrillas. Wales joins them, setting up the front credit montage and Wales' transformation from everyman to legend, plowman to gunslinger.

The front credits are a transitional device, a temporal bridge that compresses the Civil War into a monochromatic two-minute montage. The war is represented by a continuous cavalry charge and a constant barrage of bullets and cannon fire. There is no time for recollection or thought — only soldiery and survival. The montage is shot entirely through a blue filter to suggest Wales' reduction in character and spirit. The colors and the promise of spring are lost. Wales sees nothing but a blue, hazy landscape, a violent world devoid of sunlight or color. Nothing changes but Wales' wardrobe and countenance, which gets increasingly stoic with each shot. As the front credits come to a finish, so does the war and the blue filter — Surtees restores full color, but uses a palette that is dominated by blues and grays to suggest the legacy of the war and Wales' refusal to accept its end.

For Wales, the past has been sublimated into the Civil War. He cannot surrender until he confronts Capt. Terrill and the memories that have left a scar down his face (in *Unforgiven*, Munny is also scarred by his past, but the wounds are spiritual rather than physical). Fletcher (John Vernon), Wales' erstwhile superior, reminds Wales that if he refuses to surrender, "they'll be coming after you Josey. There's nowhere you can go to be away from them." Wales knows that Fletcher is referring not only to the Union troops and bounty hunters who will torment him, but the repressed images of the past that he holds deep in his psyche. Wales stays behind in long shot, crouched in the same position he was in when Bloody Bill Anderson asked him to join the Confederate cause. Tormented and consumed by the past, Wales wants to keep the war alive so he can avoid dealing with his repressed memories. Given one last chance to formally surrender, Wales responds, "I reckon not" and spits a wad of tobacco, a phrase and a gesture Wales uses throughout the film to rebuff and disarm his opponents. The terse, emblematic "I reckon not" expresses Wales' defiant belief that "there ain't no forgetting." The spitting of tobacco gives Wales an edge during a gunfight (he spits seconds before he reaches for his pistols) and provides him with an outlet for his scorn and mordant sense of humor — when Jamie (Joseph Bottoms) asks Wales if they should bury the corpses of two hillbillies who tried to ambush him, Wales spits dismissively on their foreheads and remarks, "The hell with them fellows, worms got to eat too."

It does not take long for Wales to resume his war with the Union. Senator Lane (Frank Schofield) reneges on his promise to Fletcher that his men will be granted full amnesty — after surrendering their weapons and pledging allegiance to the United States, Wales' comrades are mowed down like the cattle in *Hud* (Martin Ritt, 1963). Wales responds by riding into the Union camp and fighting an entire regiment single-handedly. Eastwood makes excellent use of his mythical roots for this scene and many to come. Wales, whenever confronted by cruelty and injustice, goes into an impregnable trance and metamorphoses into an invincible force of reckoning. He is a vessel of the Lord, a Moses-like figure who protects those who are at the mercy of the United States government and the numerous rogues and highwaymen who roam the West. Despite being misanthropic and without faith (the Indians nickname him the Gray Rider), Wales cannot accept the suffering of others. He goes into action whenever he witnesses crimes against those who cannot defend themselves. Wales interrupts his siege of the Union camp when he discovers that Jamie (Timothy Bottoms), the sole Confederate survivor, is critically wounded, Jamie rekindles Wales' paternal instincts and reminds him of the blessings of companionship and family. Wales, however, does not feel comfortable being Jamie's steward; when Jamie finally succumbs to his gunshot wound, Wales fears that his very presence causes death and misery. Later in the film, he confesses that "before I get to liking someone, they ain't around long."

Hounded by Terrill's Red Legs and every drunken backwoodsman with a deer rifle, Wales crosses into Indian territory for sanctuary. The Indian Nations see Wales as an ally, a white man at odds with his own. There, Wales meets and befriends another man displaced and traumatized by the Civil War, Lone Watie (Chief Dan George), a proud Cherokee who lost his family along the Trail of Tears. Initially, the old chief hopes to capture Wales and collect the reward money, but when Wales sneaks up behind Watie and trusts him enough to take a nap, Watie grows fond of the Gray Rider. Consigned to a reservation, Watie feels dispossessed and forgotten. He identifies with Wales and his reluctance to let go of the past. Watie exhibits an instant desire to accompany Wales and abandon the reservation. Wales' group takes on a third member when he visits a nearby trading post to buy Watie a horse and encounters Little Moonlight (Geraldine Keans), another proud and stoic Native American. Little Moonlight is at the mercy of the trading post owner, who does not hesitate to abuse her for the smallest of infractions. As Wales approaches the trading post, the proprietor is beating Little Moonlight for dropping a bottle of whiskey. Eastwood cuts to a wrathful shot of Wales, watching from afar. Wales enters the post with visual and moral authority. Backlit by the afternoon sun, Wales throws open the door and stands at the threshold — his sudden entrance brings light and decency to the dark and nefarious structure. In the rear of the store are two Red Legs, too busy raping Little Moonlight to notice Wales. When they do, Wales is ready — he shoots them and spits a wad of tobacco on their foreheads as a final insult Little Moonlight follows his trail and eventually sets up camp with Wales and Lone Watie. Wales does not like being the leader of a group of nomads. He gets even more incensed when a 'mangy hound' stays close to their camp. Wales tries to scare it off with a salvo of tobacco juice, but eventually relents and grouses that the dog might as well join the group, being that, "Hell, everyone else is."

Wales' group turns into a full-fledged wagon train with the introduction of Grandma Sarah (Paula Trueman) and Laura Lee (Sondra Locke), two survivors of a convoy overrun by Comancheros. Once again, Wales is forced to take action, despite his reluctance to do so. He appears as a lone, backlit figure on the horizon, his mythic scope magnified by the landscape. Wales' confrontation with the Comancheros is the climax of his role as a divinely inspired savior and warrior — he takes complete control of the frame and kills nearly two dozen men. By rescuing Grandma Sarah and Laura Lee, Wales' role changes. He becomes a wagon master and a shepherd. His flight becomes a pilgrimage to the Crooked River Ranch, the former home of Sarah's deceased son. Because her son died at the hands of Confederate guerrillas, Sarah takes an instant dislike to Wales despite her debt to him. Sarah cannot forgive Wales or forget the bloodshed and animosity of the Civil War. Her refusal to forego the past resembles Wales' struggle; both have to overcome their loss if they want to live without misery and despair. Jamie reawakens Wales' dormant paternalistic instincts; Lone Watie and Little Moonlight restore Wales' faith in fellowship and personal integrity. Sarah and Laura Lee help Wales revert to his former self and purge his demons. Wales has no choice but to change. The closer the wagon train comes to the Crooked River Ranch, the less indispensable he becomes. The Wales that magically vanquishes the Comancheros diminishes in importance as the wagon train nears its destination and metamorphoses into a settlement.

To reach the Crooked River Ranch, the wagon train must pass through Santa Rio, a defunct mining town. Wales strides into the Lost Lady Saloon, rings the spittoon with his tobacco, and performs a miracle — he brings whiskey to Kelly (Matt Clark), Rose (Joyce Jameson), and the other remaining citizens of Santa Rio. As Grandma Sarah socializes with some of her son's former associates, Wales sits in a faraway corner, alienated and uncomfortable. He is almost relieved when a bounty hunter enters the saloon and refers to him by name. Wales gives the man ample opportunity to leave, but the bounty hunter refuses to do so, forcing Wales to fire in self defense. With this unnecessary murder, Wales' role as a divinely inspired gunslinger-warrior-messiah fades. His encounter with the bounty hunter has none of the mythic overtones of the Comanchero confrontation. Wales is no longer the master of the horizon, backlit by the sun — in the saloon he is squeezed into a dark, spot-lit corner. Wales does not perform his customary ritual (speak, spit, shoot), but instead draws his gun with a heavy heart and fires. No one benefits from the needless death of the bounty hunter. Wales' legendary status becomes an albatross. Instead of being a guardian and benefactor, Wales becomes a liability, a magnet that attracts strife and misfortune.

Wales loses his identity as a nomadic warrior (the archetype for the Man with No Name) when the wagon train reaches the Crooked River Ranch, which is nestled in the rear of a spacious and beautiful valley. Bruce Surtees uses autumnal colors and an abundance of sunlight to suggest the Edenic qualities of the homestead and its surroundings. Although nature predominates in *The Outlaw Josey Wales*, it is chiefly foregrounded before the opening massacre and after the wagon train has reached the valley. Eastwood and Surtees do this to suggest the revitalization of Wales and his return to faith and domesticity. Throughout his journey, Wales is too withdrawn to appreciate the beauty of nature. When he tarries at the Crooked River Ranch, Wales re-experiences nature and the horrible memories that have scarred him.

Although the ranch is deserted, Wales approaches it with caution. He enters the abandoned property first, swinging the door open with the same vigilance and spatial authority he wielded at the trading post. With the journey completed, however, Wales' role as leader passes to Sarah, a matriarch who turns the neglected property into an organized and productive household. The camera does not stay with Wales, but pans with Sarah as she sets up house immediately. Wales prepares to spit on the floor, but is forced by Sarah to swallow his own tobacco juice, a sign of his diminished role. As he did in the Lost Lady Saloon, Wales keeps his distance, sitting several hundred yards away from the ranch as Sarah, Lone Watie, Little Moonlight, and the left-over patrons of the Lost Lady Saloon restore and rebuild the ranch. Sound, so important to the opening of *The Outlaw Josey Wales*, returns to bring back the past and to form an inversive circle with the beginning of the film. The rhythm of work (Little Moonlight chopping wood, Sarah beating a rug, the men mending a fence) reminds Wales of the axe and the shovel, triggering the chaotic point of view shots of the opening massacre and burial. We see a huge close-up of Wales' eyes as shots of his burning homestead and the cries of his family echo in his head. Because Wales has been in perpetual motion since the opening credit montage, he has denied the past. Now, forced to recline and watch rather than move or act, Wales re-experiences the past in painful flashes of sound and image. Wales' first encounter with his past is cut short by the sudden appearance of Laura Lee, who embodies innocence and youth, despite the fact that she was nearly raped by a band of Comancheros. Both Wales and Laura are withdrawn and alienated from others, but while Wales is bitter and angry, Laura is idealistic and eager for erotic and romantic experience.

Wales' redemption and his relationship with Laura are postponed by Ten Bears (Will Sampson), a Comanche chief who threatens the survival of the Crooked River Ranch. Wales leaves the ranch, thinking that his time has come. Laura Lee calls out to him as he rides out of the valley, her cry similar to that of his wife's earlier in the film — Wales hesitates, but refuses to turn around and acknowledge the promise of the future or the pain of the past. He chooses to ride toward adversity and oblivion. Wales assumes the bearing of a warrior prepared for battle, but his confrontation with Ten

Bears lacks the omniscience and spatial mastery of the Comanchero scene. Wales does not dominate the frame as he rides toward Ten Bears and his warriors. Surtees does not backlight Wales with the same intensity — the illumination comes from overhead rather than behind. Eastwood cross-cuts between progressive shots of Ten Bears and Wales riding toward the lens to generate suspense and stress how outnumbered and vulnerable Wales is, no matter how formidable he may be with his pistols. Both Wales and Ten Bears anticipate death — while Ten Bears wears a painted death mask to prepare for mortal combat, Wales sucks on his tobacco, spitting it in front of Ten Bears to inform him that he is a man to be respected and reckoned with. When Ten Bears learns that Wales is the Gray Rider, he tells him he may go in peace. Wales refuses:

> I came here to die with you or live with you. Dying ain't so hard for men like you and me. It's living that's hard when all you've ever cared about has been butchered or raped. Governments don't live together, people live together. With governments you don't always get a fair word or a fair fight. Well I've come here to give you either one or get either one from you. I came here like this so you know my word of death is true and that my word of life is then true. The bear lives here, the wolf, the antelope, the Comanche. So will we.

Ten Bears responds with:

> It is sad that governments are chiefed by the devil tongues. There is iron in your words of death for all Comanche to see — and so there is iron in your words of life. No signed paper can hold the iron, it must come from men. The words of Ten Bears carry the same iron of life and death. It is good that warriors such as we meet in the struggle of life ... or death. It shall be life.

Wales enters a blood pact with Ten Bears, rejecting the common law tradition of his own culture. Ten Bears consecrates the pact by intoning, "So will it be." Wales replies, "I reckon so," rather than "I reckon not," a sign of his transition from a man of violence to a man of peace. Formerly a warrior, Wales becomes a peacemaker: the difference between "so" and "not" being equal to the difference between life and death, the past and the future. With its racial and sexual equality, *The Outlaw Josey Wales* is an argument for diversity and a culture built on human rather than legal principles. A populist film, *The Outlaw Josey Wales* celebrates the American spirit and the melting pot, ethnic foundations of our culture. Throughout the film, Wales encounters carpetbaggers, merchants, and opportunists who represent the limitations of capitalism and how it perverts rather than preserves a society based upon brotherhood and equality. Grandma Sarah's ranch serves as a Utopian retreat, a place where even Wales can find solace and a sense of purpose. With the creation of the Crooked River Ranch community, true civilization comes into being — not the ramshackle silver and cattle towns that impede its progress.

After safeguarding the Crooked River Ranch and serving as a liaison between the Comanches and the settlers, Wales makes a tentative effort to become part of the community. Wales no longer watches from afar, but he cannot join the revelry, preferring to brand cattle and watch from behind a fence as the jubilant community sings and dances. He is brought out of his shell by Laura, who asks if he would like to hear a song. As a reminder of the importance of Jamie in kindling Wales' redemption (he would have been killing Union soldiers ad infinitum if Jamie had not crossed his path), Wales requests Jamie's favorite song, 'The Rose of Alabama'. He tries to waltz with Laura, but his dancing proves to be nowhere near as graceful as his marksmanship. Later that evening, Laura Lee makes love to Wales. (In many of Eastwood's films, most notably *Play Misty for Me*, *Breezy*, and *Sudden Impact*, the woman instigates sexual contact — the man responds, rather than acts; sexuality is a force men dread and dodge because it requires intimacy and a loss of self-control.) Laura's sexual advances push Wales closer to his past and the trauma he has repressed. He dreams of the massacre and wakes up next to Laura with a start, a thunderclap coinciding with the cries of his son. While shepherding the wagon train or representing the interests of the Crooked River Ranch, Wales exhibits bravery and valor, but when it comes to his own needs and desires Wales lacks the resolve to confront himself. Wales cannot free himself from the scourge of the past until he confronts his nemesis, Capt. Terrill. The purity of spirit he shares with Ten Bears cannot be applied to his own affairs. Wales believes that his very being threatens the ranch — he decides to leave early in the morning without having to say farewell to his surrogate family, but is discovered by Lone Watie, who quietly laments his departure. Sick with regret and shame, Wales remarks, "Sometimes trouble just follows a man."

What Wales does not realize is that he can no longer run. Before he can leave the valley, Wales is blocked by Capt. Terrill and his Red Legs. Surtees reinserts the blue-gray filter over the scene to remind us of the link between Wales and his nemesis, and Wales' monochromatic obsession with the Civil War. Throughout *The Outlaw Josey Wales*, Wales has come to the rescue of those unable to defend themselves. Now Wales, who has lost the power to kill two dozen men single-handedly, is backed up by Grandma Sarah and the Crooked River Ranch community. Sarah's willingness to forgive Wales for his 'sins' energizes him and gives him the strength to confront Terrill and

the bloody harvest of the past. Eastwood cuts to a close-up of Wales smil-
ing as Sarah, Lone Watie, Laura Lee, and Little Moonlight raise their rifles
and pledge their support. The blue-gray filter lifts as Wales spits for the
final time and unloads, but as a reminder that he is no longer the invincible Gray Rider, Wales is shot and falls from his horse. Wales does not kill a
majority of the Red Legs — his newfound family does, especially Laura Lee,
who kills an impressive number of Red Legs.

With his surrogate family in charge, Wales can concentrate on Terrill,
the living embodiment of his past. Wales chases Terrill on horseback, trying
to intercept and come face to face with the images and sounds that have been
beguiling him since Terrill stigmatized him with his sword. Their chase ends
at an abandoned station, a clear stand-in for Wales' deserted homestead.
Wales corners Terrill and walks toward him slowly, unloading his past by
firing the empty chambers of his pistols. Wales fires one empty chamber after
another, triggering the past with a flurry of images and sounds. Eastwood uses
montage to extend time and the revelation Wales experiences while clicking
his guns. The clicks of empty pistols invert the opening montage when Wales
fired countless rounds in anger and despair — the lack of ammunition in the
climax indicates Wales' willingness to confront and accept the past. Wales
does not need to shoot Terrill; all he has to do is peer into Terrill's eyes and
know that the hatred inside them no longer exists in his own. The images and
sounds of the past wane as Wales reaches the last empty chamber. The spell
is lifted. Having overcome his past, Wales loses his blood lust and wanderlust and smiles with relief. As a final, Biblical gesture, Wales prevents Terrill
from drawing his sword, guiding his hand so that the saber that scourged
Wales is embedded into Terrill's chest by his own hand.

With Terrill dead, Wales has no purpose nor destination. He returns
to Santa Rio, where he encounters Fletcher, who, like Deke Thornton
(Robert Ryan) in *The Wild Bunch*, has been forced to pursue Wales against
his will. Fletcher, weary of the Civil War and its ruinous legacy, is willing to
accept an apocryphal story from the patrons of the Lost Lady Saloon that
Wales has fled to Mexico the moment Wales walks into the saloon. Wales
follows Fletcher outside to the center of town — a suitable place for a climactic showdown — but neither he nor Fletcher want to perpetuate the cycle
of violence that has marred their lives. Frazzled by his gunshot wound,
Wales pretends that he does not know Fletcher and asks him what he will
do once he tracks down Wales in Mexico. Fletcher watches the blood drip
from Wales' gunshot wound and replies, "I think I'll try to tell him the war
is over." Wales' wound is an irreversible sign that he is no longer the Gray
Rider and God's emissary, just a man tired of running and fighting. Wales
answers; "I reckon so (again, a rejection of "I reckon not," the phrase he uses
when Fletcher asks him to surrender), I guess we all died a little in that

Josey Wales (Clint Eastwood) confronts the past by pointing his pistols at the man who scarred his face and massacred his wife and son.

damn war." The final shot of the film is that of Wales riding into the sunset, a reversal of the backlighting that turned him into a mythic warrior and a temporary incarnation of the Man with No Name.

In *The Outlaw Josey Wales*, Eastwood guides the Man with No Name through a journey of self-discovery and transubstantiation. While *High Plains Drifter* takes the mythic elements of *A Fistful of Dollars* and *The Good, the Bad and the Ugly* and amplifies them to such a Gothic scale that Leone's influence is mitigated and nearly forgotten, *The Outlaw Josey Wales* examines the mythic, legendary, and human legacy of the Man with No Name with a character who embodies all three elements of Eastwood's persona. Wales begins the film as a humble tiller of the soil. With the loss of his family, homestead, and faith, Wales metamorphoses into the Gray Rider, a legendary outlaw who takes on mythic overtones to bring about God's will. Wales' divinely inspired task is to lead Grandma Sarah's wagon train to the promised land. Once there, Wales loses the Lord's afflatus and returns to his former self. By putting Eastwood's western persona through such a rigorous journey of divine and human revelation, *The Outlaw Josey Wales* resolves the dilemma that is the Man with No Name by revealing the man within the myth. In many ways, *The Outlaw Josey Wales* marks the logical end of Eastwood's western persona — his next two westerns, *Pale Rider* and *Unforgiven*, are essentially variations on *High Plains Drifter* and *The Outlaw Josey Wales*.

Pale Rider makes the Stranger irreproachable, while *Unforgiven* puts No Name through another Trinity-metastasis, only to reverse the redemptive gains of *The Outlaw Josey Wales* by questioning the moral and archetypal foundations of Eastwood's persona. Having successfully redeemed his mythical persona with *The Outlaw Josey Wales*, Eastwood attempted to do the same for his Dirty Harry persona in *The Gauntlet*.

The Gauntlet, 1977

It's in *The African Queen* tradition: a love-hate thing that turns out to be a *Love Story* [Thompson and Hunter, p. 32].

The Gauntlet is the modern equivalent of *The Outlaw Josey Wales*, a film that resolves the dilemma of Dirty Harry and the Eastwoodian antihero by pitting him against the impersonal conformity of modern America. Repeating the theme of redemption, *The Gauntlet* uses a style different from *The Outlaw Josey Wales* to emphasize the importance of romance and idealism in an age corrupted by cynicism and loneliness. Rather than use the widescreen to poeticize the frame, Eastwood uses the anamorphic lens to stress how the city of Phoenix and the pessimism of the modern world are visually compressing Ben Shockley (Clint Eastwood) and Gus Mally (Sondra Locke) and ensnaring them in a pressure cooker of desperation and misplaced animosity. Because nature has been superseded by highways, architecture, and technology, *The Gauntlet* does not have the lyrical grandeur and natural vistas of *The Outlaw Josey Wales*. Instead of being an extension of nature (*The Outlaw Josey Wales*), *The Gauntlet* is an extension of the modern world — a world devoid of landscapes or legends. To capture the absurd, dislocated quiddity of modern existence, Eastwood adopts a languid style that closely resembles the works of Michelangelo Antonioni. According to cinematographer Rexford Metz :

The look of *The Gauntlet* was to be as real as possible with the color enhanced to make it on the edge of being unbelievable, as there were 250,000 squib hits and no one died. The look was the result of polarizing filters, over-exposure and color attenuators [Plaza, p. 86].

In keeping with Antonioni and his phenomenological studies of Rome in *la notte* (1961) and *l'eclisse* (1962) and Los Angeles in *Zabriske Point* (1970),

Eastwood reduces the influence Ben has over his environment by making modern architecture and technology the dominant interest of the frame. Ben's decision to drive a fortified bus into the city of Phoenix and defy the combined firepower of the entire Phoenix police force is a quixotic attempt to reassert the individual over the city and its corrupt institutions. Josey Wales' journey is from anguish to acceptance; Ben's journey is from complacency to civil disobedience. Wales prevails as the lone figure on the horizon; Ben is dwarfed by the modern world until he hijacks a Greyhound and makes a beeline for City Hall.

Ben Shockley is a clever variation on Dirty Harry; a drunken, haggard, washed-up police officer who has reached a crossroads in his wretched and disappointing life. Our first glance of Ben is during the front credits as he straggles out of a seedy bar, greeting the dawn with an ungodly amount of liquor in his blood. When Ben reluctantly arrives to work, a pint of whiskey falls out of his car, shattering on the sidewalk and spilling its loathsome contents. Ben sits disconsolately, a look of weary disgust and defeat covering his features. Woozy and negligent in his appearance and attitude, Ben is spatially and spiritually displaced, a broken man without drive or conviction. He is chosen by corrupt police commissioner Blakelock (William Prince) to escort a witness from Las Vegas back to Phoenix precisely because of his negligence and lackluster job performance. (When Ben's former partner Josephson [Pat Hingle] frets over Ben's unkempt chin and collar, afraid it might imperil his meeting with Blakelock, Ben mumbles, "Fuck 'em".) Blakelock assumes that because Ben has surrendered to alcoholism and lassitude, he will not be clever enough to guarantee the witness' safety. Ben does not know that he is expendable. To survive, he must be redeemed.

That redemption comes in the form of Gus, the witness incarcerated in Las Vegas. Gus is a prostitute who slept with Blakelock and knows of his underworld connections. Much like Ben, Gus is at a crossroads. She is aging and losing the schoolgirl looks that have enabled her to make a living as a high-placed Las Vegas call girl. Like Breezy, Gus can detect the preoccupations and shortcomings of any man she encounters — she reads Ben instantly and quips, "Terrific, my life on the line and they send me an on the ropes bum." When Ben and Gus meet, neither treats the other with much respect or restraint. Both behave like broadly drawn stereotypes: Ben is the stock down on his luck cop with a cruel streak; Gus plays the role of the stock hooker with a locker room mouth and a chip on her shoulder. Her repeated attempts to warn Ben are compromised by her rude behavior and profane language. Ben assumes she is nothing but a lying whore — when she tries to persuade him that they are in peril, Ben backhands her against the wall of her cell. For the first half of the film, Ben is thickheaded and unresponsive. He ignores Gus and falls into the traps laid by Blakelock. Eastwood uses a small repertoire of bemused expressions and double takes to convey Ben's obtuseness and impassivity. Ben blinks his eyes in mock disbelief when Gus calls him a "big prick"— Ben does not heed or take Gus seriously until he wrestles with the fact that he is a dupe and a "big prick." Eastwood gives a dead pan performance until Ben is ready to apologize for his actions, lower his defenses, and reveal his true personality. Gus puts up as many defenses as Ben, and wastes no opportunity to degrade or belittle the man who is supposed to be her bodyguard.

Gus' efforts to warn Ben are in vain. Eastwood enjoys exposing Ben's stupidity and blind obedience and playing a character who is not as intelligent or resourceful as Dirty Harry. When Gus tells him the Mafia has laid odds that they will never arrive in Phoenix, Ben refuses to believe her, even when he sees the odds posted as 70 to 1. To get Gus to the airport, Ben has her gagged and bound and placed in an ambulance. Gus persists in her derogatory analysis of Ben, snapping, "You really get off on roughing up girls, don't you ... Big man, big forty-four caliber fruit." Ben does indeed gloat over his control, shamelessly displaying the macho mentality Gus accuses him of exhibiting. That mentality is permanently shaken when Ben's rental car explodes, a suspicious limousine pulls up from behind and shooting starts. Ben commandeers the ambulance, hands Gus his pistol, and orders her to shoot back. This action, the lending of the phallus, marks a transition in their mutually antagonistic relationship. Gus repels the limousine, then turns the gun on Ben, who tries to wrestle it out of her hand as they weave down the wrong side of the highway. Their tussle is a miniature battle of the sexes, with the woman intimidating the man with his own symbol of sexual dominance. Eastwood cuts briskly from hand-held medium close-ups to low-angle shots from beneath the steering wheel to displace the camera and suggest how self-destructive and counterproductive it is for Ben and Gus to assault each other. Ben manages to gain the upper hand, but openly confesses to Gus, "I damn sure don't know where to go." It is up to Gus to devise a plan of action; Ben's macho mentality turns out to be a defense mechanism that hides his insecurities and indecisiveness.

Gus directs Ben to her home, an unimpressive tract house, where she proceeds to behave like the meretricious hooker Ben assumed her to be. She tries to seduce him, confident that after a good performance, he will let her go. Ben sees through Gus' disingenuous plan and remarks, "I get the feeling your heart is not in your work." We now have the displeasure of seeing how low both Gus and Ben can get. Gus lashes out at Ben for his ignorance and unquestioning obedience. Ben tells Gus, "I just do what I'm told," to which she answers, "Yeah, well so does an imbecile." True to her description, Ben calls Blakelock and pays for his loyalty several minutes later when a throng of policemen appear and open fire on the premises, leveling it to the ground. That fusillade has an absurd, slapstick quality recalling the synchronized mayhem of a Mack Sennett or a Buster Keaton short. In *The Gauntlet*, Eastwood heightens violence to suggest the bizarre and disconnected anomie of modern America. In *The Outlaw Josey Wales*, violence has a moral and personal dimension — Wales' blood feud is never impersonal or random, but Biblical in its conception and resolution. In *The Gauntlet*, violence is mechanical, impersonal, and heedlessly destructive. Josey Wales stares into the eyes of his opponents and senses their strengths or weaknesses. His final confrontation with Terrill is a dynamic exchange of glances and memories. The nameless, faceless police officers and assassins that fire upon Ben and Gus are random beings, hidden by helicopters, rooftops, and sunglasses. Neither we nor Ben or Gus get to know the people who are ordered to kill them — they are as indistinguishable as the bare Southwestern terrain. Ben's whole reason for running the gauntlet and driving a bus through thousands of armed and impersonal cops is to restore humanity and morality to an alienated and hysterical world. By absorbing the firepower of the entire Phoenix police department, Ben and Gus purge the city of its faceless demons. They leave the film, alone and unharmed, as thousands of police officers mill around, newly conscious of how remote and impassive they have allowed themselves to become.

Blakelock sets up Ben every time he calls for backup. Be that as it may, Ben is responsible for the fusillade that decimates Gus' home. When the police arrive and order the occupants of the house to come outside and surrender, Gus locks herself in the bathroom and crawls through a hidden passageway. Ben knocks on the door — when he receives no answer, Ben shoots the lock out, giving the trigger-happy police a golden opportunity to open fire. Ben has to cower on the bathroom floor while gunfire perforates every square inch of the house. He manages to find Gus' secret tunnel seconds before Gus' home groans and collapses. Gus waits outside of the tunnel to see if Ben has enough sense to follow her to safety. With Gus in tow, Ben kidnaps a constable (Bill McKinney) and orders him to take them to the state line. Up to this point, Ben has been a dutiful lawman who does not question his orders or superiors. He does not separate himself from his badge. When he shows it to the constable, hoping to being taken seriously, the constable replies, "You think that little piece of tin proves anything? You could have gotten that from a box of Cracker Jacks." Ben's attempts to define himself as a cop are in vain — now that he is a fugitive and a renegade, his badge has no meaning. Until he defies orders, thinks for himself, listens to Gus, and runs the gauntlet, Ben is a piece of tin that is exploited and hunted by Blakelock. The constable accuses him of "choosing sides," a misogynistic reference to Ben's willingness to trust Gus. Eastwood keeps the camera glued tightly to the interior of the car as the constable refers to Gus' genitalia and reduces her to a pornographic cliché. With his growing discontent with his badge dominating his thoughts, Ben remains silent as the constable uses crude and abusive language to objectify and outrage Gus.

Instead of being reduced to tears, Gus calmly smokes a cigarette and reverses the verbal assault, stressing how similar and yet how inferior a cop is to a prostitute:

> As I see it, the only difference between you and me is that when I
> quit work, I take a long hot bath and I'm as clean as the day I was
> born. But a cop, especially a flunky like you, the sheriff whistles,
> you squat. And what it does to you rots your brains. No amount
> of water on earth can get you clean again ... I know you don't
> like women like me, we're a bit aggressive. We frighten you. But
> that's only because you've got fluff in your brain and I'm afraid
> the only way you'll ever clean it out is to put a bullet through it.

She concludes with the explosive gibe, "Oh, does your wife know you masturbate?" The constable loses his composure and goes into hysterics, his masculinity dented and damaged. Impressed by Gus' resolve and quick-wittedness, Ben "chooses sides." His demeanor improves. He begins to wonder why every time he gives Blakelock his itinerary, a hundred cops intercept and attack him. Won over by Gus' artfulness, Ben is much more willing to trust her instincts and get out of the car when she fears that trouble might be awaiting them at the state line. The constable, unwilling to believe a woman and a cop who has chosen sides, is mistaken for Ben and Gus and riddled with automatic weaponry. In *The Gauntlet*, loyalty to your profession or an institution can be fatal — Ben must confide in Gus if he is to escape the same fate.

At nightfall, isolated from the modern world, from ambulances, telephone booths, and foregrounded cans of Tab, Ben and Gus take refuge in a cave and begin the difficult process of relating to each other as people, rather than as a cop and a whore. Neither can seem to get out of their protective shells. Ben, still unsure of himself and his predicament, harbors a lot of resentment toward Gus and tells her, "For two cents and a stick of gum I'd kick the shit out of you." He strikes Gus and receives a kick in the groin for his impudence. Gus adds to the sting of the kick by declaring, "You're a loser, Shockley, you're a nothing, a nobody." Bottle in hand, Ben hisses, "Miserable bitch," and prepares to swallow, but cannot. Something has clicked. Eastwood then match dissolves to Ben's face the next morning as he 'sees the light' and makes an effort to respect and communicate with Gus.

Eastwood wants to remind us, however, that Ben has a long way to go. Like Wales, Ben has to face his symbolic adversary (Blakelock) before he can be redeemed. When a motorcycle gang loiters outside of the cave, Ben resorts to the same dull-witted macho behavior that polluted his earlier exchanges with Gus. Ben provokes several of the bikers so that he has an excuse to confiscate one of their bikes. Clearly, Ben is getting off on being in control for the first time in the film. Gus stands at the mouth of the cave, shaking her head in disbelief. Ben's aggressive behavior does not go unchecked: later in the film, as Ben and Gus hop a moving freight train, Ben comes face to face with the consequences of his actions — riding in the car are the three bikers (Roy Jenson, Dan Vadis, Samantha Doane) he bullied in the desert. They manhandle Ben until Gus offers her body, giving Ben enough time to collect himself and retaliate. Ben learns that cocky, pistol-driven masculinity not only jeopardizes his welfare, but Gus' as well. He sits quietly, watching Gus with admiration. This woman, this supposable 'nothing witness for a nothing trial' becomes Ben's penance and salvation.

Nearing Phoenix and civilization, Ben rents a motel room so that he and Gus can prepare for the film's climax. The scene is slow and intimate; as with the scene inside the patrolman's car, Eastwood minimizes the number of camera set-ups, encouraging us to observe the characters without much spatial or temporal interference. Eastwood uses the anamorphic frame to simplify montage so that the characters can interact without too many cuts or camera angles. Although the violent sequences of *The Gauntlet* are characterized by up-tempo editing and disorienting dutch angle point of view shots, much of the film is composed of phenomenological shots and long takes. When Gus and Ben struggle with each other in the ambulance or the bikers in the railroad car, the violence is charged with panic and fear; when Ben accidentally sets off the fusillade that levels Gus' home or when Ben and Gus run the gauntlet, the violence has a surreal, lackadaisical tone that contrasts with Ben and Gus' point of view shots and reactions. This is in marked contrast with *The Outlaw Josey Wales*, in which every scene of violence is charged with an electrifying sense of tension and release. Montage and mise-en-scène are more balanced in *The Outlaw Josey Wales* because the world Wales inhabits is balanced — it is he, not his environment, that is out of whack. Ben and Gus have not only themselves, but a hostile, impersonal world to contend with as well.

Eastwood counterpoises the motel scene with the earlier scene set in Gus' house. In that unfortunate scene, neither Gus nor Ben are very considerate or sincere: Gus believes that Ben is just another John who can be led by his penis; Ben assumes that Gus is a scheming whore who will go down on any man for the smallest favor. It is fitting that the scene ends with a fusillade — Ben and Gus' first scene together in close quarters is disastrous, a calamitous conflict of interest and wills that shakes the very foundations of Gus' home. Ben and Gus are not the principal interest in the scene — the

En route to Phoenix, Ben Shocklee (Clint Eastwood) and Gus Malley (Sondra Locke) learn that a state of grace between the sexes can be a source of personal redemption.

house and its graphic destruction are the main focus. During their stay in the motel, Ben and Gus assert their presence over the surroundings and experience a romantic re-awakening. They eclipse the drab motel room, comforting and inspiring one another as they prepare to overcome Blakelock, the police force, the city of Phoenix, and the anomie of modern America. This scene is the heart of the film, a shift from fear to hope, hatred to love. Ben and Gus let down their guard — Eastwood does the scene shirtless while Locke is clad only in a bath towel. Ben has some flowers delivered to Gus, and explains to her, while she arranges and sniffs the roses, how he once was an idealist who thought he could make a difference in the streets. Eastwood softens his acting style — instead of resorting to a collection of reactions and double takes (the Las Vegas scenes), stoic silences (the ride in the constable's car), or hostile stares (the cave), Ben re-discovers how sensitive and optimistic he once was before he lost his enthusiasm and his self-respect. When Gus asks Ben why he is hell-bent on confronting Blakelock, Ben replies, "At least someone will know I tried." "Who," she asks, "Blakelock?" "No," Ben answers, "me." Gus shows her faith in Ben by calling her mother and informing her that she plans to marry Ben, settle down, and raise children. She then calls her bookie and puts her entire life savings on Mally No

Show (now 100:1). Gus is willing to gamble on Ben and put her fate in his hands. The hijacking of the bus and the fortification of it with steel plating is a romantic gesture in a film that is essentially a tall tale and a fable about the need for integrity, individuality, and imagination in the modern age (a theme that would reappear in *Bronco Billy*). Ben and Gus want Blakelock to know that the individual is not doomed; that love and a hard-fought reconciliation between man and woman can triumph over any institution, no matter how corrupt.

Ben and Gus run the gauntlet and survive. Ben is shot in the leg and can only drive several blocks before he succumbs to fatigue and passes the helm to Gus, who manages to maneuver the decimated bus to the steps of City Hall, where Blakelock and a chorus of police officers await. When Ben and Gus emerge from the incapacitated bus, the policemen lower their firearms and take off their sunglasses. As long as Ben and Gus stay hidden in the bus, the policemen do not question Blakelock's authority and fire without restraint. Confronted by the bleeding, exhausted faces of Ben and Gus, the policemen ignore Blakelock's order to kill on sight and regain their humanity. What was an impersonal display of power and corruption becomes an intense *guerre à mort* between Ben, Gus, and Blakelock. The police form a circle around the three as Gus manages to kill Blakelock before he can fatally wound Ben. Because they are able to function as a team and work out their differences and individual shortcomings, Gus and Ben can now take control of their lives. Ben has reformed himself and his department; Gus is free of danger and the rut of prostitution. Apart from one another, Ben and Gus can only survive; together, they can live, prosper and raise a family. The gamble pays off: at 100 to 1, the dividends of Mally No Show promise infinite returns. *The Gauntlet* can be seen as an argument for equality and solidarity between the sexes — Ben and Gus reach Phoenix and are truly reborn.

The Gauntlet belongs to the paranoia cycle of the 1970s (*Serpico* [Sidney Lumet, 1973], *Chinatown* [Roman Polanski, 1974], *The Parallax View* [Alan Pakula, 1974]), but the true inspiration of the film is *It Happened One Night*, Frank Capra's seminal screwball comedy. Both films are love stories in motion in which two selfish, stubborn individuals are forced to rely on one another for comfort and security. The central place where both couples begin to appreciate and learn about each other is a motel. By journey's end, both protagonists have grown and matured, their views of life and love profoundly altered. With *Bronco Billy*— another fable about the modern world from the perspective of a disaffected artist — Eastwood would appropriate the form of the screwball comedy and use Capra's later films, *Mr. Deeds Goes to Town* (1936) and *You Can't Take It with You* (1938), as a central inspiration.

Bronco Billy, 1980

If ever I had a message to get across, you'll find it in *Bronco Billy* [Buerif, p. 15].

Bronco Billy is Eastwood's *Mr. Deeds Goes to Town* and *You Can't Take It with You,* a film about idiosyncrasy, integrity, and personal fulfillment in a world of conformity and disappointment. If *The Gauntlet* presents us with a modern, arid, and impersonal world hostile to the individual, *Bronco Billy* presents us with an artist hostile to modern society. Bronco Billy McCoy (Clint Eastwood) is a modern Don Quixote, an inveterate dreamer who transforms his childhood fascination for circuses and Roy Rogers into a nomadic career and lifestyle. Billy's Wild West Show is a refuge from urban malaise, a throwback to the turn of the century and the cowboy ethos that dominated Hollywood in the 1930s. In Eastwood's words:

> He is a favorite of mine. Because of the idealism. The guy is simply out of touch with the world as it is today. But he has a dream of the world he wants — traveling around with a broken-down carnival act, which is totally obsolete [Hentoff, p. 29].

Billy is a working-class existentialist hero, an artist courageous (and foolhardy) enough to replace his rueful past with a living fantasy. A former convict who went to prison for seven years for attempted murder (he shot his wife after catching her in bed with his best friend), Billy tries to make myth real in an age where fantasies are consumed and experienced vicariously. Billy pretends for real. In his words:

> I was raised in a one-room tenement in New Jersey. As a kid I never even saw a cowboy, much less the wide-open spaces, except when I could scrounge up a quarter for a picture show. I was a shoe salesman till I was thirty-one years old. Deep down in my heart I always wanted to be a cowboy. One day I laid down my shoe horn and swore I'd never live in the city again. You only live once, got to give it your best shot.

As with *The Gauntlet,* the city is hostile to the individual. Imagination and personal fulfillment are the frontiers of the modern world — Ben Shockley and Bronco Billy its pioneers. Billy's Wild West Show is a quintessential American phenomenon. It is a restless convoy to nowhere; a persistent example of self-promotion and self-indulgence. Billy's show is made up of a group of former convicts (Doc Lynch [Scatman Crothers], Lefty LeBow [Bill McKinney] and Chief Big Eagle [Dan Vadis]) and misfits (Leonard James [Sam Bottoms] and Lorraine Running Water [Sierra Pecheur]) who share Billy's antipathy toward the modern world and enthusiastically adhere to his idiosyncratic *Weltanschauung*. They use the same anachronistic idioms and sayings that Billy has borrowed from turn of the century dime novels and B westerns. Billy immerses himself so deeply into his persona that when any member of his troupe shows doubt or discontent, he raises his voice and loses his temper. Billy's determination to preserve the spirit of the Wild West Show makes him tyrannical and slightly psychotic. In true screwball fashion, he is an oddball, a "character" not unlike Katherine Hepburn in *Bringing Up Baby* (Howard Hawks, 1938) or John Barrymore in *Twentieth Century* (Hawks, 1934). Billy is so sensitive about being the head honcho that he berates his crew for informing him that they have not been paid for two months. Billy has an emotional, financial and spiritual investment in his traveling Wild West Show; without it, he has no reason to exist. His art is his life.

For Billy, the adult world offers nothing but pessimism and desperation. Children provide Billy with the inspiration he needs to keep his show on the road. Without the "little pardners" who attend Billy's show and watch it with wonder and amazement, Billy would become an embarrassment, a middle-aged man masquerading as a man of the West. What Billy cannot tolerate is the modern adult world's disdain for fantasy and the innocence of childhood. While cashing a check, Billy finds himself the victim of a bank robbery. He shows little interest in thwarting the robbery until one of the thieves pushes a child aside, causing him to fall on the ground and break his piggy bank. Billy takes on the hostile expression of the Man with No Name and reclaims the child's innocence by disarming the bank robbers with a flurry of gunfire. Initially heartbroken, the child watches Billy's display of marksmanship and mouths a silent "wow."

Billy is no fool. He knows that children are not only his inspiration, but his source of income. Eastwood emphasizes this in a self-referential scene when Billy sneaks up on a group of youngsters inspecting his custom-made convertible. Framed in a low-angle full shot, Eastwood strides into the right side of the frame, backlit by the sun. The construction of the shot, and Eastwood's dominance of it, brings us back to the mythological omniscience of *High Plains Drifter* and *The Outlaw Josey Wales*. Billy's spatial hegemony ends, however, when he asks the children why they are not in school. One child sheepishly informs Billy that it is Saturday — Billy loses his composure and control of the frame and apologizes for his error by muttering, "I've been riding late last night. A man's mind gets kind of fuzzy when he's been on the range." His aura considerably diminished, Billy switches from a childhood legend to an entrepreneur, giving away free tickets to the children so that they will pester their parents into going to the show that evening. Eastwood ends the low-angle coverage of Billy, attenuates the backlighting, and cuts to neutral two-shots of Billy fraternizing with the children to highlight his sudden loss of stature. Like Eastwood, Billy is both an icon and a huckster; to some, a man and to others, a legend. Billy would like to think that he is a paragon of virtue who will redeem the modern world and an inspiration to the next generation, but he is not too self-deluded to admit that what he is doing is selling and promoting rather than living a dream. At best, Billy is a struggling artist who manages and headlines a down at the heels carnival act. As *Bronco Billy* begins, Billy's show is running out of inspiration and capital. The Wild West Show is floundering despite Billy's best efforts to keep the show solvent and his employees content. The show is losing money, and badly in need of new blood. The pressure is making Billy irritable and dictatorial. Like Ben Shockley, Billy needs a woman to restore his spirits and preserve his dream.

In *Bronco Billy*, Eastwood returns to a circular construction of narrative (*Play Misty for Me, High Plains Drifter, The Gauntlet*) in the form of an opening and closing act to show the decline and revitalization of Billy's show. *Bronco Billy* opens with an aerial, time-lapse shot of the Wild West Show's tent being raised as afternoon dissolves into night. Billy sets up his tent in a safe, rural setting, situated far from any city or metropolis. He prefers to tour in Wyoming and Utah, states that do not remind him of the Northeast. Eastwood uses the lens and certain angles to show us that Billy's show is heading down the road toward bankruptcy and obsolescence. According to cinematographer David Worth:

> We shot the first performance with a longer lens to accentuate the sparseness of the audience and the fact that it was a seedy, run-down kind of circus act, and the last performance we shot with wide angle lenses, to emphasize the fact that the circus tent was now crowded and made of American flags. The tent ... picked up a lot more light, and gave it a much more upbeat feeling [Plaza, p. 112].

The first performance of the Wild West Show is intentionally awkward. The timing is off and the acts lack pizzazz or novelty. The tent is dark, the bleachers sparsely populated, and the spotlights intrusive and unflattering. The lack of an audience enervates Billy and his crew. There is no magic, only sweat, labor, and mediocre applause. Doc's introduction lacks flair. Chief Big Eagle gets bitten by his own snake and issues forth a disquieting shriek. Billy's entrance is marred by a skipping phonograph player that accompanies his act with John Philip Sousa marches. Eastwood restrains from cutting to a flattering close-up of Billy to preserve the impersonal, awkward tone of the opening act. The shots do not flow with the Sousa march which is heard in the background instead of on the soundtrack. Eastwood cuts to arbitrary long shots to decentralize our perspective and encourage us to observe rather than participate. Billy's act is "off" both spatially and rhythmically — we are not given the best seat in the house. The Sousa march ends with an abrupt screech when Billy dismounts from his trusted horse Buster. Billy's act comes to a mortifying close with the entrance of Mitzi (Tessa Richarde), his new assistant. Mitzi cowers in fear when she throws plates into the air, tentatively reads her lines, and is so nervous during the knife throwing act that her ankle falls out and gets pierced. What more could go wrong? On the road the next morning, Billy promises, "I'm going to find us an angel who will make us all proud to be in the show." Billy needs something more than a mere assistant. He needs a woman who is a cowgirl at heart, a woman who will challenge and inspire him.

In *Bronco Billy*, Eastwood borrows from the central conflict of the screwball genre — the commingling of the working and privileged classes — by pairing the plebeian Billy with the patrician Antoinette Lily (Sondra Locke), a spinster who must marry before the age of 30 to retain her inheritance. Her marriage to John Arlington (Geoffrey Lewis) is one of necessity and convenience. She treats him with the same disdain she has for life in general. While Billy transcends the banality of the modern world, Antoinette has succumbed to it. Billy has faith in humanity; Lily is a misanthrope. *Bronco Billy* reverses the basic conflict of *The Gauntlet*. Instead of the woman redeeming the man, Billy redeems Lily by separating her from New York City and making her a part of his Wild West Show. Billy understands Antoinette's dilemma. He too has known disappointment and depression, but refuses to allow it to cripple his childhood dreams and his savvy for show business. Although a much older man, Billy is a child at heart, while Antoinette, not yet 30, bitches and complains constantly. Her behavior is supercilious and insufferable. After only one evening with Antoinette, Arlington flees, leaving her destitute with no transportation or wardrobe. Antoinette is forced to ask Billy for a dime to use the phone. In typical screwball fashion (e.g., *It Happened One Night*), she is forced to accompany Billy to the next town. Antoinette shakes her head and tells herself, "This isn't happening."

Like Gus and Ben in *The Gauntlet*, Billy and Lily are a combustible couple-to-be who constantly trade barbs. Their personalities clash and collide. Antoinette does not miss an opportunity to undercut Billy and his Wild West Show. While riding with Billy in the cab of his truck, she tells him, "You are nothing but an illiterate cowboy," causing Billy to come to an abrupt stop and hammer on a steering wheel until he regains his senses. Billy cannot tolerate any sallies against his ego or his dream — attack his show or his identity, and you have a petulant, vindictive child on your hands. Like Ben, Billy must contend with a woman who sees his limitations and short-comings and has no qualms about using them as the butt of a joke or an insult. Billy, however, does not have Ben's bitter disposition which lasts until he renounces the bottle and stops calling Gus a "lousy bitch" — he is a for-giving man who maintains a positive veneer and attitude and supports a sur-rogate family who respects and reveres him. Billy spends most of his time worrying about the survival of his business, not Antoinette's bitter obser-vations of how silly or pitiful his life has become.

Billy gives Antoinette a tryout as his assistant, and is surprised to learn that this unimaginative and pessimistic woman has talent. Antoinette responds to Billy's cues instinctually. Not only can she throw plates effort-lessly, but she can shoot as well as Billy. This discovery makes Billy self-con-scious and insecure. Like Ben, Billy's reliance on his guns is a major part of his image. From *The Outlaw Josey Wales* to *Bronco Billy*, women take hold of the gun and dispute its meaning and significance: in *The Outlaw Josey Wales*, Granny supersedes Wales' pistols with a broom and a branding iron; in *The Gauntlet*, Gus threatens Ben with his own gun, in *Bronco Billy*, Antoinette manipulates a pistol with as much confidence and stagecraft as Billy does. Stripped of the masculine mystique of the gun, Wales, Ben, and Billy must re-evaluate what constitutes manhood: the gun or the man wield-ing it. Antoinette's arrogant and acerbic presence is a direct challenge to Billy's ego and his vision. By including her in his act, Billy wages a war of wills with her that tests his patience and sanity. During her debut as Billy's assistant, Antoinette improvises her lines, something an assistant has never done. By introducing new dialogue into Billy's show, Antoinette forces Billy to be more flexible and spontaneous. Self-reliant for too long, Billy cannot fathom any other way but his own. With no regard for her state of undress, he walks into Antoinette's dressing room and bellows, "I'm the head ram-rod here. I give the orders." When Billy detects mutinous feelings among his crew, he goes into hysterics, stops the convoy, and yells at them in the rain until their grievances grow silent. Billy needs a woman as dynamic and head-strong as himself to inject life into his show and to relieve the mounting pressures that cause him to explode into paroxysms of fury and frustration.

Antoinette is in no rush to return to New York City. She comes across a newspaper headline declaring her dead (Antoinette's stepmother, Irene Lily [Beverlee McKinsey], and her lawyer, Edgar Lipton [William Prince], devise a scheme to frame Arlington for Antoinette's murder and keep the fortune for themselves) and decides to remain incognito. Although she per-forms in the show and shares in the group's activities, Antoinette does not make an effort to be civil or understanding. When the troupe goes to a bar to celebrate Running Water's pregnancy, Antoinette matches them beer for

Antoinette Lily (Sondra Locke) tests the pride and patience of Bronco Billy (Clint Eastwood), a showman who lets his dreams and imagination define his art and life.

beer, but does her best to dampen their *joie de vivre*. Her gloomy presence eventually scatters the table. She is left sitting across from Billy, who encourages her to cry and to open up. After being told by Antoinette that "people are such idiots," and "folks just want to take," Billy remarks, "Girl, you sure are mixed up." Full of Budweiser and impatience, Billy tries to end Antoinette's maudlin display by demanding that she dance with him. Antoinette's pessimism poisons the spirits that animate and sustain the Wild West Show. Billy's efforts to redeem Antoinette are metonymic — if he can exorcise her evil spirits, he can redeem a modern world bereft of kindness or creativity. When Billy tries to kiss Antoinette, she responds by smacking him in the face, a smack that puts a curse over Billy and the Wild West Show. The slap starts a barroom brawl that sets into motion a domino-like series of unfortunate events: Antoinette is nearly raped in the parking lot, Leonard is arrested for public drunkenness and accused of being a Vietnam deserter, and Billy's tent burns to the ground when a restless group of teenagers set off a pack of firecrackers.

In less than 24 hours, Billy sees his dream unravel. He is left impoverished and crestfallen, but he refuses to give in to despair or defeat. His first priority is not the show, but his family, and he sacrifices his pride and principles to keep it together. Billy forgives Leonard for being a Vietnam deserter and sacrifices his life savings to release him from jail — not only does Billy bribe Sheriff Dix (Walter Barnes, who played an equally unimpressive law-man in *High Plains Drifter*), but he allows the sheriff to unmask him as a "fake" cowboy. This scene — a pivotal one in the film — shows us that Billy is not immune to the modern world and the contempt that men like the sheriff have for someone who does not lead a normal, nine to five existence. Billy's meeting with the overweight, self-important Sheriff Dix is a modern standoff, one in which Billy has no recourse but to be silent and accommodating. Dix is eager for a bribe, but what he really wants is to humble Billy and to mock his western persona. He is the antithesis of the children Billy admonishes earlier in the film — unlike the children, the sheriff has no imagination or wonder, only resentment. Billy is never given a backlit low-angle shot, nor is he able to leaven the scene with some self-deprecating humor. The sheriff owns the scene, thanks to a series of over the shoulder and reverse shots. Billy cannot act nor respond to the sheriff's threats. After being asked, "Aren't you Bronco Billy, the fastest gun in the west, the toughest hombre this side of Dodge City?" all he can say is "Look, I'm just making a living like everyone else." Dix accuses Billy of being a coward and a "yellow-bellied egg sucker" and demands that he admit that the sheriff is faster on the draw. In a medium close-up, Billy does so, a sad resignation passing over his features. For a few minutes, we see Billy separated from the security of his Wild West Show. Billy drops his Western lingo and does not draw and twirl his pistols. He has no snappy comebacks. As much as Billy detests humbling himself in front of Sheriff Dix, he must accept the world as it is or lose what little independence he has left.

Antoinette's curse tests Billy's grip on reality and his allegiance to his surrogate family. Billy chooses not to banish Antoinette, even after Lefty and Doc Lynch try to persuade him that she is cursing the show. Billy's unwillingness to do so shows his patience and forbearance and his unselfish desire to heal Antoinette of her emotional and spiritual wounds. Overwhelmed by adversity, Billy decides to retreat into his fantasy world and rob a train, something even Doc Lynch sees as impracticable and harebrained. The holdup is a comic disaster: Billy and his posse cannot even force a freight train to slow down, let alone stop. Eastwood cuts to a child inside the train, pointing at Billy pursuing it on horseback, and enchanted by what he sees. The child tries to wake his mother, but she sits with her eyes closed, impervious to Billy and his posse. Once again, it is children to whom Billy appeals and from whom he gets his inspiration. The child believes. He sees Billy and chortles with delight, "Cowboys and Indians." Minutes before the arrival of the train, Antoinette tries to dissuade Billy from robbing it by informing him, "You're living in a dream world; there are no more cowboys and Indians, that's all in the past." In the modern, adult world, Billy is misunderstood and maligned. Only children and adults who have not lost their imagination or sense of play believe in Billy. Without his tent, Billy loses his perspective and tries to bring fantasy to life. Instead of kowtowing to the modern world and curmudgeons like Sheriff Dix or Antoinette, Billy does the exact opposite, resorting to a romantic, foolish gesture to sustain his dream. Billy realizes, however, that he must have a tent to be Bronco Billy. Without it, he has no context for his living fantasy.

For many years, Billy has been giving complimentary shows for orphanages and other charitable institutions that could not afford to reimburse him. Now Billy seeks aid from one of his old acquaintances, Dr. Canterbury (Woodrow Parfrey), the director of a home for the criminally insane. The doctor agrees to sew a tent out of the American flags he manufactures for the government, provided that Billy teach him how to twirl and shoot a six-shooter. By placing Billy and his fellow misfits in an insane asylum, Eastwood focuses on the Wild West Show's estrangement from reality and the fact that if Billy's brood were diagnosed by Dr. Canterbury and his staff, they would be labeled as mentally incompetent. Their refusal to conform to the 1980s would be seen as a withdrawal from reality and an inability to cope with modernity. When Doc asserts, "Some of these people in here are as sane as you and I," Lefty remarks, "That ain't saying much." Billy and his family know that, without their show, they could be back in prison or committed to an asylum like the Home for the Criminally Insane.

The company's prolonged stay at the home gives Billy an opportunity to devote his attention to Antoinette, who still bristles at his touch. After another vituperative argument in which Billy laments, "There must be 13-year-olds who are more woman than you," and Antoinette retorts, "Well at least I'm not a phony cowboy from New Jersey," Antoinette does something completely out of character — she goes to Running Water for advice and companionship. Running Water informs Antoinette that Billy's show is a source of empowerment and self-improvement: "You can be anything you want, all you've got to do is become it." Antoinette realizes that if a man like Billy can overcome his criminal past and bring his dreams to life, then she should be able to rediscover her youth and redeem herself. Antoinette drops her pretenses, marches into Billy's trailer and demands that he make love to her. Billy and Antoinette fall in love, but their reverie is short. Just as Billy warms to the idea of teaching Antoinette all of his tricks and expanding her role in the show, the FBI learns that she is alive, shows up en masse, and demands that Billy and his company accompany her to New York City for an inquest. Billy cringes in terror — he refuses to return to the city that reminds him of his sordid past and his former life as an ex-con shoe salesman. Billy can cope with crooked sheriffs, fires and employee mutinies, but he cannot stomach returning to the city. He suddenly dismisses Antoinette as bad luck and takes his show into hiding.

Antoinette returns to her penthouse apartment in New York City while Billy hides in a bar somewhere in Idaho. Separated from one another, Billy and Antoinette give in to self-pity and melancholia — Billy sits humped over a collection of empty beer bottles, drunkenly repeating to himself, "Bronco Billy ain't afraid of no tin-horn sheriff," a sign that his encounter with Sheriff Dix and his disastrous attempt to rob a train has exposed him to the truth that his identity is nothing more than a ridiculous fantasy brought to life. Antoinette is no better. In a fit of suicidal self-pity, she stuffs a handful of sleeping pills in her mouth and debates whether to swallow them. Eastwood does not allow Billy or Antoinette to feel sorry for themselves for long — Billy grows tired of his self-imposed exile, gets up (albeit clumsily and drunkenly) and proclaims that the show must go on with or without an assistant. Antoinette's thoughts of swallowing the sleeping pills disappear when Running Water calls, informing her that Billy needs her badly. She spits the pills onto her nightstand and heads for the nearest airport to rejoin Billy and the show.

The second and climactic performance of the Wild West Show is a rousing, kinetic display of talent and enthusiasm. David Worth's use of shorter lenses emphasizes the capacity audience and the red, white, and blue flags that make up Billy's new tent. The hue of the stitched together flags gives the tent a luminosity that was lacking in the first act. As Billy is introduced, we hear the tinny recording of the Sousa March. With Antoinette's unexpected appearance, however, Billy gets inspired and the source music becomes part of the soundtrack. The newly amplified music sets the pace and rhythm of the shots, which cover the performers from lower and more complimentary angles (the opening sequence uses high angles and asymmetrical, spatially ambiguous shots to make the performers seem awkward and unfocused). The timing of the performers are exact; there are no awkward transitions, no accidents, and no children looking sullen and distracted. Eastwood cuts quickly from performance to performance, adding a carnival atmosphere to the show. He gives Billy an exhilarating 360 degree pan as he rides Buster; then, to intensify the momentum and excitement, shoots a 360 degree pan from Antoinette's perspective as she spins on the wheel waiting for the blindfolded Billy to throw his knives.

Redemption has been reached — Antoinette has liberated Billy from his anal-retentive need to be the head honcho 24 hours a day; Billy has converted Antoinette into a "rootin-tootin" cowgirl from the Rio Grande'. Antoinette regains her humanity; Billy loses his dogmatism. The show is revitalized, and with Antoinette's considerable wealth, is guaranteed to endure for years to come, no matter how anachronistic it may be. Eastwood finishes the film with a Brechtian flourish by having Billy address the viewers, bestowing his parting blessing: "So we come to the end of our show, ladies and gentlemen, thank you for being so kind to us." Eastwood, faithful to his love of circular construction, cuts to an aerial pullback of Billy's tent, only now the sun is rising rather than falling, and the tent, rather than being somewhere rural and provincial, is near the outskirts of a medium-sized city. His faith in love and the power of imagination and childlike wonder restored, Billy can coexist more easily with the modern world. He is willing to set up his tent near the suburbs. Men like Sheriff Dix may still threaten Billy's independence, but the multitude of children and healthy adults who applaud the Wild West Show at the end of the film give Billy all the positive reinforcement he needs.

Contrary to Dave in *Play Misty for Me* and, later, Red Stovall in *Honkytonk Man*, Charlie Parker in *Bird*, and John Wilson in *White Hunter, Black Heart*, Billy's obsession with his artistic career does not plant the seeds of his destruction. Billy's intentions are noble; he does not use art to go into emotional hibernation (*Play Misty for Me*) or to rebel against time or personal responsibility (*Honkytonk Man, Bird, White Hunter, Black Heart*). Billy and his employees perform for positive, life affirming reasons. Billy is not a beatnik (*Play Misty for Me*), a prodigy (*Bird*), or a maverick expatriate (*White Hunter, Black Heart*), but a blue-collar man who believes in hard work and sacrifice. He devotes his life to his show and manages it with an energy and a determination that can only be admired. His odd mannerisms and western trappings make him endearing and precious in a world where sad, lonely people like Antoinette drift through life.

Bronco Billy is the culmination of the artistic cycle. In *The Outlaw Josey Wales, The Gauntlet,* and *Bronco Billy,* Eastwood heals his persona of its emotional and psychological wounds. The Man with No Name and Dirty Harry are no longer alienated from society or themselves — they are humanized and redeemed. Billy is vindicated and celebrated as a symbol of reinvention and the American spirit. The artist offers a healthy alternative to a life of quiet desperation. The path to salvation in *The Outlaw Josey Wales, The Gauntlet,* and *Bronco Billy* is long and arduous, but it does come. For the remainder of his second phase, Eastwood would concentrate on loners who come to terms with themselves without the security of a surrogate family or a supportive girlfriend (*Firefox, Honkytonk Man*). The high spirits of *Bronco Billy* would give way to grimmer, more melancholy story lines. Having celebrated life, Eastwood would confront the inevitability of death.

Firefox, 1981

He's (Mitchell Gant) a professional, and before his arrival, he has no idea of how important his mission is for the dissidents. He

doesn't know much about the politics that take place behind the
scenes. And once he's there, he's constantly uneasy. Except when
he flies the plane, because that's when he's in his element [Plaza,
p. 126].

With *Firefox*, Eastwood spoils the egalitarian promise of *The Outlaw
Josey Wales*, *The Gauntlet*, and *Bronco Billy*, and brings the redemption cycle
to an inappropriate close. There is no community, only the subterfuge and
inhumanity of the Cold War. Mitchell Gant (Clint Eastwood), the tortured
protagonist of *Firefox*, is a Vietnam veteran who suffers from delayed stress
syndrome. He is wracked with epileptic memories of being a prisoner of war
and watching a young Vietnamese girl being consumed by a blast of napalm.
His war trauma turns him into a psychological invalid — unlike Hemlock
in *The Eiger Sanction*, who is able to readjust to civilian life, Gant goes into
seclusion to escape from the past and the dehumanizing effects of modern
technology. *Firefox* does not have the aerobatic camaraderie and code of fellowship found in Howard Hawks' *Only Angels Have Wings* (1939) and *Air
Force* (1943). Gant is alone and isolated. He finds salvation not in the arms
of a woman and/or a close community of fliers, but in the cockpit of an elite
fighter jet. Gant adjusts to the modern world by symbolically joining with
the machine — the Firefox becomes an extension of his thoughts and reflexes,
and Gant, an organic extension of the Firefox. Contrary to Ben Shockley,
who defies the faceless conformity of the modern age, Gant overcomes his
weaknesses by reconciling with technology and conforming to the needs of
the machine.

Firefox rushes through the front credits and takes us right into Gant's
psychological distress. A helicopter combs the landscape for Gant, who is
jogging near his home in the Alaskan wilderness. Gant sees the copter, runs
back into his cabin, clutches a rifle and suffers a debilitating seizure as it
lands outside of his window. Gant has a paranoid fear of planes and of modern technology — he tries to flee from his past career as a pilot, but the rever-
berations of the helicopter's blades take Gant back to Vietnam and the image
of the child disappearing in a sea of napalm. At the beginning of *Firefox*, Gant
has renounced his past by embracing nature. He concentrates on his
physique and his organic link to the earth, rather than his mind or his former link to the sky. Outside of the plane, Gant is a part of the ecosystem;
inside a plane, Gant is cut off from his body and the earth. We see Gant from
the vantage point of the helicopter: a small, telluric figure eclipsed by the
din and size of the helicopter hovering overhead. By the end of *Firefox*, Gant
ceases to be terrestrial and overcomes his paralyzing fear of technology by
plugging into the machine. His aging body is supplanted by the gadgetry of
the Firefox — once airborne, Gant must forego his body and become pure

thought. He mutates into a head shot, a series of medium and tight close-ups that nullify his body, emphasize his head, and minimize Eastwood's cinematic presence. The first image Gant (and we) see after his seizure-flashback is a close-up of a pilot, his face hidden behind a helmet. Gant comes face to face with his alter ego, the pilot he once was before he became a prisoner of war and witnessed the grisly aftermath of one of his bombing raids. That man is one without fear or guilt, a man without nightmares or misgivings, more comfortable with the complexities of technology than with those of guilt and human feeling.

Like Hemlock in *The Eiger Sanction*, Gant is blackmailed by the government and forced to take a dangerous and distasteful mission. If he does not cooperate with the CIA, his cabin will be seized. He is ordered to enter the Soviet Union surreptitiously as Boris Glazunov, an American businessman, rendezvous with Russian dissidents Pavel Upenskoy (Warren Clarke) and Pyetr Baranovich (Nigel Hawthorne), and steal the Firefox just as the First Secretary (Stefan Schnabel) is to arrive to conduct a final inspection of the plane. Gant is not a professional spy. He is picked to fly the plane because of his expertise and his fluency in the Russian language. Gant is not an ideal candidate for the mission; he panics and is prone to seizures at the most inopportune moments. What he does have is a conscience. He watches with horror and outrage as members of the Russian underground are sacrificed so that he may elude the Soviet authorities and gain access to the Firefox. When Gant ambushes Lt. Colonel Voskov (Kai Wulff), the pilot of the second Firefox prototype, he mutters, "Hell, you didn't do anything," and allows him to live. Gant's transgression preserves his humanity and separates him from the cutthroats who run the KGB and the CIA.

Gant loses his compassion and empathy, however, once he climbs into the Firefox. To fly the aircraft and negotiate Soviet airspace, Gant must surpass his body and become one with the plane. Before he steals the Firefox, Gant sees the Cold War as a needless waste of human life. Once airborne, he loses his morality and terrestiality and becomes as amoral and impassive as Jonathon Hemlock. Gant is much more sympathetic when he is standing in the shower, waiting to board the Firefox. Clad only in a towel, he is powerless and crippled with fear. Once he boards the Firefox, he learns to let go of his memories, fears and regrets and to concentrate his energies on targeting and destroying the aircraft carriers and Migs that try to intercept him. Gant is outpaced by Voskov, who reciprocates his earlier show of humanity. Caught in a tense dogfight, Gant suffers another debilitating seizure, forgets to think in Russian (the plane's controls are controlled by thought), and goes into a nose-dive. Voskov does not attack until Gant regains consciousness and is combat ready. Voskov's act is a Hawksian gesture of professional respect, much like that between Christopher George

Shell-shocked Vietnam veteran Mitchell Gant (Clint Eastwood) overcomes his fear of technology by commandeering and piloting the Firefox, a Russian fighter jet.

and John Wayne in *El Dorado* (1967). Gant's response is to suppress his humanity, clear his mind of guilt and compassion, and annihilate the second Firefox. By killing Voskov, Gant rejoins the Cold War and returns to his former self — the helicopter pilot he sees after his first seizure-flashback. The recurrent image of the Vietnamese girl being engulfed by flames disappears as Gant shatters the sound barrier.

Gant achieves freedom not by dwelling on the earth and resolving his psychological difficulties with the help of a loved one or a community, but by disappearing into the void and renouncing what little humanity he had when he returned from Vietnam. The transformation of Gant from a distraught, earthbound veteran to a supersonic man-machine is a disquieting refutation of the relationships and communities that characterize *The Outlaw Josey Wales*, *The Gauntlet*, and *Bronco Billy*. In *Firefox*, redemption is dehumanization: to become healthy Gant must rid himself of everything that makes him human. A product of the modern age, he accepts the machine as his destiny and his true self. The body and the soul give way to the synapses of the mind and the microchip. Technology, so hated by Ben Shockley and Bronco Billy, takes over Mitchell Gant and the entire film.

Despite its terse opening and antonymic construction (earth vs. sky; body vs. mind; human vs. machine), *Firefox* is laden with too much narrative and too little visual inventiveness. Eastwood intended *Firefox* to be a widescreen epic, an espionage film that turns into a state of the art video game, but the film is compromised by too many scenes of the American and Soviet high command deciding what to do next. *Firefox* has solid production values and special effects, but little else. It lacks momentum and a human center. Eastwood gets to play a defenseless man on the brink of a nervous breakdown, but he fails to find a style that compliments his performance. The numerous close-ups of Eastwood talking to his headset are so dehumanizing they become tiresome and repetitive. When he climbs into the Firefox, Eastwood as we know him ceases to exist. He becomes a disembodied voice and a helmeted face assimilated by technology. The climactic dogfight with Voskov is an afterthought, a sad, lonely confirmation of Gant's inhumanity and the film's growing stolidity. *Firefox*, oddly enough, feels weighted down as soon as Gant reaches the heavens.

Honkytonk Man, 1982

> Red Stovall is based a bit on some self-destructive people I've
> known. He's wild and funny, but he's been a coward in his time.
> He won't face up to his ambitions. He's not that great a singer,
> but he writes some interesting things. When he gets his moment,
> he's already destroyed himself [Plaza, p. 134].

Honkytonk Man is Eastwood at his best. Set during the latter years of the Great Depression, it is his purest, most pacific film, a picaresque comedy that develops into a gentle tragedy of reconciliation and regret. Red Stovall (Clint Eastwood), the film's nomadic protagonist, is a doomed artist-musician who does not have the wherewithal or willpower to redeem himself. Stricken with tuberculosis, Red does not take life or his health seriously until it is far too late. He is deathly ill, but full of spirit. Red is not a well-heeled dilettante like *Play Misty for Me*'s Dave Garver, a skilled entrepreneur like *Bronco Billy*'s Billy McCoy, or a globetrotting nonconformist like *White Hunter Black Heart*'s John Wilson. Much like *Bird*'s Charlie Parker, Red is willfully self-destructive and undisciplined. Dave, Billy, and Wilson reach a stage in their lives when they must put their careers in perspective: Dave realizes the importance of love and a stable relationship, Billy learns to be less dogmatic and more accommodating, and Wilson discovers that his devil may care approach to filmmaking is actually a way to stave off his fears and responsibilities. All three evolve into kinder, more responsible people. Red and Bird never reach this stage; both compromise their talents by abusing their bodies and rejecting the advice of doctors and loved ones. Eastwood prefaces *Bird* with a quote from F. Scott Fitzgerald: "There are no second acts in American lives." For Red and Bird, that holds true. Both live and express themselves through their music — when they can no longer perform, they languish and die. Whit (Kyle Eastwood), Red's nephew and protégé, entreats Red to enter a sanitarium, but Red insists, "I intend to live life out on my own terms or I ain't going to live at all."

Red, like Bird, cannot take care of himself. He is charismatic, but frustratingly irresponsible and capricious. Red does not overcome the obstacles that prevent him from settling down and becoming a success. The tuberculosis inside Red makes him temperamental and sends him into spasmodic coughing fits that get worse as the film proceeds. As Red himself admits, "Damn fever, when it comes on, it makes me as snappish as a pair of sheep shearers." When Whit finds himself at the receiving end of one of Red's fits, his mother — Red's sister, Emmy (Verna Bloom) — tells him, "It's not your fault. It's not his fault either, can't blame him more than you can blame a crippled man for hobbling. He's only human." Contrary to Bronco Billy, Red does not draw any sustenance from the road. The highway consumes Red and leaves him alone and exhausted. His inability to settle down prevents him from developing good habits or establishing a relationship with a woman. Red once loved a "raw-boned Oakie girl" named Mary and got her pregnant, but he could not stay faithful, and deserted her. Now he wanders, too old to meet another woman, too stubborn to stop smoking and drinking and enter a sanitarium. Red is so impulsive and impractical that his dream of playing at the Grand Ole Opry is just that — a pipe dream he can enjoy while throwing back another pint of whiskey. When Red finally does get an opportunity to audition for the Opry, his voice has been ravaged by tuberculosis, cigarettes, and whiskey. His death has a dignified sense of resignation, an understanding of how important, and yet, how fleeting life is. *Honkytonk Man* affirms life but accepts death as something everyone must confront, no matter how well- or ill-prepared one may be.

Honkytonk Man begins effortlessly with the barest of exposition. The front credits pass by almost unnoticed as we see images of Whit's family abandoning their field before a dust storm smothers their crops. Eastwood's inconspicuous placement of the credits in *Firefox* and *Honkytonk Man* anticipates *White Hunter, Black Heart*; *Unforgiven*; *A Perfect World*; and *The Bridges of Madison County*, in which he dispenses with them entirely. Red's arrival through a cloud of dust prefigures the end of the film, when he is laid to rest and his coffin is covered by dust and dirt. When Red is introduced he is already close to the grave — he is "dead drunk" and feverish when he drives headlong into a weather vane and comes to a clumsy stop in front of Emmy and her husband, Virgil's (Matt Clark), homestead. Red is taken inside, stripped to his underwear and laid flat on a bed, an image that will re-appear two hours later when Red is on another bed, covered with sweat, suffering from consumption and regret as he slowly but inexorably dies. Red is associated with death and disease (the dust storm and tuberculosis), but he is also associated with the polished guitar that Whit strums and admires. In *Honkytonk Man*, Eastwood repeats certain motifs but changes the circumstances so that we get a linear and circular ending — linear in the sense that Red must die (Eastwood on Red's demise: "Somebody said, 'Why didn't you make him live?' But self-destruct — that's the way that guy is, and you can't make a sudden change at the last frame" [Thomson, p. 71]) — but circular in the sense that Whit will inherit Red's legacy and Marlene (Alexa Kenin) will give birth to Red's child. Red's convalescence and recovery is a refutation of the Man with No Name's resurrection in *A Fistful of Dollars* and *The Good, the Bad, and the Ugly*, and the later resurrections in *Sudden Impact* and *Unforgiven*. In *Sudden Impact* and *Unforgiven*, Eastwood is reborn: the mortal becomes mythic. In *Honkytonk Man*, Red is resuscitated, only to die later in the film. There is no redemption and resurrection, only the recognition of death and the desire for reconciliation.

Whit's family is beset by poverty and misfortune. Trapped in the Oklahoma Dust Bowl, Emmy and Virgil have little choice but to abandon their farm and emigrate to California. Prior to Red's arrival, Eastwood shows us Whit's family huddled in their decrepit farmhouse, waiting for the dust storm to subside. The family looks listless and exhausted. Only Whit and his Grandpa (John McIntire) seem to have any spunk. Tired of being a cotton picker, Whit sees Uncle Red as a welcome alternative to his father, who spends most of his time glowering and bemoaning the loss of his crops. Virgil's melancholia throws a pall over the entire household. However slow-witted and consumptive Red may be, he is still a good-natured person with a hankering for adventure and a keen sense of humor. Whit sees two paths ahead of him: 1) pick cotton and be miserable like Virgil or 2) play guitar and be fancy-free like Uncle Red. While Emmy and Virgil prepare for future drudgery in California, Red recuperates so that he can accept an invitation to audition for the Grand Ole Opry. If given a choice, Whit would much rather go east with Red than west with his family.

The first time Red comes into contact with his nephew, he asks Whit to hand over his guitar case. Instead of taking hold of his guitar and singing a tune, Red whips out a pint of "dust cutter" and takes a swig. Red's priorities are skewed — his first impulse is to drink, not play. Red's whole life is full of bad choices brought on by hardheadedness and poor judgment. It does not take long for Whit to realize that Red is not a very capable person. Red cannot smoke one of Virgil's homemade cigarettes without dropping the live ashes onto his lap. His driving is even worse. While taking Whit's family out for an afternoon drive, Red loses control of the wheel when he tries to smoke another of Virgil's cigarettes. Red gives the excuse that "I'm not exactly at my best with a fire under my ass," but it is painfully clear to the audience and everyone in the car that Red has no business carrying a driver's license. Red's lamentable driving skills are a metaphor for his inherent lack of self-control and direction. His driving is so bad that later in the film a highway patrolman (Tim Thomerson) orders him to hand the wheel over to Whit, who proves to be a much better motorist than his uncle.

Worried about her brother's health, Emmy permits Whit to drive his uncle to Nashville. Their first jaunt is to a nearby honky-tonk called the Pair of Dice Cafe. Red takes a seat on the stage and performs "When I Think About You", a slow and easy love song. In *Clint Eastwood: Filmmaker and Star*, author Edward Gallafent points out that Red does not have the temperament and lifestyle to be a country and western star: "The bar in which Red sings at the opening of the film is an entirely benign setting, the place where country folk come to listen and dance ... The opposite is true of Nashville, or rather of the Opry, where entertainment is commercial — a show with a national radio hook-up and subject to censorship" (Gallafent, 1994, p. 195) Red thrives in an informal setting. He is in fine form on the road or in a blues bar in Memphis, but when he arrives in Nashville, he cannot handle the pressure of performing live on the radio. He barely makes it through his first and only recording session. Red does not have enough self-restraint to be a celebrity. He prefers to be a small-time hustler. After his performance at the Pair of Dice Cafe, Red enlists Whit's help in stealing some chickens from a barnyard. Red is so drunk and inept that he knocks over the chicken coop and nearly gets himself and Whit killed. Whit has to play Huck Finn to Red's Jim and break him out of jail the next morning, earning his respect and trust.

Red is eager to leave the state the next day, as is Grandpa, who wants to return to his home state of Tennessee. Three generations come together as Red, Whit, and Grandpa hit the road. Red composes "Honkytonk Man" in the back seat of his car while Grandpa plays the harmonica and Whit improvises some lyrics. Because Red is in no hurry to reach Nashville, *Honkytonk Man* has a leisurely pace and a phenomenological charm. Eastwood has time to diverge and develop several warm and comic vignettes. The change in location and setting gives Eastwood the opportunity to introduce a multitude of quirky types (Tracey Walter is a standout as Pooch, a backwoods mechanic) and supporting characters, including Marlene, a teenage stowaway and aspiring singer who falls in love with Red and believes that their destinies were meant to be intertwined. Marlene tries to get Red to like her by singing "My Bonnie Lies Over the Ocean", but her voice is so God-awful that he snaps that only in an amateur contest with a "braying

In costume as Red Stovell, Clint Eastwood performs his dual roles as actor and director on the set.

jackass" would she have a chance of winning. When Red's car breaks down in a secluded part of Arkansas, both Red and Grandpa decide to take the bus to Tennessee. Red, true to form, misses the afternoon bus and wakes up naked in a alcoholic fog next to Marlene, who claims she has conceived. Red leaps out of bed, hops on the early morning bus, and instructs Whit to book Marlene on the next westbound bus and to meet him at a Memphis Beale Street blues club.

In *Honkytonk Man,* Eastwood uses an aspect ratio of 1:85 to 1 (as he does in *Play Misty for Me; Breezy; Bronco Billy; Heartbreak Ridge; Bird; White Hunter, Black Heart;* and *The Bridges of Madison County*), balanced composition, medium close-ups, and tight two-shots to emphasize character over space. He relies on location shooting (mostly in and around California, Nevada and Tennessee) to add texture and atmosphere to the visuals, but he does not let them intrude on the close, personal space of his characters. In his 2:35 to 1 films (*High Plains Drifter, The Eiger Sanction, The Outlaw Josey Wales, The Gauntlet, Firefox, Sudden Impact, Pale Rider, The Rookie, Unforgiven,* and *A Perfect World*) Eastwood uses space to magnify or alienate his characters. In the artistic cycle (*Play Misty for Me; Bronco Billy; Honkytonk Man; Bird; White Hunter, Black Heart;* and *The Bridges of Madison County*), space is immediate and intimate.

For the first two-thirds of *Honkytonk Man*, Eastwood uses a variety of camera placements and location shots to give the film a broad and easy tone. After Whit says good-bye to Grandpa and reunites with Red in Memphis, Eastwood's coverage tightens and the film's tone shifts from comedy to tragedy. The transition takes place as Whit and Red are driving late at night from Memphis to Nashville, the last leg of their journey. Whit shows concern for Red's reliance on whiskey as cough syrup, but is sharply rebuked for it: "Look Hoss, if you want to be my sidekick and chauffeur that's fine, but if I want a nursemaid and a wife to bitch at me, I'll go and get myself one." Eastwood uses intimate framing and low-key selective lighting to bring us closer to Red as he confides in Whit and tells him of his ill-fated love for Mary, his "raw-boned Oakie girl." Eastwood alternates between close-up angle and reverse angle profiles and diagonal two shots of Red and Whit to put us in the midst of Red and Whit's conversation (he repeats this device in *Bird* and *A Perfect World*). Cinematographer Bruce Surtees keeps the scene dark, the only available light coming from the headlights and the dashboard. He spotlights Whit and Red's faces, keeping us close to Red's expressions and as he quietly recalls the past. The world outside the moving car ceases to exist. Red recollects how Mary left her husband to be with him, how he got her pregnant and deserted her when his freedom was threatened. He admits that he felt something tangible for Mary, but did not have the strength of character to make their relationship work: "I got drunk and started feeling sorry for myself as usual, and I got to thinking what a no-good bastard I was and what a decent girl Mary was. Maybe I loved her all the time." Later on, Red tried to see Mary and their baby daughter, but decided otherwise when her family threatened to break his fingers: "Nah, she's better off not knowing about me. Mary was right to go back to her husband. What the hell did I have to offer a kid? Just honky-tonks and flophouses. That's a life of a country singer, Hoss. Sound good to you?" Whit answers, "Don't sound too hot when you put it like that, but it sure beats picking cotton and living in a sharecroppers shack." Eastwood ends the scene with a long take of Red staring into the dark distance, musing, "Maybe you're right, boy." Because of Whit's curiosity, Red comes to terms with the past, something he is loathe to do, but something he must do if he is to die honestly. For perhaps the first time in his life, Red wonders if he should have stayed with Mary and abandoned his singing career. As Red smokes a cigarette, his face registers fear and hope, loss and desire. Red's past catches up with him; he ceases to be a drifter without a care. With this confession of guilt and regret, Eastwood shows the emotions hinted at in Red's songs and the source of his inspiration and lyrics. Once Red gives in to his feelings, he no longer needs music to translate his feelings. Red does not need his guitar to die. All he needs to do is reach out and weep.

After Red makes his confession to Whit, he cannot repress his memories of Mary. He arrives at the Opry unprepared for his audition, most of his material being unfit for a "clean, wholesome family show." Red's voice is taut and strained. He tries valiantly to sing "Honkytonk Man", but is cut off by a painful coughing fit. Prior to his audition, Red flashes Whit a broad smile. After the audition, Red loses his sense of humor and succumbs to tuberculosis. He exits the stage a different man, more dead than alive. Red is given one last shot at posterity when Henry Axle (Joe Regalbutto) offers him a modest recording contract with Burnside Records. Any energy Red has is converted into the microphone. With each recording session, Red dwindles and doffs a critical part of his wardrobe — his voice gets wispy and his eyes get teary. By the last session, Red is without his trademark tie, jacket and hat; he becomes a haggard and disheveled old man with one foot in the grave. His voice finally gives out during the recording of "Honkytonk Man" — he falls to the floor and coughs out his lifeblood as Smoky (Marty Robbins), a tenderhearted studio musician, finishes his song. Eastwood tracks slowly toward Red's face as he realizes that his career and life are over. Red dies in a delirium, bedridden as he was at the beginning of the film. He hugs Marlene and cries out for Mary, the memory of that "raw-boned Oakie girl" more real than anything else in his life.

The ending of *Honkytonk Man* has both closure and continuity: Red returns to the dust from which he came; Whit inherits Red's guitar, clothes, and Stetson; Marlene shows up pregnant with Red's child. For his first performance, Whit sings "Swing Low, Sweet Chariot" over Red's grave. He tosses Red's car keys on top of the casket ,and with Marlene as his traveling companion and musical accompaniment, heads down the road toward his own destiny. Whit looks back once, but then keeps going. In *Honkytonk Man*, life and death overlap; age and innocence meet. "Honkytonk Man" becomes a hit, playing on a nearby car stereo as Whit and Marlene walk into the distance. In spite of his self-destructive tendencies, Red is a sympathetic character and an artist of great sensitivity and spirit. Red is not a caretaker like Josey Wales or Bronco Billy — he is every adolescent's dream come true: a mentor who teaches responsibility by behaving irresponsibly. Red is an inspiration, a chance for Whit to experience the world of country and western music firsthand. Whit's uncle lets him hang out in honky-tonks, blues clubs, the Grand Old Opry, and a Nashville recording studio. He teaches Whit how to play a guitar and introduces him to such luminaries as Bob Wills and the Texas Playboys. Red exposes Whit to all the vices a man needs to write country songs: drinking, thievery, and sex — in addition to recruiting him as his criminal accomplice, he encourages Whit to partake of his whiskey and make himself at home in a whorehouse. He also forces Whit to come to terms with death, suffering, and the gravitational pull of the past. Near the end, Whit has to function as Red's personal manager and nurse him through the final stages of his illness. Whit does not judge Red — he appreciates him for what he is and cherishes the time they share together. By casting his own son as Whit, Eastwood gives Red and Whit's relationship added poignancy and depth.

Honkytonk Man is a gentle, understated film that celebrates life, even as it acknowledges the finality of death. Red accepts death with grace and honesty. His willingness to let go and surrender to the past and the grave mistakes he made is tantamount to a religious confession. It results in his posthumous fame and Whit's desire to continue his dream and career.

Sudden Impact, 1983

> The hard-core fans, I could just bombard them with the same
> kind of character for the rest of my career. But that wouldn't be
> interesting [Thomson, p. 66].

By dying on screen as Red Stovall in *Honkytonk Man*, Eastwood widened the boundaries of his cinema and became less dependent on his persona to give meaning and structure to his work. His audience, however, felt otherwise. Both *Bronco Billy* and *Honkytonk Man* fell short at the box office. To preserve his commercial standing, Eastwood had to bow down to his audience and reacquaint himself with Dirty Harry and the Man with No Name in *Sudden Impact* and *Pale Rider*. After the catharsis of *The Outlaw Josey Wales* and *The Gauntlet*, Eastwood found himself at an impasse — how could he make another No Name-Dirty Harry film without reversing the redemptive spirit of his second phase? Eastwood's solution was to make himself the subsidiary interest of *Sudden Impact* and *Pale Rider*. Eastwood is the *raison d'être* of *The Outlaw Josey Wales*, *The Gauntlet*, *Bronco Billy*, *Honkytonk Man*, and *Firefox*. His presence is central to each film. In *Sudden Impact* and *Pale Rider*, Eastwood chooses not to be the *raison d'etre*, even though he is the *deus ex machina* of both films. He tries to be a minor player in two star vehicles designed to capitalize on his charisma and persona. Inspector Harry Callahan (Eastwood) is of marginal importance to *Sudden Impact*; in *Pale Rider*, the Preacher is a guardian archangel who stays in the background until the final shootout. Eastwood remains aloof until he has no recourse but to foreground his persona and conform to his audience's expectations. Both films suffer from a lack of conviction and concinnity — *Sudden Impact* is lurid and discursive; *Pale Rider* languid and leaden.

Sudden Impact is not so much a Dirty Harry film as it is a film in which Harry makes an occasional appearance. The Harry of *Dirty Harry*, *Magnum Force*, and *The Enforcer* ceases to be in *Sudden Impact*. The icon of modern anomie and angst becomes a faceless, backlit specter who comes to the rescue of Jennifer Spencer (Sondra Locke), a rape victim who returns to the seaside community of San Paulo to confront and execute the small-town riffraff who sexually assaulted her and her younger sister, Elizabeth (Liza Britt), beside a carousel and underneath a roller coaster many years ago. Bruce Surtees' cinematography is dense, dark, and speckled with primary colors and long lenses that turn backgrounded objects into hazy, phantasmagoric patterns. The inky and expressionistic camera work takes us into the disturbed psyche of Jennifer, the film's interior narrator. It is her memories and fears, not Harry's, that we share. Eastwood brings us into Jennifer's private drama and psychic space by transplanting Harry from the macrocosmic streets of San Francisco to the microcosmic boardwalk of San Paulo. Harry is drawn into Jennifer's psychodrama and stumbles into her Doppelgänger, Mick (Paul Drake), the ringleader of the group that raped Jennifer and her sister.

In *Dirty Harry*, Scorpio served as a synecdoche for the sociopolitical turmoil of the late 1960s and early 1970s. He is a misanthropic Id-creature, an outcast who thrives on destabilizing the social order. Mick is as irrepressible as Scorpio, but he is not a manifestation of social chaos and unrest. He is an intimate projection of the Id, a leering psychosexual predator who violates and torments women, and lives and thinks through his phallus. Because *Sudden Impact* is a psychological film in the same vein as *Play Misty for Me*, Mick and the other principal antagonist, Ray Perkins (Audrey J. Neenan) — a hideous, foul-mouthed lesbian — are libidinous demons that dwell in the recesses of Jennifer's consciousness. Jennifer relocates to San Paulo to renovate the dilapidated carousel and kill her assailants. By repainting and restoring the carousel and tracking down her rapists, Jennifer purges her ghastly memories and gives her past a new veneer. As Jennifer stalks and ritualistically shoots her rapists in the crotch and the head, Mick emerges from the past and her psyche, ready to violate what remains of Jennifer's dignity and sanity. Harry is of marginal importance until he sleeps with Jennifer, grapples with Mick, and shares the shame and indignation of being beaten, assaulted, and raped.

With its psychological subtext and its private, rather than public, milieu, *Sudden Impact* is a reversal of the first three Dirty Harry films in which Harry wages a crusade to keep San Francisco and American society from slipping into an abyss. Scorpio is Harry's Doppelgänger in *Dirty Harry*, but he is also a synecdoche of urban and moral decay and a society whose priorities and institutions have gone completely awry. In *Magnum Force* and

Inspector "Dirty Harry" Callahan (Clint Eastwood) receives little solace from brandishing his .44 Magnum and daring a street criminal to "make my day."

The Enforcer, Harry risks his life and career to prevent San Francisco from being overrun by a renegade squad of motorcycle police and an opportunistic band of urban terrorists. Harry is a public crusader in all three films. His conscience, dedication to his job, and his intolerance for lawlessness and bureaucratic indifference supply him with enough ammunition to wage war against sociopolitical chaos. By *Sudden Impact*, the years of struggle have taken their toll. Harry changes into an ill-mannered and dyspeptic "dinosaur". He loses the righteous fury of *Dirty Harry*, the casual watchfulness of *Magnum Force*, and the cool resilience of *The Enforcer*. Surtees lights Eastwood's face so that it looks weather-beaten and aged. The gray tint in Eastwood's ruffled hair is emphasized, as are the crevices in his forehead. Harry is still at odds with the judicial system and *The Enforcer*'s Captain Briggs (Bradford Dillman), but his idealism has calcified into a short-tempered intransigence. Briggs tells Harry that it's a whole new ball game out there, and in a sense he is correct. The criminals Harry comes into contact with are simple-minded hoods without any symbolic or sociopolitical value. Harry's part-time campaign against the mob is futile and self-indulgent. He cannot thrive without a crisis or a nemesis.

In the first three Dirty Harry films, San Francisco and its denizens play a major part in the mood and texture of the films. The streets give *Dirty Harry*, *Magnum Force*, and *The Enforcer* a sociopolitical subtext — by being a visible denizen of the streets, Harry qualifies as a man of the people. East-wood begins *Sudden Impact* with an aerial view of the city, but he quickly dissolves to a car parked outside of San Francisco. He then takes us inside the automobile as Jennifer puts her pistol in her former rapist's trousers and performs a ".38 caliber vasectomy." By moving from the city to a secluded spot, Eastwood stresses the private over the public. In *Sudden Impact*, society disappears. San Francisco loses its thematic and visual importance. Midway through the film, Eastwood uproots Harry and trans-ports him to San Paulo, depriving him of his purpose and identity. Forced to define himself in a new context, Harry investigates Jennifer's trail of corpses and becomes intertwined in a private and psychological, rather than a public and sociopolitical, conflict. *Dirty Harry*, *Magnum Force*, and *The Enforcer* are outside films. All three of the climaxes occur in daylight, as the sun sets in the horizon. *Sudden Impact* is dark and claustrophobic, in keep-ing with its psychological subtext and private milieu. Even when shot out-side in daylight, Eastwood's tenth film has the black-and-white gloom of Fritz Lang and Robert Siodmak's post-WWII film noirs.

Rather than confront society's ills and contradictions through a police officer's day to day struggle with crime and corruption (*The New Centuri-ons* [Richard Fleisher, 1972], *Serpico*, *The Super Cops* [Gordon Parks, 1974], *Hustle* [Robert Aldrich, 1975], *Fort Apache, the Bronx* [Daniel Petrie, 1981]), the cop film in the 1980s lost its sociopolitical edge and devolved into a for-mulaic showcase for facile racial bonding and acrobatic stunt work (*48HRS* [Walter Hill, 1982], *Running Scared* [Peter Hyams, 1986], *Lethal Weapon* [Richard Donner, 1987], *Lethal Weapon 2* [Donner, 1989], *Lethal Weapon 3* [Donner, 1992]). Harry and his public crusade were becoming passé. Amer-ican cinema began to close in on itself and become self-referential, a reflection of the growing polarization and fragmentation of society. The civic, socially dynamic cinema of the 1970s was replaced by a post-modern fascination for recycled mass media, psychosexual repression, and com-puter technology. Moviegoers still wanted Eastwood to narrow his eyes and wave his .44 Magnum and flout the establishment, but they also wanted him to kick indiscriminate butt, not challenge the status quo. *Sudden Impact* reflects this sea of change in attitudes and aesthetics — Eastwood torques up the violence, curtails Harry's crusade to salvage the city, takes him out of his sociopolitical milieu, and forces him to experience the most egregious of private crimes: rape.

Eastwood shows rape as a crime so heinous and vicious that it cannot be sublimated without severe psychological and neurological distress (Jen-nifer's sister is in a permanent state of shock). Jennifer's occupation as a painter is not therapeutic enough to free her of the past. Harry harasses the Mafia out of habit; Jennifer returns to San Paulo to regain her sanity. In

Sudden Impact, crime is personal — it ruins individual lives, not society as a whole. Once Harry meets Jennifer and gets caught up in her personal drama, he takes on her seething indignation and channels it through his AutoMag. Harry's handgun gets a thorough workout in *Sudden Impact*— the body count is ludicrously high. *Sudden Impact*'s violence does not have the gritty immediacy of *Dirty Harry*, the gruesome brutality of *Magnum Force*, or the exploitative audacity of *The Enforcer*. Eastwood makes the violence more surreal and over the top to complement Jennifer's overwrought state of mind and Surtees' neurasthenic camera work. In *Dirty Harry*, *Magnum Force*, and *The Enforcer*, violence drains Harry emotionally and psychologically. Each film ends with an aerial view of Harry staring in disbelief or walking away in disgust. In *Sudden Impact*, Harry is more immune to violence. The only time he seems youthful and energized is when he is pointing his Magnum at a suspect and daring him to make his day. Harry has a blasé attitude toward violence and its effects on the psyche until he spends a night with Jennifer. Separated from San Francisco and his collection of two-piece suits (to stress Harry's displacement, Eastwood wears casual clothes and pairs him with a bulldog named Meathead), Harry is drawn to Jennifer's smoldering anger and resentment. He encounters a kindred soul, a woman who is obsessed with balancing the scales of justice. Harry quickly realizes that her crusade far surpasses his own. The personal outranks the sociopolitical.

The highlight (and purpose) of *Sudden Impact* is the climax. Mick and his two lackeys ambush Harry and throw him into the sea. Harry experiences Jennifer's feelings of pain and terror. Like Jennifer, Mick wants to revisit the past. He kidnaps Jennifer and takes her to the same place where he raped her years before. Jennifer puts up a valiant struggle before Harry is resurrected; for six minutes, she kicks, punches, and evades her attackers, never losing her cool or her dignity. We watch Jennifer defend herself for so long we forget that Harry has emerged from the sea and retrieved his AutoMag. Harry's emergence as a backlit specter is reminiscent of the Stranger's return in *High Plains Drifter*— for several minutes, the angry, embittered antihero becomes an elemental force of vengeance. When he reappears, Harry is as implacable as his AutoMag — he calmly dispatches Mick's henchmen and keeps his pistol fixed on Mick, who with Jennifer as his hostage, climbs to the top of the roller coaster. Mick is knocked off balance by Harry's AutoMag, plummets through the glass ceiling of the carousel, and lands on a unicorn. Jennifer's latest work of art is complete — her Doppelgänger is impaled by the very object that defined him.

In *Dirty Harry*, *Magnum Force*, and *The Enforcer*, Harry is committed to the law — even when he breaks it, he does so to strengthen the rule of law and order in a chaotic society. In *Sudden Impact*, Harry renounces the law and his crusade to save America from itself. He does the unthinkable and exonerates Jennifer of murder. Harry's participation in Jennifer's personal drama takes him outside of San Francisco, the law, and himself. We wonder, as Harry sleeps with Jennifer and establishes a tentative relationship, if he will ever be able to go back to San Francisco and carry his badge again. Has Harry exorcised his own demons as well as Jennifer's? The last shot of *Sudden Impact* is an aerial pullback — a standard for the series — but instead of Harry being alone we see him accompanied by a woman and in the troubling position of a persona without a purpose, an antihero who is now only so much antimatter. By resurrecting Harry and making him a backlit, mythological icon, Eastwood reduces him to an essence, a persona without substance. Harry is redeemed, but reduced to nothingness. His crusade is over. All that made Dirty Harry is stripped away. *Sudden Impact* minimizes Harry, resurrects him into something supernatural, then reduces him to a tabula rasa. Harry regains his humanity, but loses the qualities that made him iconic. Eastwood successfully eliminates Harry without having to alienate his audience.

Eastwood has been eager to sabotage the Dirty Harry series since *The Gauntlet*. His deconstruction of Harry in *Sudden Impact* is so thorough, that in *The Dead Pool*, the fifth Dirty Harry film, Eastwood's characterization bears little, if any, resemblance to the Callahan of the first four films. Harry is reduced to an aging homicide detective placed on a list of celebrities whose obituary is soon to be written. *The Rookie*, Eastwood's last cop film as a director, would finally retire Eastwood's contemporary persona and make him part of the establishment. Harry trades in his Magnum for a starched white collar and a nameplate. The renegade would become a bureaucrat.

Pale Rider, 1985

I'm not a Biblical scholar, but I've always been fascinated by the mythology of those Biblical stories and how they relate to the mythology of the western [Plaza, p. 158].

After sanctifying his Western persona in *High Plains Drifter*, and humanizing it in *The Outlaw Josey Wales*, Eastwood had two choices: deify or deconstruct the Man with No Name. In *Pale Rider* Eastwood tries the former, but does it so half-heartedly that the mythic elements seem forced and underdeveloped. Eastwood wanted to mitigate the influence of his persona in *Sudden Impact* by stripping it down to its barest elements. *Pale Rider* attempts to do the same, but does so with such little energy or stylistic rigor that nothing is added to or subtracted from Eastwood's mythic persona. Throughout the course of *Sudden Impact*, Harry is marginalized until he is deconstructed into a specter without an identity, an icon without a purpose. In *Pale Rider*, Eastwood marginalizes the Preacher as well, but abstains from any iconoclastic tendencies. The Preacher — a pantheistic archangel who stays in the shadows, passively awaiting the moment when he must remove his collar and don his gun belt — is so ephemeral, he seems indistinct even when he is the focal point of the film; a fatal flaw, given that *Pale Rider* is built around the omniscient myth of the Man with No Name. Irrespective of Bruce Surtees' striking cinematography (the film was shot on location in Sun Valley, Idaho), *Pale Rider* is neither structurally nor stylistically adventurous — it fails to broaden or reduce the scope of the Man with No Name and borrows too heavily from *Shane* (George Stevens, 1953). *Pale Rider's* constant allusions to *Shane* and the slack narrative despoil Eastwood's iconic richness and prevent the film from being as pure and hypnotic as *High Plains Drifter* and *The Outlaw Josey Wales*. Eastwood does not just use *Shane* as a source of inspiration — he copies the film's story line and conflict. Instead of being set in a valley, *Pale Rider* takes place in a canyon. The conflict between a community of farmers and a lone rancher is turned into a struggle between a group of independent miners and a greedy strip miner. In *Shane*, the hero is an Apollonian guardian angel; in *Pale Rider*, he is an older and kinder version of the Man with No Name.

Rather than leave the identity of the Preacher an enigma as he did with the Stranger in *High Plains Drifter*, Eastwood sets him forth as a representative of the Lord's wrath. When the Preacher rides into the miner's camp for the first time, Megan Wheeler (Sidney Penny) is reading from Revelation, chapter six, verses five through eight:

> And when he opened the fourth seal, I heard the voice of the
> fourth beast say come and see and I looked, and behold, a pale
> horse, and his name that sat on him was death, and hell followed
> with him.

Eastwood cuts to a foreboding, back-lit, low-angle medium close-up of the Preacher inspecting the camp as Megan finishes with the phrase "and hell followed with him." The Preacher is the fourth horseman of the apocalypse, an archangel who, oddly enough, considering the eschatological references to Revelation, is much gentler than the Stranger, who is the true hell raiser. Despite its theological content, *Pale Rider* is much less Gothic than *High Plains Drifter* and much less concerned with deliverance and damnation.

Clint Eastwood as the Preacher, a kinder and more pantheistic archangel than the Stranger in *High Plains Drifter.*

Pale Rider not only borrows the basic story line and conflict of *Shane* (independent farmers [miners] versus corporate ranchers [miners]) but its allegorical use of nature, too. In *High Plains Drifter*, the town of Lago seems to be nestled in a hinterland, an elemental place where God keeps a watchful and wrathful eye. *Pale Rider* is less abstract and more dependent on a variety of rugged locations to suggest the moral conflict between Coy LaHood (Richard Dysart) and the independent miners. How each group treats nature is a measure of their character and faith. The independent miners do not deface or alter the landscape — they pan for gold by waiting for nature to bring it downstream. LaHood's strip mining operation destroys the land, uproots the trees, and devastates everything in its path. By working with the land, the independent miners show their respect for the environment and God's creation. By destroying the land, LaHood shows his contempt for nature and God's sovereignty. The miner's encampment, a crazy-quilt assemblage of lean-to shacks and tents, is in direct contrast to the high-altitude stillness and symmetry of LaHood's town. The miner's cabins and belongings do not clash with the canyon; LaHood's town and mining operation are an imposition on the landscape and an effrontery to the mountainous horizon.

As with *High Plains Drifter*, we have a town that has forsaken God, but in *Pale Rider*, the town is not inherently wicked; LaHood and his hydraulic mining equipment are wicked. The Preacher does not burn down LaHood's town; he dynamites that which is most unholy: the mining operation. Nature in *Pale Rider* is an extension of God. Those who treat it with respect reap spiritual benefits; those who rape the land risk stern punishment. Bruce Surtees' cinematography foregrounds nature and makes it so visually captivating that it minimizes Eastwood's cinematic presence.

While the Stranger is the *deus ex machina* of *High Plains Drifter*, the Preacher is less central to *Pale Rider*, even though he is the film's lodestar. The Preacher responds to a prayer; the Stranger is summoned by a curse. The Preacher's mission is to consecrate a community and to vouchsafe God's creation; the Stranger's assignment is to consign a town and its wicked inhabitants to hell. The Stranger materializes out of a fiery netherworld; the Preacher descends from a frozen, austere peak. Unlike the Stranger, the Preacher does not determine the film's mise en scene and montage until the climax — nature is the nexus of most of the film. The Preacher takes on the form of a man who has been ambushed and murdered (in his former life, the Preacher was shot six times in the chest by Stockburn [John Russell]), but that crime has no moral or thematic link to the central conflict, hence the anticlimactic tone of the Preacher's showdown with Stockburn, a subplot that is not effectively integrated with the moral conflict between the miners and LaHood. Eastwood's inability to link the Preacher's private conflict with the central conflict diffuses *Pale Rider*'s narrative thrust and reduces the Preacher's mythic dimensions. Despite being an archangel in name, the Preacher is really just a quiet spirit haunting the landscape.

One of the main differences between the Stranger and the Preacher is that of temperament: the Stranger is a virile, sentient being who relishes his reincarnation into human form; the Preacher is an older, more sanctified version of the Stranger who experiences sexual desire, but with much more decorum and restraint. The Preacher is a noble steward of the Lord, fond of parables, labor, and good works. He wears his collar not as an embellishment, but as a reminder of his holy mission. The Stranger is not outwardly pious; he is a compendium of carnal and earthly desires. He carries out the Lord's orders, but does so begrudgingly with a sadistic streak that shows zero tolerance for the weak and wicked citizens of Lago. The Preacher does admire himself in a mirror, drink whiskey, and make love to Sarah Wheeler (Carrie Snodgrass), but he does not relish being in human form as much as the Stranger does. In *High Plains Drifter*, sex is paganistic — the Stranger bestows grace or damnation through intercourse (women receive the phallus, not the pistol). For the Preacher, sex is a blessing, a reminder to Sarah that Hull Barrett (Michael Moriarity) has earned the right to be her husband. The

Stranger exhibits a lustful desire for female companionship. He knows no fear or anxiety. After hearing Stockburn's voice beckoning him in the distance, the Preacher experiences loneliness and spends the night with Sarah. The Preacher refrains from donning his guns until Hogue and the camp face imminent annihilation. Only then does he destroy LaHood's mining operation and challenge Stockburn. His showdown with Stockburn and his deputies is as ritualistic as the Stranger's showdown with Stacey Bridges, but it lacks momentum and dramatic intensity. In a series of slow pans and precisely orchestrated shots, the Preacher shoots the six deputies (S.A. Griffin, Jack Radosta, Robert Winley, Billy Drago, Jeffrey Josephson, John Dennis Johnston) one by one until only Stockburn is left, standing dumbstruck in the middle of the street as the Preacher calmly approaches him and fires a half dozen rounds into his chest and a seventh into his forehead. The Preacher climbs on his horse after killing his nemesis and leaves before Megan can thank him for answering her prayer. The Stranger waits until the next morning before he makes his theatrical exit through Lago—he makes it a point to inspect his handiwork one last time before returning to the netherworld from which he came. Because *Pale Rider* lacks the circular construction and the simple structure of *High Plains Drifter*, the Preacher's departure has no connection to the narrative. He leaves with little mystery or symbolism intact.

In *Pale Rider*, the Preacher remains passive and peripheral as long as he wears his collar—when he goes into a Wells Fargo office and retrieves a safety deposit box containing his pistols, he unfastens his collar and lets it fall into the box. This same scene and placement in the narrative occurs in *Sudden Impact* when Harry opens a drawer, retrieves his AutoMag, and, with a malevolent sneer, loads it. Both *Sudden Impact* and *Pale Rider* revolve around the central image of Eastwood picking up a pistol and preparing for violence. Despite the redemptive elements of *The Outlaw Josey Wales*, *The Gauntlet*, *Bronco Billy*, and *Firefox* and the benevolence and humanity of *Honkytonk Man*, Eastwood could not evade the expectation that he be hostile, armed, and dangerous. The loaded-gun imagery of *Sudden Impact* and *Pale Rider* makes violence the *raison d'être* of both films, nullifying Eastwood's efforts to reform and redeem his persona. The anticipation of violence is the lynchpin that holds *Sudden Impact* and *Pale Rider* together—without it, the films have no reason for being. The showdowns are empty, dispirited rituals that provide a fetishistic thrill for Eastwood's unrepentant diehard action fans.

With his third phase, Eastwood would overstep the loaded-gun image and replace it in *The Rookie* and *Unforgiven* with two recurring shots: a low-angle close-up of Eastwood loading and aiming his weapon, as his victim, seen in high-angle close-up, waits to die. The ambiguous image of Eastwood pointing a gun at close range from a threatening angle involves the audience in a cinematic interplay of helplessness and dominance. Violence is no longer a fetish or a vicarious thrill — it is a disturbing shift in perspective and audience identification that throws doubt upon the Man with No Name and Dirty Harry's excessive use of force. By placing the audience in the middle of the montage, Eastwood makes us fear, rather than anticipate, violence.

5

Third Phase, 1986–1994

There are two American art forms, the Western and Jazz. It's funny how Americans don't support either of them anymore [Plaza, p. 48].

I don't think violence sells. It has to be in the right story or the right situation. You can't just do action scenes and tack them together [Frank, p. 51].

In *Breezy*, Eastwood believed it was necessary to make two cameo appearances to remind us of his directorial presence. By *Bird*—Eastwood's second "off-screen" film — he does not have to do a walk-on to remind us that he is the film's director. Eastwood does make a brief appearance in *Bird*, sitting in the rear of a nightclub, drinking a mug of beer as Charlie Parker performs "Lester Leaps In," but angles the depth of field shot so that his profile is almost indistinguishable from the other patrons. Like Charlie Chaplin in his director-only film *A Woman of Paris* (1923), Eastwood makes a non-cameo so that the audience will not be diverted by his physical presence (Chaplin appears on the screen for several seconds in heavy makeup as a careless porter). Instead of calling attention to himself, à la Alfred Hitchcock, Eastwood prefers to be incognito. With his third phase, Eastwood would finally surmount his persona and re-define the overall aesthetic and thematic perimeters of his work. His tongue-in-cheek description of his work — "to me what a Clint Eastwood film is, is one that I'm in" (Johnstone, p. 138) — would prove to be more self-deprecating and deceiving than ever before.

Eastwood's third phase introduces the theme of retirement, a welcome transition in his work. Having already redeemed his persona (*The Outlaw Josey Wales*, *The Gauntlet*) and reduced it to its archetypal roots (*Sudden*

Impact, Pale Rider), Eastwood decided to withdraw it from the screen. In *Heartbreak Ridge, The Rookie,* and *Unforgiven,* Eastwood superannuates his persona so that a new generation of protégés can take his place. The torch is passed to Stitch Jones and David Ackerman in *Heartbreak Ridge* and *The Rookie,* but in *Unforgiven,* William Munny teaches his protégé to kill, only to be relieved when the Schofield Kid rejects his grisly legacy. For Eastwood's characters, retirement is a positive life choice: Highway can finally stop phallus gazing and start learning how to communicate with a woman; Nick Pulovski, who is promoted from grand-theft-auto detective to lieutenant (a de facto retirement from the streets), can finally recline in an office and eat donuts all day. *Unforgiven* stresses the need for Eastwood's characters to retire — as soon as Munny resumes his erstwhile career as a bounty killer, he degenerates into a cold-blooded killer.

With *The Rookie* and *Unforgiven,* Eastwood intensifies his study of violence by making it less palatable for the viewer. Each film ends with a disturbing exchange of tight high angle and low angle close-ups that blur the line between victim and aggressor. In *Unforgiven*— a grim morality play that exposes the underside of the Man with No Name — Eastwood resurrects No Name one last time to show us the overriding horror of violence and the gulf that exists between the human and the mythic parts of his persona. Part mortal, part legend, and part myth, Munny is a walking critique of the Trinity that has defined Eastwood's persona and cinema. No Name's cool exterior hides an Id as monstrous as Micky (Woody Harrelson) and Malory (Juliette Lewis) in *Natural Born Killers* (Oliver Stone, 1994). By dissecting and deconstructing No Name, Eastwood raises doubts about an archetype he helped create and popularize: Munny is touchingly human, but he is also shockingly inhuman. In *The Rookie,* Eastwood leaves the Dirty Harry series in a cul-de-sac and robs Harry of his mystique by making Nick part of the very bureaucracy that Harry shuns and despises. To further subvert the Dirty Harry series, Eastwood strips the violent content of the film of any depth and meaning. Both *The Rookie* and *Unforgiven* let us know in no uncertain terms that No Name and Dirty Harry no longer define Eastwood's cinema, opening up new horizons for his directorial work.

Eastwood not only overcomes his persona during his third phase as a starteur; he also broadens the scope of his style and uses it to enhance his study of death, mortality, and the true essence of humanity. He brings the artistic cycle to a close with two films that highlight different elements of his aesthetic: *Bird,* which is elliptical and experimental; *White Hunter, Black Heart,* which is linear and austere. While *Bird* is an inclusive character study in which there is no distance between the viewer and Charlie Parker's consciousness, *White Hunter, Black Heart* keeps us at arm's length until the final moments, when John Wilson stops acting and starts being. In both films,

Eastwood strives for a holistic union of time, space, and character. As with Red's recognition of his impending death in *Honkytonk Man*, Eastwood pushes toward a phenomenological catharsis that gives the film its narrative and graphic thrust.

With *Unforgiven* and *A Perfect World*, Eastwood redoubles his study of humanity and morality by asking us to identify with two antiheroes: William Munny, a legendary outlaw, and Butch Haynes, a sociopathic fugitive. Although both men are confirmed murderers, Munny and Haynes, through their futile attempts to overcome their flaws, exhibit more humanity than their victims or pursuers. Eastwood takes us out of the Manichean world of *High Plains Drifter*, *The Outlaw Josey Wales*, *Sudden Impact*, and *Pale Rider* and guides us into a forbidden zone where guilt and innocence, good and evil, and sin and salvation are hard to pinpoint or determine. Instead of presenting us with an indestructible super hero, Eastwood gives us criminals and artists who are as inexplicable as life itself. In *A Perfect World*, the capstone of his third phase and the triumph of Eastwood the director over Eastwood the star (as Red Garnett, he manages to be a supporting actor in his own film), he brings together all of his thematic and cinematic elements into an epiphany, a circular summation of all that is unmistakably Eastwoodian, a summation he has been striving for since the bird's-eye opening of *Play Misty for Me*.

Heartbreak Ridge, 1986

Tom Highway in *Heartbreak Ridge* is proud of his military
achievements, but there's a statement in the film about machismo
and a certain anti-pseudo machismo, in a way. It's portrayed in
the outrageous things this guy does [Gentry, p. 22].

In the mid-1980s, the war genre was a fading phenomenon. The specter of Vietnam had denounced and deconstructed the post-WWII image of the clean-cut GI. The moral division of right and wrong and the themes of duty and sacrifice that defined such films as *Sgt. York* (Howard Hawks, 1942) and *They Were Expendable* (John Ford, 1945) went by the wayside. Films such as *The Deer Hunter* (Michael Cimino, 1978), *Apocalypse Now* (Francis Ford Coppola, 1979), *Platoon* (Oliver Stone, 1986) and *Full Metal Jacket* (Stanley Kubrick, 1987) indicted war and associated it with genocide, suicide, and madness. Virtually no film in the 1980s used World War II or Korea as a backdrop, and the few contemporary war films that succeeded at the box office were routine action-adventures that featured men without depth or tenderness obsessed by the memory of Vietnam (*Rambo: First Blood Part II* [George P. Cosmatos, 1985]; *Missing in Action* [Joseph Zito, 1984]). *Heartbreak Ridge* is not representative of the Vietnam cycle or the Rambo clones of the mid-to late 1980s. Eastwood had already played a shell-shocked Vietnam veteran in *Firefox*. He had already dealt with the traumatic legacy of war in *The Outlaw Josey Wales*. In *Heartbreak Ridge*, the disappointments of Korea and Vietnam haunt Gunnery Sergeant Thomas Highway (Clint Eastwood), but what weighs heaviest on his heart is not his combat record, but his inability to communicate with his ex-wife Aggie (Marsha Mason), a woman he loves, but misunderstands and takes for granted.

Highway is similar to Bronco Billy and Dirty Harry. His devotion to the Marines is as steadfast as Billy's commitment to the Wild West Show and Harry's belief in a code of universal justice. Highway has no tolerance for bureaucracy or mediocrity and cannot conform to civilian life. He believes "that a lot of body bags get filled if I don't do my job." A martial Dirty Harry, Highway goes by the book until the book becomes too constrictive and prevents him from ensuring the proper training and safety of his men. Highway's mantra is "you improvise, you overcome, you adapt." He relies on this mantra while in uniform but fails to make use of it in his personal life or his relationships with women. In Eastwood's words:

> He's innocent in a scarred-up kind of way, even though he shouldn't be innocent at all. I like that quality in him ... He is fighting the enemy within him ... He is a strange paradox. Nowadays in the marine corps, recruits are represented as computer operators having a great time. Highway is from the old school. He's been in the trenches and fought in the jungles. He doesn't think the realities of war should be hidden or covered up ... On the other hand, he feels tremendous anxiety about his personal relationships. The whole idea of reading *Harpers,* [sic] *Bazaar* or *Cosmopolitan* to learn the secrets of a relationship is really naive, but he actually is naive about women. He has never been understanding or emotional in his entire life, even though he may have wanted to be. He simply never took the time. His love life probably amounted to a gal in Bangkok or a woman in Taiwan now and then. His only serious relationship had been with Aggie, and he didn't know how to handle her. Actually they didn't know how to handle each other ... Highway's whole life is a tragedy [Plaza, p. 166].

Highway's foolish attempts to memorize catchwords from women's magazines to become a sensitive male are as wrong-headed as his macho drinking binges. When Highway asks Aggie, "Did we mutually nurture each other? Did we communicate in a meaningful way in our relationship?," Aggie responds incredulously, "Hell, I thought we were married." Aggie does not want an emasculated Highway. What she wants is a Highway who knows that she is "not one of your troops who can be bullied." Eastwood does not see the male ego as a disease that needs to be cured. What Eastwood decries, and what Highway suffers from, is machismo, and how it prevents men like Highway from establishing meaningful relationships with men or women. Like Josey Wales, Highway must let go of his memories and join the rest of society. To do so, he must acknowledge that his devotion to the Marines has been an excuse to be an overgrown adolescent instead of a loving husband.

Highway's praiseworthy attempts to reconcile with Aggie and reverse the severe limitations of the Marine's exclusive code of masculinity discredit John Wayne, an icon Eastwood has been compared with since the late 1960s. Although Wayne personified the postwar American male in westerns directed by John Ford (*Stagecoach, Fort Apache* [1948], *The Searchers, The Man Who Shot Liberty Valance* [1962]) and Howard Hawks (*Red River, Rio Bravo, El Dorado*), his major contribution to American culture was *Sands of Iwo Jima* (Alan Dwan, 1949) and the archetype of the gung-ho American: "not until John Wayne created the role of Sergeant Stryker in *Sands of Iwo Jima* and then merged his own personality with the character did Americans find a man who personified the ideal soldier, sailor or Marine" (Suid, 1978, p. 92). With *Heartbreak Ridge*, Eastwood pokes fun at Sgt. Stryker and Wayne's code of masculinity. The film is a comic refutation of *Sands of Iwo Jima*, a burlesque critique of a male universe that dares to marginalize women.

The beginning and end of *Heartbreak Ridge* inversely establish and resolve Highway's need to retire from the Marines and reconcile his differences with Aggie. The film opens with stock black and white footage of the Korean War, the formative period in Highway's life and military career. As the front credits end, we move gradually into the present (1983) and an aerial view of a detention center. Cinematographer Jack N. Green slowly inserts color as we track toward Highway, who is spending the night in jail for urinating on a police car and being drunk and disorderly. The slow transition from black and white to color and the confluence of the Korean War footage with a drunken, incarcerated Highway suggests that he is imprisoned by the past, that the martial brotherhood of John Wayne and *Sands of Iwo Jima* has deteriorated into boastful besottedness. By dissolving into the present without automatically switching from black and white to color, Green and Eastwood emphasize Highway's rudimentary, monochromatic mindset and his estrangement from the sexual normalization of the post-Vietnam era. It is apt that our first encounter with Highway should be inside a jail cell full of

overweight drifters and reprobates listening in as he tells some of his salacious war stories to an eager young inmate. When one roughneck has the
temerity to question Highway's masculinity, Highway responds with a heavy
dose of bravado ("Be advised that I'm mean, nasty and tired. I eat constan-
tino wire and piss napalm, and I can put a round through a flea's ass at 200
meters.") and a precise series of blows that trounce his opponent. His manhood verified and validated, Highway returns to his story, a raw condem-
nation of some Indonesian whores who had the effrontery to give him and
several other Marines gonorrhea. Highway's notion of masculinity is severely
limited — outside of this narrow, enclosed world of shit talking and fist fighting, Highway is a nuisance and an embarrassment. He cannot grow out of
the machismo that has kept him gung ho for 30 years.

When he meets his troops for the first time — an unimpressive and
insubordinate bunch of grousers and goldbricks — Highway brags, "I've
drunk more beer and pissed more blood, banged more quiff and busted
more ass than all of you numb-nuts put together." In Highway's world, the
penis and the vagina predominate. His two favorite subjects are fighting
and fucking. Highway relies on his vast arsenal of off-color one liners to train
and discipline his men. He loves to undercut the affection or respect another
man may feel for him by making crude, homoerotic wisecracks ("I'm not
doing this because I want to take long showers with you assholes."). Toward
his African-American protégé, Stitch Jones (Mario Van Peebles), Highway
is critical and callow (when Stitch jokes, "What's twelve inches and white —
nothing," Highway responds, "I'll show you what's black and bleeding if it
don't shut its face") until he is convinced that Stitch can fend for himself on
the battlefield. Highway's pornographic view of the world enables him to
be a peerless drill sergeant, but once he leaves the base, Highway is adrift.
Aggie is ready to spar with him the moment he finagles his way into her
home. Until he matures, Highway is a priapic parody of John Wayne, a dip-
somaniac obsessed with his own manufactured masculinity.

In *Heartbreak Ridge*, the invasion of Grenada is an afterthought, an
excuse for Highway to gracefully exit from the Marines. The true highlight
of the film is when Highway listens to Aggie and realizes that his inability
to communicate and his fear of commitment caused the failure of their marriage. Highway shows a new willingness to discard his phallo-centrism and
respect Aggie's emotional needs. Eastwood does not portray Grenada as a
tactical victory, but simply a golden opportunity for Highway to retire without any regrets or dishonor. Highway leads the platoon to its first skirmish,
but is forced to take cover and play dead while Stitch Jones takes command
and completes the assault. Jones' combat readiness and ability to "improvise, overcome, and adapt" alleviate Highway's fears that the Marines will
not find a few good men to replace him. Highway's declaration that his

Gunnery Sergeant Thomas Highway (Clint Eastwood) relies on his braggadocio and machismo to transform Stitch Jones (Mario Van Peebles) into an elite Marine. Highway's code of masculinity works well in the barracks, but not in the home of his ex-wife Aggie (Marsha Mason), who has little patience for Highway's adolescent behavior.

record is now 1-1-1 (Korea: tie, Vietnam: loss, Grenada: win), is a sly wink to the audience — Grenada is Highway's psychological victory, and little else. Eastwood portrays Grenada as a second-rate military operation, an unspectacular Marine landing spoiled by poor logistics and gross mismanagement (Jones has to use his calling card to call in an air strike). Highway shows much more bravery in Aggie's living room than he does in the Caribbean.

The climactic homecoming of *Heartbreak Ridge* is a wonderful refutation of the opening credits. No longer confined by the black and white images of the Korean War, Highway is emancipated by the red, white, and blue images of the American flag and the hundreds of bright, loving faces that are eager to welcome the troops home. Highway does not have to die in combat like Sgt. Stryker in *Sands of Iwo Jima*. He does not need to be a noble sacrifice and a testament to the male ego and the martial spirit of the armed forces. In *Heartbreak Ridge*, that sacrifice is no longer necessary. A greater, more necessary sacrifice is Highway's determination to renounce his machismo and reunite with his ex-wife. Highway leaves the film arm in arm with Aggie. A state of grace between the sexes replaces the Cold War and Highway's fascination with his penis.

Heartbreak Ridge has all the benchmarks of a traditional war film, but at heart, it is really a racy throwback to the service comedies of the 1950s and 1960s ("Gomer Pyle," "McHale's Navy"). The combat sequence is out of sync with the rest of the film. Eastwood cannot make up his mind whether the invasion of Grenada should be taken seriously or played for laughs like the first two-thirds of the film. The lack of a consistent tone or a gritty climax makes the film overlong (it could lose about 20 minutes of footage) and uneven. Except for the opening and closing images — which give *Heartbreak Ridge* an antonymous unity — most of the film seems rushed and under-rehearsed. Mise-en-scène and montage are not integrated enough to give the film a balanced rhythm. Eastwood never gives us a distinct sense of time or place. He tries to give the film a loose, phenomenological feel, but he does not use space, composition or the lens to compliment the long takes, resulting in episodic scenes that hit or miss. Many of the film's shots are cut short and not given adequate time to breathe. The film seems to have been edited with a rusty pair of hedge clippers.

Next to *The Rookie, Heartbreak Ridge* qualifies as Eastwood's sloppiest film. Eastwood seems to equate comedy with slapdash technique. Except for *Bronco Billy* (the only comedy Eastwood has directed with a sure hand) and *Every Which Way But Loose* (a film that somehow benefits from being sloppy), some of the worst Malpaso films have been comedies (*Any Which Way You Can, City Heat, Pink Cadillac*). *Heartbreak Ridge* functions mainly as a comic vehicle for Eastwood. Eastwood is ideal as Highway, but apart from Marsha Mason and Arlen Dean Snyder as Choozoo, the acting is alarmingly amateurish. Mario Van Peebles' physique is much tighter than his peacockish performance. Another serious drawback is Green's cinematography, which is entirely too dark. Green takes Eastwood's preference for backlighting to an extreme — during the combat sequence, it is difficult to determine who is who. It would take one more film (*Bird*) for Green to inherit Bruce Surtees' legacy and master the nuances of backlighting and location shooting. Despite its many problems, *Heartbreak Ridge* does has two virtues: Eastwood's virtuoso performance and Jim Carabatsos' screenplay, an inexhaustible source of outrageous put-downs and salacious Parthian shots. Eastwood shit talks with the speed and dexterity of a rap artist. Carabatsos' script was considered to be so salty that the Department of Defense withdrew its support for the film. *Heartbreak Ridge* is not an advertisement for the armed forces. Highway even shoots a Cuban mercenary in the back, a scene the military ruled as a serious no-no.

With *Heartbreak Ridge*, Eastwood gets a welcome break from the Man with No Name and Dirty Harry and another opportunity to show the virtue of an adult understanding between a man and a woman. The film, however, lacks the visual and thematic unity of the redemption cycle. With *Bird*, Eastwood would return to the visual and thematic unity of *Bronco Billy* and *Honkytonk Man* and embark on an odyssey of films that would re-define and enlarge his cinescape.

Bird, 1988

If they get it, they get it. If they don't, maybe someone who knows will point it out. I couldn't just make it for the lowest common denominator [Plaza, p. 183].

Bird and *White Hunter, Black Heart*, the final two installments of the artist cycle, mark a return to balanced form for Eastwood. Although both are detailed character studies, *Bird* and *White Hunter, Black Heart* are polar opposites: they form a diptych that extends the boundaries of Eastwood's cinema without compromising its core elements. *Bird* is an expressionistic labyrinth, a circular and elliptical journey into a tortured musician's soul; *White Hunter, Black Heart* is a straightforward examination of a filmmaker possessed by hauteur and hubris. With *Bird*, Eastwood discards narrative and plunges into phenomenology; with *White Hunter, Black Heart*, Eastwood remains faithful to a narrative in order to achieve a phenomenological catharsis. In *Bird*, nearly a half-dozen characters serve as a collective, interior narrator; in *White Hunter, Black Heart*, the narrator is Peter Verrill, a third-person raconteur whose memories and feelings do not define or interrupt the narrative. *Bird* asks us to identify directly with Charlie "Bird" Parker (Forest Whitaker) and tap into his life force; *White Hunter, Black Heart* distances us from John Wilson by preserving an objective narrative structure. *Bird* asks us to participate; *White Hunter, Black Heart* to observe. Both films make use of backlighting and intimate framing (a staple of the artistic cycle), but instead of *White Hunter, Black Heart*'s use of reverse masters and extensive location shooting, *Bird* relies on subterranean lighting and transmutable montage. A nocturnal, underground film, *Bird* rarely ventures outside of Bird's psyche. When it does, Bird is either unconscious or dead. *White Hunter, Black Heart* is the opposite: Eastwood replaces *Bird*'s transitional form dissolves with movement within the frame to assert the primacy of nature and achieve a cogent sense of time and place. The absence of light and narrative define *Bird*; the prominence of the African sun and the

Eastwood makes use of an elliptical narrative and a bebop mixture of memories and formal montage to bring us into the psyche of Charlie Parker (Forest Whitaker), a musician who cannot reconcile his heroin addiction with his *joie de vivre.*

Aristotelian resolution of Wilson's egotism define *White Hunter, Black Heart.* Charlie Parker is an open book; John Wilson, a self-conscious enigma. Eastwood varies each film's style to capture the essence of Bird and Wilson's respective mindsets. According to Eastwood, Bird "was responsible for so many innovations with rhythm, harmony, melody, intonation, improvisation and just on and on" (Gentry, p. 16) however, Bird "was a man of unusual sensibility and feeling. Along with that he didn't know how to curb things, to do things without excess. He would do things in extremes" (Gentry, p. 21). Because Parker is such a raw, unfocused life force, *Bird* itself is an episodic paradox, a Gordian knot of dichotomies and ambiguities. Because Wilson is a master manipulator, *White Hunter, Black Heart* has a controlled, economical narrative that comes to a tragic end when Wilson discovers the enormity of his hubris.

In *Bird*, life is mercurial and incomprehensible. The film is a lifelong, freeform fusion of bebop jazz and backlighting, movement and stasis, sound and silence. Eastwood uses various camera angles, tracking shots, compound moving shots, arc track-crane pans, double exposures, lap dissolves, sound dissolves, natural wipes (the cymbal and the iodine bottle), and fades to give *Bird* a fluid sense of time, place, and consciousness. He brings us inside bebop's "distended chords, esoteric scales and melodic extensions" (Megill and Devlory, 1984, p. 120) and Bird's stream of consciousness by adapting them into cinematic terms. Instead of rhythm, melody, timbre, and harmony, Eastwood relies on mise-en-scène, montage, and the transitional, associative, and abstract powers of cinema. The intervals between octaves are filled in with long takes or angle-reverse angles; pitch becomes the degree of lighting or the angle of the lens. The final cadence is not a musical piece, but a climactic montage that splices together the major motifs and characters of the film. For Eastwood:

> *Bird* is reflective of the music. It floats back and forth between
> these periods of his life and I didn't want to do condescending
> things like start a scene with 'July 10, 1944' or something like that.
> You just go there. By and large, you're moving in and out of the
> time changes, just by the visuals or the general feel [Gentry,
> p. 17].

Eastwood uses backlighting and extremely low-key lighting to bring to the surface the mysterious forces that both inspired Bird's genius and hastened his destruction:

> The usual lighting on an actor is a key light, a fill light, and a
> backlight. A lot of times, especially on Forest, we used only a key
> light. Sometimes the light came in straight from behind him, so
> he was just a silhouette backlit against smoke. There was hardly·
> anything there. One of the reasons we did this was to underscore
> his isolation. *Bird* is very much a one-light picture. I told Jack
> Green that I wanted to approach *Bird* as if it were a black and
> white film. We've done that before, like with Tightrope. You light
> the film for surfaces and spatial depth more than for color tex-
> ture. Even with costumes, they tended to be dark and light rather
> than too colorful [Gentry, p. 19].

Cinematographer Jack N. Green saw the backlighting as a way to emphasize the symbolic beauty and texture of black skin and the tensions underlying Bird's interracial relationship with Chan Richardson (Diane Venora):

I knew the film was a cameraman's dream — it was full of wonderful visuals, seedy, dark nightclubs, dark alleys, lots of night
scenes, and all with a cast of dark people mixed with very light
people. The main difficulty — and I was trying to be consistent
about this — was to maintain my first approach to the lighting in
this film, and to do exactly the opposite of everybody I'd seen
light the combination of a white actress and a black actor before,
which is to put the key light favoring the black person, and let the
spill, or fill light the white person, which makes sense, because it
has good balance. But I did exactly the opposite, I lit my key light
to her, and let him take a back edge light, or what was left of fill
light — and there was very little of that, because I don't use much
fill light ... black skin does something with that kind of light that
white skin can't do, it reflects the light so well and so bright as its
angle skips across the skin [Plaza, pp. 176-7].

Although Pauline Kael complained that *Bird*, "looks as if (Eastwood) hadn't
paid his Con Edison bill," (Biskind, 1993, p. 56) the low-key lighting creates a myriad of dichotomies that lend substance and structure to the film:
light and dark; black and white; past and present; life and death; success and
failure; jazz and heroin; memory and reality. Eastwood keeps *Bird* dark from
the beginning (the stark front credits) to the end (the overcast funeral service) to sustain the dichotomies that make up Bird and his nocturnal, moody
existence.

Bird's front credits pass by quickly, setting up the central dichotomies
of the film by eliminating any need for exposition or continuity. Eastwood
alternates from dark stationary credits to two postmeridian, outdoor tracking shots, establishing a dichotomy of movement and light, stasis and dark.
The first track pan features Bird as a child riding a pony and playing a pic-
colo. The second features Bird as a teenager, practicing the saxophone. Both
are compound moving shots that intersect and pull away from Bird as a
foregrounded object (laundry rustling in the breeze, the side of a house)
obscures the lens and sets up a transitional fade. Eastwood does not introduce us to Bird. He abbreviates Bird's childhood and adolescence (it is said
that Bird did not remain innocent for long: he was a heroin addict at age 15
and married a year later) so that he can plunge directly into his adult life
and consciousness. Cross-cutting across time eliminates the need for
chronology or correlative clarity. With the bridging shot of an airborne
cymbal, Eastwood contrasts Bird's rise (1944) and fall (1954) at the beginning of the film to stress dichotomy over narrative, mood over continuity.
Through intimate framing and selective lighting, Eastwood places us in the
middle of Bird's thoughts, relationships, and performances, and lets us
become an unconditional part of his life. Because it is reflective of bebop,

Bird introduces motifs and dichotomies early in the film so that they can be played in different keys (i.e., cinematic arrangements) throughout the film. The past and present are decussated, repeated, and revisited. Eastwood takes events out of context to bring us closer to Bird and the dichotomies that make him both irresistible and insufferable.

As the credits end, the camera moves out of darkness into the year 1944 and the Three Deuces club, where Bird is in the midst of "Lester Leaps In". Bathed in a lustrous blue light that highlights Bird and his performance, the Three Deuces is cavernous, yet cozy. The camera forms another rightward track pan, craning close to Bird as it follows the fixtures of the club, the symmetry of the shot and the centrality of place a sign that Bird is in his element, that he is tune with his instrument and his audience. The preponderance of moving shots in *Bird* suggests that Parker is airborne — he is "on the wing". His life is a suspended cymbal toss. Bird's flight is suggested by the repetition of the cymbal that takes us out of 1944 and into 1954 and the continual arc pans and camera tracks that initiate scene transitions. The cymbal's right to left movement (left to right is considered to be normal — right to left movement is traditionally associated with disorder and disorientation) contrasts with the front credit and 1944 track pans, which suggest an ascendance. The cymbal signals Bird's short life span and his eventual downfall. When it finally lands, *Bird* ends with a stunning finality.

Thunder crashes and rain falls as the cymbal crosses the frame and bridges the temporal gap between 1944 and 1954. Following a disastrous performance at Birdland, Parker stumbles into his home, disoriented by stomach ulcers, heroin, alcohol, and melancholia. Eastwood gives us two sides of Bird: the public genius and the private junkie. By showing Parker before and after his prime, Eastwood constructs a whole series of dichotomies that give us a well-rounded portrait of Bird. We see the public Bird captivating an audience in 1944; ten years later, we see the private Bird, distraught and alone. In 1944, Bird is healthy, well-dressed, and intoxicated by the fervor of bebop; in 1954, he is incapacitated by substance abuse, poor health, and strong thoughts of suicide. During the Three Deuces performance of "Lester Leaps In," everything fits; ten years later, Bird complains that his solo clashed with his string section. Inside the Three Deuces, Parker is illuminated by a complimentary hard-edge blue light; inside his home, Bird is edge-lit by thunder cascading in the evening sky. Unlike the patrons of the Three Deuces, Chan does not greet Bird with applause. She watches him with a stoic disinterestedness that belies years of pain and disappointment. Bird cannot avoid the subject of death; he tells Chan that he has drafted a will, swoops into the bathroom, contemplates his reflection, and then attempts suicide by swallowing a bottle of iodine. Drained by Bird's self-destructive mood swings, Chan spends several seconds watching Bird languish on the floor before she wearily remarks, "That was stupid. Now I'll have to call an ambulance."

By way of a sound dissolve — a voice-over of Dr. Heath (Arlen Dean Snydor) reading Bird's psychological profile — Eastwood takes us to Bellevue Hospital, where the film changes course and becomes a circinated, interconnected series of flashbacks. The first two flashes of memory belong to Bird: Eastwood tracks toward a medium close-up of Bird and dissolves back to 1935, when Bird began shooting heroin, and 1938, when he began to hone his style by taking part in Buster Franklin's (Keith David) Cutting Contest. The first flashback serves as an omen: Dr. Caulfield (Bill Cobbs), the doctor who delivered Bird, warns young Parker (Damon Whitaker) that heroin will kill him prematurely. When asked, "What are you going to do about it?", Bird replies, "What am I supposed to do about it?," a phrase he repeats when the flashback dissolves away, a sign that he never forgot, but nonetheless never heeded Dr. Caulfield's warning. The 1938 flashback — a prelude to Buster Franklin's flashback within a flashback — briefly shows Bird a year before he discovers his style. Eastwood moves down a hallway of aspiring saxophonists, ending the track in front of Bird, who waits anxiously to test his skills against Buster. In 1935, we see what will destroy Bird; in 1938, we see what will redeem and immortalize him. Bird shows both courage and cowardice, ambition and apathy. We see hints of his genius and the seeds of his destruction. After the 1938 flashback, Eastwood returns to 1954 via the airborne cymbal, a reminder of Bird's dual nature and his inescapable fate.

After entering Bird's consciousness for a short time, Eastwood cuts to Chan, who rejects Dr. Heath's recommendation that Bird be given shock treatment: "We're talking about a very special, creative man. His livelihood depends on his ability to improvise and compose music." Dr. Heath asks Chan whether she wants a musician or a husband. Chan's reply? "They do not separate." Chan loves not only Bird, but his music. She cannot conceive of Bird without his talent. Because Chan's father was a successful nightclub owner and jazz entrepreneur, Chan knows jazz and loves it dearly. Her knowledge and love of jazz enable her to understand the magnitude of Bird's artistry and tolerate his many shortcomings. To trace how and why Chan became so enamored of Bird, Eastwood segues into the first extended flashback of the film, a complex, concentric network of events and perspectives generated by Bird and Dizzy Gillespie's (Samuel E. Wright) eight-week engagement at the Three Deuces.

Eastwood uses an evocative lap dissolve reminiscent of Jed Leland's flashback to the breakfast table in *Citizen Kane* (Orson Welles, 1941) to take us back to 1944. He keeps Chan in the right side of the frame as he fades out the interior of Dr. Heath's office and fades into 1944, the year Chan met Bird.

In the left side of the frame we see a sprightly Chan, lighting a cigarette and dashing across the street. Eastwood lingers on the superimposed face of the older Chan before he slowly dissolves her out of view. With this dissolve (and many others), Eastwood moves between counterbalanced shots to suggest a transference of time and space. By lap dissolving or match cutting with reflective, symmetrical shots, Eastwood gives the flashbacks a seamless sense of balance and flow: memory becomes a fluid exchange of concrete, composed images. Such counterbalance of form lends structure to a seemingly chaotic mélange of events and perspectives.

The camera cranes upward as Chan crisscrosses toward 52nd Street, the home of bebop. As Chan makes her way to "the Street", jazz music seeps into the soundtrack. Eastwood lovingly recreates 52nd Street in its heyday, tracking behind Chan as she walks with a hip, jaunty step, invigorated by the numerous strains and styles of jazz wafting from the clubs. Chan greets Pinkus, the Mayor of 52nd Street (Hamilton Camp) with a hug and darts into the Three Deuces. The tracking shot that dutifully trailed Chan becomes a running long take led by Pinkus, who takes us on an impromptu tour of the Street as he hustles for his next tip. Eastwood switches to a third narrator when Pinkus' running take is interrupted by Buster Franklin, who steals Pinkus' shot with a reverse angle cutaway.

Pinkus raves about Bird, but is rebuked by Buster, who erupts into laughter when he recalls Bird's disastrous "debut" in 1938. Eastwood dissolves from Buster back to the 1938 cutting contest, once again using a close-up of a face (Buster is on the left side of the frame, as opposed to Chan, who sits on the right side) as a reference point. Once on stage, it does not take long for the teenage Bird to dissect the melody and stray away from the tempo. Buster and his band, accustomed to the easy rhythms of blues and swing music, do not know how to respond to Bird's melodic extensions. His atonal sound alienates the audience and inspires Buster's drummer to unscrew his cymbal and toss it contemptuously on the floor. Eastwood cuts to a low-angle shot of Bird, looking pensive and unnerved as the band and the audience laugh him off stage. Only Buster's laugh has a nervous twinge of dread and envy — deep down he knows that Bird is not a clever performer like himself, but a prodigy who will redefine jazz music. Buster's anxious laugh serves as a convenient bridge back to 1944 — by dissolving from Buster laughing in 1938 to him laughing in 1944, Eastwood suggests that for six years Bird has been a joke and a mere anecdote or memory to Buster. That changes as soon as Buster wrests the camera from Pinkus and enters the Three Deuces, bringing us back to Bird's opening performance of "Lester Leaps In". Buster's face grows increasingly solemn as Bird cuts loose: confronted by his own obsolescence, Buster doubts his own musicianship. Eastwood cuts away from Buster to a medium shot of Chan, who is entranced by Bird's wizardry. Chan is elated; Buster is devastated. As she claps, we hear her voice-over, a reminder that she is the original narrator of the flashback. It is here that *Bird* resembles the pattern of bebop: Chan's memory branches off into a collective experience that transposes shots and memories as if they were bebop melodies. Eastwood moves from narrator to narrator and memory to memory without losing the flow or meaning of the sequence. Before closing out the flashback, Eastwood cuts back to Buster, who is alone on a bridge, a symbol of his displacement. Relegated to a relic, Buster mumbles, "What do you think of Yardbird," and throws his sax into the river. It is here, as the sax slowly sinks and disappears from view, that Eastwood superimposes Chan's head and dissolves back to 1954. During Chan's flashback, we see Bird's public side and his musical genius and influence. Instead of entering Bird's consciousness, we experience the trepidation and exhilaration that his music evoked. Because of this, Chan's flashback does not stay with one narrator nor does it have the desperate mood swings of Bird's three extended flashbacks. Bird is not the dominant interest of Chan's collective flashback; it is his music that binds it together. When Eastwood concentrates on Bird's memories, we grow closer to the private Bird and the dichotomies that tear him apart.

Chan's elliptical flashback leads automatically to Bird's first extended flashback, which encompasses the years 1944 through 1947. Riding home in a taxicab after being discharged from Bellevue, Bird revisits the past when Chan hands him a birthday card from Dizzy Gillespie. Eastwood moves toward a medium close-up of Bird and fades to black, the camera panning backwards to 1944 as Dizzy answers his door at four in the morning, brought out of bed by Bird, who is inspired, loaded, and full of song. Bird's early morning visit sets up several dichotomies that divide and unite Bird and Dizzy. Benny Tate (Jason Bernard), a jazz émigré whom Bird parties with in Paris, helps Bird codify the spectrum that he and Dizzy represent: "Diz and Duke (Ellington) on one side, and junkies on the other." Diz is a stable, responsible band leader who honors his engagements and makes provisions for the future. Bird is irresponsible, aimless, and constantly in motion. Although thrice married, Bird cannot lead a domestic existence. Bird envies Dizzy's apartment and stable home life, but he does not have the discipline or will power to make a franchise out of his own music. Dizzy is usually associated with stable, stationary camera setups, while Bird's shots swerve and oscillate, a reflection of his capricious personality and restlessness. Later in the film, when Bird and Dizzy meet at a beach-side cocktail lounge in Los Angeles, Eastwood positions them in angle-reverse angles so that they form a reflection of one another. Both are shot in medium close-up from behind the shoulder: Dizzy framed toward the left, Bird to the right. Dizzy confirms this dichotomy when he tells Bird:

I'm a reformer, you're trying to be a martyr ... Why am I a
leader? Because they don't expect me to be. Because deep down
they like it if the nigger turns out unreliable. Because that's the
way they think its supposed to be. Because I don't give them the
satisfaction of being right ... My secret is if they kill me, it won't
be because I helped them.

Confronted by racial stereotypes, Dizzy undermines the status quo by
being virtuous and reliable. Race complicates Bird's relationship with Chan,
but it is heroin and Bird's lack of self-control that mar his marriage and cripple his career. Dizzy's nemesis is external; Bird's is from within. By not taking responsibility for his absenteeism and drug addiction, Bird embodies the
very stereotypes that Dizzy tries to contradict. Bird's inability to understand the consequences of his actions damages not only his reputation, but
that of the entire African-American community.

Bird's flashback moves from Dizzy, his public collaborator, to Chan, his
private confidante. Bird and Chan's relationship is open and free, yet dark
and unbalanced, symbolized by the stark, high contrast backlighting that
makes up most of their scenes together. Bird cannot express his love to Chan
normally. He either behaves like a mock courtier, making grand romantic
gestures (the Valentino serenade, lip syncing to opera) or a pitiful child,
pleading for understanding and forgiveness. Bird courts Chan by following
her to her brownstone, which, in actuality, served as a haven and salon for
many local jazz musicians. Fond of dropping the word "man" at the end of
any available sentence, Chan takes Bird to the Suicide Room, an ironic choice
given that our first glimpse of Chan and Bird is prior to his suicide attempt.
Chan is both attracted to and repulsed by Bird. When Parker tries to kiss
her, Chan resists his advances by informing him, "You're not my type man."
Bird eventually convinces her otherwise, but perpetuates the backlit, high
contrast dichotomy of attraction and rejection by deserting Chan after making love to her — when Chan informs Bird that she is pregnant by another
man, Bird leaves her shrouded in darkness, a pattern he will repeat throughout the film. Bird never illuminates Chan with his love: she spends most of
her time waiting in the darkness for him to come home, patiently accepting
his limitations as a father and husband. Parker cannot remain faithful to
Chan — he does not have her patience or resolve. The only scene in *Bird* that
shows Parker and Chan coexisting without any tension or misunderstanding is during Bird's third flashback when he is forced to seek work in Los
Angeles after losing his cabaret card. Chan drives Bird to LaGuardia Airport. En route, they share a quiet moment of reflection and clarity as King
Pleasure's version of Parker's "Kansas City" plays on the radio. Because Bird
is in motion, he can relax. The easy melody and the soothing sound of rain

"I just make it. If people want to come and see it, fine. If they don't, that's their prerogative" — Clint Eastwood on location directing *Bird*.

brushing against the car calms Bird and allows him to be comic, sensitive, and nostalgic. As with *Honkytonk Man*, an evening car ride seems to placate Eastwood's characters and allow them to open up and revisit the past. In *Bird*, as with *Play Misty for Me*, *Bronco Billy*, and *Honkytonk Man*, Eastwood achieves intimacy via a series of close angle-reverse angle shots that place us solidly and unobtrusively within Chan and Bird's conversational space.

For *Bird*, Eastwood decided upon a 1:85 aspect ratio to give the film intimacy — unlike *High Plains Drifter*, *The Outlaw Josey Wales*, or *The Gauntlet*, Eastwood is not interested in the widescreen use of distance and space. *Bird* is a private film. Atmosphere is achieved not by taking advantage of natural locations (an Eastwood specialty), but by manipulating the confines of a studio set. The expressionistic lighting and artificial sets take us out of the real world of space and nature and into Bird's chaotic, fragmented world. In keeping with the elliptical nature of the narrative, Eastwood refrains from establishing shots or visual exposition of any kind — there is no progressive montage, just close, tightly framed, carefully composed, and selectively lit shots that place us immediately into the emotional and psychological space of the characters. Eastwood varies each shot, moving from stationary symmetrical setups to restless tracking shots to suggest a constant flow of moods and feelings. *Bird* is indeed similar to jazz in that it varies its focus and tone without losing sight of the overall structure, traveling from one time frame to another, or swooping from one narrator or flashback to another to capture a new perspective or emotion. Eastwood does not emphasize natural, external space until the end of the film, when a road is associated with death and oblivion.

The first part of the 1944-47 flashback features Bird's dichotomous relationship with Dizzy (public) and Chan (private). We are also introduced to Red Rodney (Michael Zelnicker), a Jewish trumpeter who idolizes Bird. The remainder of the flashback degenerates into heroin addiction and madness as Bird stays in Los Angeles and goes into temporary exile to avoid seeing Chan, who gives birth to Kim, the child by the nameless white musician who got her pregnant. Bird sleeps with Audrey (Anna Levine), a wealthy dilettante, goes into withdrawal when he cannot secure a steady supply of heroin, and suffers a mental breakdown while recording "Lover Man." He spends six months recuperating at the Camarillo State Hospital before he brings the flashback to a close by reuniting with Chan in Central Park and meeting her newborn daughter, Kim. To bring us back to 1954, Eastwood cuts from the newborn Kim to her as a seven year old, welcoming her stepfather home.

Parker's second flashback (1949-50) takes its cue from Birdland, the nightclub named after and headlined by Bird. As soon as he steps out of the taxicab, Bird deserts Chan and his family after being harassed by Estevez (James Handy), a corrupt vice cop who reminds Bird that "you're sick, you're an alcoholic, you're a junkie and your mind is hanging by a thread." Unable to handle the pressure, Bird gets drunk and refuses to go home with Chan when she finds him in the rain, languishing on a park bench. He stumbles into an alleyway across the street from Birdland and returns to the past. The short flashback associated with the opening of the club gives Bird a respite from the downward spiral of the previous flashback, but after his triumphant appearance at the International Jazz Festival in Paris and a Jewish Orthodox Wedding in Brooklyn with Red Rodney, Eastwood quickly segues into Bird's third and final flashback (1950-54) when he leaves Birdland and visits the apartment of Rodney, his old band mate. Rodney is the initial inspiration for Bird's third flashback, but when he calls Chan to inform her of Bird's whereabouts, she is identified as a subsidiary interior narrator. Eastwood uses reflective match cuts of Chan and Rodney on opposite sides of the frame to suggest once again a balance and transference of memory and perspective — Bird's close friends and loved ones give meaning and context to his recollections. They give his life structure and flow.

Bird's third flashback repeats the basic structure and tone of the first flashback — it begins with promise and hope, but ends with depression and failure. Disguising Red Rodney as his mulatto trumpeter, Bird assembles a once in a lifetime quintet and embarks on a gratifying tour of the deep South, only to be heartbroken when he discovers that Rodney has emulated him and become a junkie. The quintet folds when Rodney is arrested for possession of heroin. Forced to regroup, Bird moves in with Chan and records a critically acclaimed strings album. Parker yields to his heroin addiction, however, and loses his self-control, *joie de vivre*, cabaret card, and his daughter Pree (one of Bird's two children with Chan) to pneumonia. After Pree's funeral, Eastwood uses a natural wipe of the iodine bottle to bring us back to Dr. Heath's voice-over and the high-angle shot of Bird being rushed to Bellevue, an indication that *Bird* is closing in on itself, that the remainder of the film will be a slow rendezvous with death.

The rest of *Bird* eschews the elliptical construction of the first two hours of the film and settles into a chronological course. Bird can no longer balance the dichotomies that define him, triggering a tragic loss of control and coherence that demoralizes and eventually kills him. He loses his ability to play music, throwing the last half hour of the film into a tailspin. To suggest that Bird's wing has broken, Eastwood curtails the use of elaborate flashbacks and temporal ellipses by de-emphasizing camera movement and scaling down his montage (direct, chronological cuts replace abstract match-cut and form dissolves). Chan and Bird move to Bucks County, Pennsylvania, to give Bird a chance to recover, but his condition worsens. Without his muse, Bird's source of illumination diminishes. A piano sits in the living room, but only Chan plays it in the distance as Parker sits languishing in the foreground (Eastwood uses this same split-field diopter in *White Hunter, Black Heart* and *A Perfect World* to stress, respectively, the gulf between John Wilson and Peter Verrill, and Red Stovall and his associates).

Unable to find peace in a rural setting, Bird gives Chan her last embrace and returns to New York, where he is surprised to encounter Pinkus hustling flesh in front of a line of strip joints. Pinkus points Bird toward the Paramount, the source of the Street's decline. Bird wanders into the theater and sees Buster Franklin performing rock and roll to an appreciative young audience. The roles are reversed: Bird is now the Johnny-come-lately, displaced by a new style he finds alienating and unsophisticated. Bird experiences Buster's reaction of 10 years before, but unlike Buster, Bird feels ostracized not by a superior art form but a bastardization of rhythm and blues and swing jazz. Eastwood uses rock and roll as a metaphor for change: instead of intricate patterns and chords, rock relies on a simple repetition of rhythm, melody, and harmony (Eastwood has openly admitted that he does not like rock and roll, hence the absence of it in most of his films). Bird remarks that Buster's playing does not fit, that his stage show has little integrity or technical ingenuity. When Buster leaves the stage, Bird steals Buster's saxophone and gives his last impromptu performance, the camera tracking ahead of him as he plays a defiant bebop melody. Buster reclaims the instrument that he rejected 10 years before, but is shaken when Bird gives his reason for taking the sax: "I just wanted to see if it could play more than one note at a time." Buster, despite his new-found success, is humbled once again by Bird, who serves as his musical conscience and confessor, reminding him that his success comes not so much from talent, but a protean ability to conform to the times. Virtuosity is Bird's gift and burden. Buster is able to adapt. Bird — debilitated by heroin, the death of his child, the deterioration of his marriage, and the decline of bebop — cannot.

Parker never touches an instrument again. He fails to show up for an audition set up by his manager, Brewster (Michael McGuire), to assuage rumors that he has become completely unreliable. When Bird finally does arrive, drunk and disoriented, everyone has left. The recording studio is dark and deserted. There are no instruments except for a piano, which Bernie absent-mindedly plays. Eastwood contrasts the empty, barren studio with the Paramount to emphasize Bird's isolation and estrangement from his instrument and talent. All Bird can do is complain about his ulcers and reminisce about the past. His genius has been squandered and devitalized. Before leaving the studio, Bird has his last conversation with Chan over the phone. Chan is both relieved and saddened by Bird's late-night phone call: she is relieved to know that he is still alive, but saddened by the fact that his days are numbered. She finally tells him "I hate to hang up," to which he answers, "You didn't always."

Bird leaves the studio and staggers into the stormy night, the camera wobbling behind him as he collapses in front of the Hotel Stanhope, temporary home of jazz matron and connoisseur Baronness Nica (Diane Salinger). Thunder crashes as Bird passes out, throwing the film into darkness until a head-on shot reveals Nica helping him onto a couch. It is here, as Bird watches the Tommy Dorsey Show and goes into convulsions of laughter, that his heart finally gives out. An all-inclusive, climactic montage, a cadenza of events and faces pass by as Bird lies on the couch and accepts his death. We see Dizzy introducing him at the Three Deuces, Buster laughing, Benny Tate laughing, Audrey, Chan, Red masquerading as Albino Red, Pree's coffin, Dr. Caulfield's warning, the Iodine bottle landing on the bathroom floor, and finally, as a conclusive dichotomy, an image of Chan introducing herself to Bird at the Three Deuces (a shot previously unseen) followed by a static shot of a needle and a spoon. Which did Bird love more? Heroin or Chan? Seconds after Bird's death, Eastwood cuts to Buster's drummer in 1938, tossing his cymbal directly into the camera. He then returns to the leitmotif of the airborne cymbal, the natural wipe that contrabalances the hope and promise of the opening pans of the film. With Bird's death, the cymbal finally lands on the ground, spins, and stops.

The film ends with a coda that marks the end of Bird's consciousness. Eastwood uses a natural vertical fade-wipe to transport us to Bird's funeral. Instead of moving into Chan, Dizzy or Red's consciousness, Eastwood's camera stays neutral and distant. Without Bird's spirit, we have no frame of reference. Eastwood's camera refuses to be a participant in Bird's funeral. It gradually pans away to a tree-lined street as a backdrop for the end credits. Like *Honkytonk Man*, *Bird* ends in front of a road, a metaphor for the cycle of life and death (Eastwood substitutes that metaphor with a tree in *Unforgiven* and *A Perfect World*). Without Bird, *Bird* has no cinematic viewpoint or purpose. Death marks the end of the cinematic devices Eastwood relies upon to liberate time and space. Without Bird's memories or contradictory personality, the last shot is just an objective camera eye with nothing to focus on — all we see are passing figures, walking across a rain-swept street.

White Hunter, Black Heart, 1990

He glanced up quickly and grinned, and immediately I felt what I had felt so often on seeing him again: Here was a truly wonderful fellow, the best friend I had, delightful, entertaining, wise, perceptive, warmhearted. I even forgot that I had often had exactly the same feeling toward him before, only to want to escape him desperately not more than two weeks later [Viertel, 1953, p. 114].

I had known him for such a long time, and yet his moods and his thoughts were unpredictable to me. He behaved like a kind, fatherly fellow so much of the time, and then he would suddenly change, and become a torturer, a man bored with himself and bored with his fellows. At other times he became a clown, a bum who allowed himself to drift along uselessly, who seemed to want everyone around him to take advantage of him. Still, he was really never fooled by anyone. But the thing that puzzled me most was the huge gulf that seemed to separate what he had experienced personally and what he wanted to produce as a writer. His stories were always about tough men of action, lost in fruitless adventures, when actually he was a complete stranger to that life. He was a bum and a snob, an intellectual and a frustrated country boy, and he seemed never to be interested in the reality that surrounded him. Perhaps that was the source of his talent, the fact that he only saw the life he wanted to see, the strange romantic existence that did not exist around him, that he brought along himself, and used to color what he ran into [Viertel, 1953, p. 110].

The fever gets hold of you. It turns you every way but loose [Viertel, 1953, p. 149].— Peter Verrill, *White Hunter, Black Heart*

... its OK for you to judge me, and condemn me, and even laugh like crazy if an elephant stomps me to death. But make goddamn sure you learn something from me, kid. Make goddamn sure of that [Viertel, 1953, p. 314].— John Wilson, *White Hunter, Black Heart*

In *Honkytonk Man, Bird, and White Hunter, Black Heart*, Eastwood's artists are consumed by a fever that jeopardizes their work and entire well-being. Because of their lack of discipline and restraint, Red Stovall and Charlie Parker squander their health and talent. The tuberculosis festering inside Red undermines his long-awaited audition at the Grand Ole Opry and ruins his voice just as he is offered a recording contract. Heroin poisons Bird and rids him of his ingenuity and vitality. In *White Hunter, Black Heart*, John Wilson's (Clint Eastwood) obsession with big-game hunting threatens his well-being as well, but unlike Red and Bird, Wilson does not perish — his African guide, Kivu (Boy Mathias Chuma), dies instead. While Red and Bird are "on the wing", Wilson is planted firmly on the ground. Eastwood designs *Honkytonk Man* and *Bird* so that the deaths of Red and Parker are integral to the overall structure of the film. Their deaths give the films meaning and structure. Wilson is not as fragile as Red or Bird. His death is not predetermined. Peter Verrill (Jeff Fahey), Wilson's confidante and critic, describes Wilson as a fighter, "a brilliant screw you all type of filmmaker who continually violated all the unwritten laws of the motion picture business, yet had the magic, almost divine ability to always land on his feet." It is not Wilson's mortality that is integral to *White Hunter, Black Heart*— it is his pachydermatous ego, and how it tramples everyone and everything in its path.

As a filmmaker, Wilson is similar to Bronco Billy. He must rely on the labor, ingenuity, and creativity of others to bring his art to life. Although Billy demands that he be head honcho, he is a caring, loving man who cherishes his troupe and appreciates the sacrifices they have made to keep his dreams alive. Wilson is not as magnanimous as Billy. He expects his crew to adapt and cater to his every whim. An imperious man, Wilson uses people and places as props for his scorn and amusement, particularly Paul Landers (George Dzundra), his long-suffering producer. He agrees to direct *The*

African Trader not for artistic or commercial reasons, but the opportunity to tour Africa and impersonate Ernest Hemingway. The film is an afterthought, a pretext to go on safari and play the role of the Great White Hunter. Wilson invites Peter Verrill to accompany him to Africa to help revise the screenplay, but his real intention is to have Peter be his traveling companion and a kindred soul who will share his appetite for drama and intrigue. For Wilson, movie making is not just a profession; to him it must be as exciting and provocative as the film itself, a test of endurance and accountability, an adventure within an adventure.

Throughout *White Hunter, Black Heart*, Wilson tries to be Errol Flynn, not a real-life director with debts and responsibilities. Of all the protagonists in the artistic cycle, Wilson is the least comfortable with his craft. Instead of shooting a film, Wilson wants to shoot an elephant. Like Billy, Wilson forgets the limitations of being an artist. When Wilson nearly succumbs to fatigue after a day-long safari, Peter helps him to his feet and remarks, "Come on, let's face it. This country's too tough for us ... We're not two heroes out of one of your films." Wilson's response is a defiant blend of fact and fiction:

> You know kid, we're going to end up together, when we're old
> that is. Probably live in a cabin up in the Sierras and pan for gold.
> Have a couple of mules. Sit around the campfire at night, tell lies
> to each other. All the things we've done. The wars we fought, the
> books you've written, the movies I've made.

Wilson cannot accept being a mere film director — he must be a rugged extension of one of his films. After his disastrous attempt to rob a train, Billy learns that his role as a cowboy has no meaning outside of a circus tent. Wilson has to learn that his place is behind the camera, not in the jungle staring down an elephant. He takes Billy's comic blunder and magnifies it into a mortal sin. Wilson's cult of self, his manic need to invite certain disaster and take extreme risks puts not only his life in danger, but the lives of those who accompany him as well.

While *Bird* has a circular and interconnected structure, *White Hunter, Black Heart* has an antonymic structure that progresses from motion to stasis. Eastwood begins the film without front credits or an exposition to establish the basic conflict of the film: Wilson versus nature (In *Unforgiven* and *A Perfect World*, Eastwood truncates the front credits to bring us directly into the narrative and a central milieu or place that encircles the entire film). Our first glimpse of Wilson is of him on horseback crossing the English countryside. Through the use of point of view shots and compound moving shots, Eastwood associates Wilson with movement and action. We do not see Wilson's face as we hear Peter's opening voice-over, just a pair of boots landing defiantly on the ground at the end of his ride. In spite of his brief voice-over, Peter is not the narrator of *White Hunter, Black Heart*. Eastwood does not want us to dive into the stream of consciousness that flows throughout *Bird*. He wants us to stand next to Peter and observe Wilson with a critical and objective eye. In *Bird*, Eastwood uses elaborate montage to enter the emotional and psychological space of Parker and a half-dozen other characters. The film is not fixed in time or space until Bird dies. Because *White Hunter, Black Heart* derives its meaning and structure from Wilson's struggle with nature, Eastwood emphasizes time and space. He does this by reducing camera movement and the elasticity of form that characterizes *Bird*. While *Bird* is an interior studio film — a dark journey into an ailing musician's soul — *White Hunter, Black Heart* is an exterior film in which the journey is an actual trek through Africa. Wilson is self-conscious, but not introspective. Much of *White Hunter, Black Heart* is made up of tightly arranged conversations and confrontations that give the film a relaxed and literal pace. Instead of bebop jazz and the abstract powers of montage, *White Hunter, Black Heart* relies on words and the phenomenological allure of the African landscape.

When we first encounter Wilson, he is staying as a guest in an ornate mansion — the elegant architecture and furnishings are indicative of his chateau-sized ego. Wilson dresses and behaves as if he were an aristocrat instead of an American expatriate $300,000 in debt. Everything about Wilson is exaggerated and ostentatious, from his colonial garb and grandiloquent speech to his brash and haughty manner. Whether he is on horseback racing across a meadow or in a chartered plane careening over the Congo, Wilson must remain in constant motion. Eastwood suggests Wilson's restless nature by staging his and Peter's first conversation in the many rooms, hallways, and staircases of his borrowed mansion. Eastwood does not use an elaborate tracking shot (i.e., the Pinkus shot in *Bird*) to follow Wilson's impromptu tour of the estate — he merely cuts from room to room to suggest Wilson's unrest and limited attention span. For every sentence he utters, Wilson must take two steps. Hired to revise the screenplay, Peter tries to discuss the film's story line, but is stonewalled by Wilson, who refuses to take *The African Trader* seriously. His reasons for working with Paul Landers, a producer that he openly dislikes, are cavalier and consciously contradictory: "There are times when you can't wonder whether it is the right or the wrong thing to do, not for guys like you or me. You just have to pack up and go." Making a film is not daunting enough for Wilson. Despite the fact that he plans to shoot the film in color on location — a Sisyphean task for the most organized of film crews — Wilson must have an existential reason for going to Africa. He must tempt fate and shoot an elephant. Wilson's obsession is

Obsessed with killing an elephant, maverick filmmaker John Wilson (Clint Eastwood) withdraws from his crew and assumes the role of the Great White Hunter. Like Red Stovall in *Honkytonk Man* and Charlie Parker in *Bird*, Wilson searches for inspiration by courting disaster — his hubris becomes dangerously self-destructive.

kindled as soon as he shops for a rifle. He cannot sit still during his early-morning script sessions with Peter. Instead of rewriting the screenplay, Wilson prefers to philosophize about art and his love-hate relationship with his craft. He tells Peter that he will never be a good screenwriter because:

> You let 85 million popcorn eaters pull you this way and that way. To write a movie you must forget that anyone's ever going to see it ... I figure there are two ways to live in this world. One is you can crawl, kiss ass, and write their happy endings, sign their long-term contracts and never take a chance on anything, never fly, and never leave Hollywood. Save all your goddamn money, every cent of it and when you're a healthy 50 you die of a stroke because whatever was wild in you has eaten away the muscles of your heart. The other way is to let the chips fall where they may, refuse to sign their contracts and tell off the guy who can cut your throat and flatter the little guy who's hanging by a thread that you hold ...

The only reason Wilson is willing to meet and negotiate with Landers and the British investors is to ensure that he will have carte blanche to do as he pleases in Africa. Wilson assumes that Peter will repair the script and his crew will solve any technical and logistic problems once the unit lands in Africa.

Wilson arrives at the Entebbe airport in the guise of the Great White Hunter. During his sporadic script sessions with Peter, Wilson sits with his rifle in his hand, poised to go on safari. He resumes his lecture about the art of screenwriting, extolling the virtues of simplicity as he practices his aim. Once he is in Africa, Wilson no longer sees himself as a film director — he is a hunter in search of prey. For Wilson, the elephant is the white whale. Shooting it would be an insolent, romantic gesture, an expression of his Ahab-like defiance of nature, responsibility and the droll reality of existence. For Peter, the elephant "makes one believe in God and the miracle of creation … they're part of a world that no longer exists, a feeling of unconquerable time." Wilson's obsession makes him feverish and incommunicative. He tires of Peter's company when he refuses to join him on safari. Eastwood uses a tight split-screen shot to suggest their estrangement from one another. Wilson stands in front of the lens, smoking a cigarillo. Peter walks into the left midground of the shot and castigates Wilson for his blood lust and selfish lack of interest in the film:

> You're either crazy or the most egocentric, irresponsible
> sonuvabitch that I have ever met. You're about to blow this pic-
> ture out of your nose John. And for what? To commit a crime. To
> kill one of the rarest, most noble creatures that roam the face of
> this crummy earth. And in order for you to commit this crime,
> you're willing to forget about all of us and let this whole god-
> damn thing go down the drain.

Wilson's response is blunt, yet ambiguous:

> You're wrong, kid. It's not a crime to kill an elephant. It's bigger
> than all that. It's a sin to kill an elephant. You understand, it's a
> sin. It's the only sin that you can buy a license and go out and
> commit. That's why I want to do it before I do anything else in
> this world. Do you understand me? Of course you don't, how
> could you? I don't understand myself.

By emphasizing Wilson's head in the shot and having him stare fixedly into the distance, Eastwood shows us how monomaniacal and headstrong Wilson has become. His ego is literally in the foreground. Several scenes later, Eastwood cuts to a similar setup, a five second depth of field shot of Wilson looming in front of the lens, alienated from the rest of the crew.

Alienated from Peter, Wilson gravitates toward Kivu, his guide and hunting partner. Wilson and Kivu form an instant bond that transcends language and culture. When Kivu is first introduced to Wilson, he is back-lit by a corridor, making him as brown and translucent as the African land-scape. Kivu smiles when he meets Wilson, perhaps the first white man he can relate to and trust. Wilson moves into Kivu's village and demands that the whole production be relocated there and in Zibelinsky's hunting lodge so that he can continue to go on safari. When he finally gets close enough to an elephant to see its eyes and get a clean shot, Wilson loses his blood lust and gains an appreciation for the mystery and majesty of nature. Wilson discovers, however, that his hubris cannot go unpunished: to protect its offspring, the elephant charges the hunting party. Kivu pushes Wilson aside and tries to divert the elephant. Wilson can only lie helplessly on the ground and shout, "No!" as Kivu is gored by the elephant. In the beginning of *White Hunter, Black Heart*, Wilson is a blur, an ego force that cannot be stopped. All we see of Wilson are his defiant boots landing on the ground. Once the master of the narrative and his own destiny, Wilson lies stock-still while the elephant kills Kivu, his face no longer hidden or obscured. The ele-phant is not the obedient horse that Wilson rides through the English coun-tryside; it is a beast that can decide a man's fate. Wilson realizes that life can-not be choreographed — Kivu's death cannot be re-shot or edited out of the film. While revising *The African Trader* screenplay with Pete in London, Wilson insists that the two leads should be killed at the end of the film. He refers to himself as a cinematic God who can decide the fate of his charac-ters. When Wilson is finally confronted with the enormity of death and the depth of his own arrogance, he gamely admits to Peter, "You were right, the ending is all wrong," a statement with a double meaning (the ending of *White Hunter, Black Heart* is "all wrong," too). Weighed down by guilt and shame, Wilson returns to the set of *The African Trader* and slumps into the director's chair, his silence, lack of movement, and willingness to start prin-cipal photography a sign that his ego has finally been eclipsed. The final close-ups of Wilson do not foreground his ego, but rather, his catharsis. Wil-son diminishes from a self-made God to a lowly film director, so crushed by the realization that his hubris has caused the death of an innocent man that he can barely whisper the word "action."

The villagers use their drums to voice their sorrow and outrage when they hear of Kivu's death. They repeat the same phrase — "white hunter, black heart" — a searing indictment of Wilson and his egomania. Through-out *White Hunter, Black Heart*, Wilson goes to great lengths to defend blacks and Jews. When Harry (Clive Mantle), the manager of the Lake Victoria Hotel, beats his black waiting staff, Wilson does not hesitate to challenge him to a fist fight. Wilson would like to believe that he is a humanitarian, a benevolent American who does not take advantage of Kivu or his people. In reality, Wilson is no better than Harry or the other racist Europeans who exploit the continent. Like any true liberal, Wilson is a hypocrite — although he claims Kivu is his friend, he treats him more like a servant. The loyalty he craves and receives from Kivu (the kind of loyalty he wanted from Peter) causes the huntsman's death. Wilson is just another Westerner, bringing death and chaos to Africa and its people.

Eastwood concludes *White Hunter, Black Heart* with a gradual track toward Wilson's face, then fades to a peaceful montage of three African land-scapes, a suggestion that a new state of balance exists between Wilson and nature. Wilson's runaway ego no longer determines the film's events. Nature, represented by the elephant, excuviates the narrative and Wilson's unruly ego. No longer mobile and disrespectful to a land and a people he took for granted, Wilson and the film recede so that *The African Trader* and nature can take over.

White Hunter, Black Heart is based on Peter Viertel's novel of the same name, which was loosely based on Viertel's stormy relationship with direc-tor John Huston during the making of *The African Queen* (1951). Viertel helped write the screenplays for three of Huston's films (*We Were Strangers* [1949], *The African Queen*, and *Beat the Devil* [1954]), as well as introduce Huston to Kipling's *The Man Who Would Be King*, which Huston filmed in 1975. Huston was not only the central inspiration for *White Hunter, Black Heart*, but he also suggested to Viertel that the novel should end with Kivu's death, proof that the novel was not so much a *roman à clef* as it was a cri-tique of artistic vanity and hubris.

What distinguishes the book from the film, apart from the usual emen-dations (to simplify the narrative, screenwriters Viertel, James Bridges, and Burt Kennedy limited the film to four key places: the mansion, the Lake Vic-toria Hotel, Zibelinsky's hunting lodge, and Kivu's village), is the climax. In the novel, Wilson's obsession results not only in Kivu's death, but the ele-phant's as well. Wilson does not return to the set of *The African Trader*. He sits in a jeep and listens to the drums vilify his character. Viertel, via Ver-rill's first person narration, gives us a paragraph-long overview of the film and Wilson's fate:

> It is strange when I think of that moment now, now that's it all in
> the past, all the hard bitter work that followed, with Wilson a
> changed man, a gaunt silent scarecrow, moving among the actors
> and the lights and the crew, doing his job, and his job only, the
> job that he hated to do, the movie he had to start when every-
> thing else was over, creating the foolish make-believe when his
> mind was still burdened by the reality he could not stamp out;
> a gaunt empty man who never spoke to anyone unless it was

Buoyed by the Malpaso crew, Clint Eastwood sets up a shot on the set of *White Hunter, Black Heart*.

> necessary, never smiled, never looked anything but haunted and
> troubled. And that moment seems even stranger now when I
> think back and remember the success that greeted the release of
> the picture, the success that everyone connected with it basked
> in. Everyone except Wilson, that is, for he never saw the film
> [Viertel, 1953, p. 367].

Viertel does not absolve Wilson. He curses him, concluding the novel with the malediction "white hunter, black heart". Eastwood does not consign Wilson to a spiritual hell. Kivu's death weighs on Wilson's shoulders, but it does not break him. It forces him to rest in the director's chair and look within. Eastwood gives the film closure by ending the film with the word "action"—as *White Hunter, Heart Black* comes to a phenomenological end (Eastwood relies on longer takes and shot-reverse shots to focus on the sedentary Wilson), *The African Trader* begins. We see the real Wilson, not the outlandish daredevil who jumps out of bed to greet Peter. Wilson is finally able to sit down and be himself. The closing shot of *White Hunter, Black Heart* gives the film a peaceful resolution — Wilson's ego is erased and replaced with the impression of "unconquerable time."

White Hunter, Black Heart is not meant to be a dramatization of the making of *The African Queen*. Eastwood does not try to impersonate John Huston. When *White Hunter, Black Heart* was released in the fall of 1990, many critics complained that Eastwood was not believable as Huston, that he did not capture Huston's larger than life personality. Much like Viertel, Eastwood uses Huston as a source of inspiration, but he does not try to imitate him:

> I never knew the man and I felt it was not really necessary to know him ... I had a pretty precise idea of the way he thought and acted. He was fantastic, disconcerting, a mixture of contradictions. One moment he'd fight physically to defend a young black boy, the next he'd behave disgracefully to his collaborators. He was excessive in everything he did but that was because he believed that stimulation came from constantly taking risks. He was also a skilled manipulator who loved to disconcert people. However, I didn't really want to create an accurate portrait of Huston. What was important was to suggest him rather than ape him, which would anyway have been impossible because he was so complex [Clinch, p. 200].

> I just looked at a lot of Huston's delivery and thought in terms like that. He had a certain patronizing quality and a certain paternal quality, and I just thought about that and let it happen ... I didn't want to do an impersonation. Huston himself would have probably been much more exacting. He would have highlighted the characteristics — I just sort of took on the feeling [Thompson, p. 143].

Eastwood's affected monologues and exaggerated gestures are closer to the descriptions of Wilson in Viertel's novel than Huston's actual mannerisms. Throughout *White Hunter, Black Heart*, Eastwood works against his latent acting style to suggest Wilson's delusions of grandeur and his dissatisfaction with being an artist and intellectual. Eastwood changes his acting style to circumvent his image and achieve an alienation effect — a gnawing sense that Wilson is not who he appears to be, that he is man of numerous guises, whether it be a manor lord or a Great White Hunter. Eastwood uses a mock British accent and a declamatory tone to suggest that Wilson is always acting and putting on a facade to hide his insecurities or discontent. It is only when Wilson is silent that we get a glimpse of the hurt and confusion that he has been able to hide. Eastwood returns to his laconic acting style to bring out Wilson's true self.

For Wilson, masculinity is a romantic code that must be preserved by holding a gun or throwing a punch. Because of his age and his bluster, however, Wilson turns out to be inept at both, particularly when he challenges Harry to a fist fight. In this marvelous, revisionist scene, Eastwood defies his two-fisted *Every Which Way But Loose* persona and allows himself to be knocked out. Wilson's ignominious defeat shows us that masculinity is both a state of mind and body: Wilson has the desire and the drive, but not the youth or physical stamina to keep standing. The same conflict occurs when Wilson goes on safari — despite his will power, Wilson does not have the strength or endurance to make it through the day without wheezing and coughing. Unwilling to accept his age, physical condition, or true self, Wilson is a vessel through which Eastwood can address his own mortality, and his need to retire a persona that does not comply with his advancing age. As Wilson grows closer to the elephant, Eastwood narrows his performance and tightens the character's dialogue so that, in the end, all that remains of Wilson is a whisper and a tearful glance inward.

For Bird, death is both seductive and unthinkable. Even though Parker poisons his body with heroin, he has an illimitable zest for life. When death finally does come, he does not know whether to laugh or cry. For John Wilson, death means not the end, but the beginning of consciousness. *White Hunter, Black Heart* uses death as a point of departure rather than a journey's end. It does not end with *Bird*'s static long shot, but a series of landscapes that mark Wilson's catharsis and reconciliation with nature. When Parker dies, *Bird* comes to an end; when Kivu is gored by the elephant in *White Hunter, Black Heart*, Wilson experiences an emotional release, bringing the film to an expansive close. Kivu's death forces Wilson to understand himself and his craft and assume responsibility for his reckless, egomaniacal behavior. By ending the film with a phenomenological moment of clarity and a series of landscapes, Eastwood emphasizes the mystery of nature and the breadth of Wilson's transformation from a man of hubris to a man of humility.

The Rookie, 1990

I think the days of me doing what I have done in the past are gone ... To be saying smart lines and wiping out tons of people — I'll leave that for the newer guys on the scene [Breskin, p. 108].

After *Bird* and *White Hunter, Black Heart*, Eastwood returned once again to the *de rigueur* diptych of *The Outlaw Josey Wales–The Gauntlet* and *Sudden Impact–Pale Rider* with *The Rookie* and *Unforgiven*. *The Outlaw Josey Wales* and *The Gauntlet* redeemed Eastwood's persona and cleansed it of its spiritual and psychological wounds. In *Sudden Impact* and *Pale Rider*,

Eastwood attempted to minimize the importance of his persona by compressing it and underplaying its role in the narrative. With *The Rookie* and *Unforgiven* Eastwood reveals his growing desire not to be the on-screen gist of his films by marginalizing *and* retiring his persona. Nick Pulovski (Eastwood) is held hostage in *The Rookie* and William Munny falls gravely ill in *Unforgiven* so that the audience cannot rely upon Eastwood as the *primum mobile*. In lieu of Eastwood, the audience is asked to identify with Nick's protégé, David Ackerman (Charlie Sheen), and Munny's old comrade, Ned Logan, and would-be protégé, The Schofield Kid.

The Rookie has none of the modern angst and absurdity of *The Gauntlet* or the barely controlled bedlam of *Sudden Impact*. It barely belongs to the Dirty Harry series and its variants (*The Gauntlet*). Nick is nowhere near as professional or conscientious as Harry Callahan or Ben Shockley. Pulovski has no interest in healing the city of its metaphysical disorders — he is too busy teaching David how to flout the law, intimidate the local citizenry, and behave like an all-around louse. With *The Rookie*, Eastwood lets his persona, style, and trademark morality go by the wayside, allowing hyperbole to take over. Sloppy, overlong, and overwrought, *The Rookie* lacks a coherent setting and characters of any depth or subtlety. While *Breezy*, *The Eiger Sanction*, *Firefox*, *Sudden Impact*, *Pale Rider*, and *Heartbreak Ridge* suffer from a lack of balance, *The Rookie* is so unbalanced it seems both turbulent and lymphatic. Because it is so unbalanced, *The Rookie* takes precedence as the one Eastwood film that is not outwardly Eastwoodian. Except for extensive location shooting (*The Rookie* is set in Los Angeles, a topographical rejection of San Francisco and the Dirty Harry series) and a reliance on reverse masters, there is no circular construction (the scenes in Lt. Garcia's [Pepe Serna] office are too inconsequential), latent acting or sustained mood, image or place. Shots and scenes are either too protracted or abridged to allow the film to keep an even pace or flow. The villains have no symbolic value: in *The Gauntlet*, Blakelock and the law enforcement community are an extension of the modern age and its threat to individuality; in *Sudden Impact*, Mick and Ray are creatures of the subconscious. In *The Rookie*, Strom (Raul Julia)and Liesl (Sonia Braga) are flat villains who have no determinable sociopolitical or psychological significance whatsoever.

With *Bird* and *White Hunter, Black Heart*, Eastwood tests and expands the boundaries of the style that he perfected in the mid-to late 1970s. *The Rookie* does not elaborate on Eastwood's style — it is a lark, an exercise in self-parody that goes completely and heedlessly out of control. In an attempt to escape the waning influence of Dirty Harry (already constricted by *Sudden Impact* and *The Dead Pool*), retire his persona, and flex his creative muscles, Eastwood rejects the very elements and principles that distinguish his cinema. How else can *The Rookie* be interpreted when Eastwood surrenders to the pyrotechnic overkill of *Die Hard* (John McTiernan, 1988), *Die Hard 2* (Renny Harlin, 1990), and *Die Hard With a Vengeance* (McTiernan, 1995), and casts Raul Julia (Puerto Rican) and Sonia Braga (South American) as Germans? Irresponsible and absolutely indefensible in its treatment of violence and police brutality, *The Rookie* undercuts Eastwood's persona by rejecting morality and personal responsibility and takes *Sudden Impact* one step further — it is a willful act of self destruction, a *Lethal Weapon–Naked Gun* (David Zucker, 1988) hybrid that runs amok till the end, when Eastwood realizes how far he has strayed with an image that would prepare the way for *Unforgiven*.

Eastwood's portrayal of Nick Pulovski is as much a lark as the rest of the film. As Nick, Eastwood rejects the restrained mannerisms of Dirty Harry, resorting instead to uninhibited caricature. In temperament and behavior, Pulovski is closer to *White Hunter, Black Heart's* John Wilson than he is to Dirty Harry. Nick is loquacious and boastful. He does not dominate the screen or navigate space like Harry in *Sudden Impact*. Unlike Harry or Ben Shockley, Nick has no moral crusade or quixotic dream to guide his actions. His pursuit of Strom lacks any urgency or moral insight. Strom is not a symbol of America gone awry or a psyche gone haywire; he is a stock villain whom Nick envies and despises. Eastwood makes himself look old, tired, and dyspeptic on purpose to stress the waning importance of his modern persona and to draw attention to the last scene in the film, which marks Eastwood's de facto retirement from Dirty Harry and the cop genre (because *In the Line of Fire* is not a Malpaso film, the references to *Dirty Harry* do not apply).

Until Nick's promotion, Eastwood makes himself look slovenly and long in the tooth. His wardrobe is intentionally drab and badly in need of an iron, particularly a pair of unsightly corduroy trousers that Eastwood wears during the last half of the film. The end of *The Rookie* marks the transformation of Dirty Harry from an outsider to an insider. Nick figuratively dies when he is shot by Strom. When we see him next, he has been promoted to lieutenant. By accepting a promotion and donning a tie, Nick ends the archetypal struggle between Harry and the establishment. Eastwood trades his Magnum for a nameplate. Instead of ossifying Nick, the promotion gives him a new lease on life. He looks trim, healthy and well-groomed. Throughout *The Rookie*, Nick can never find a match to light his cigars; it is only when he is promoted that he receives a lighter of his own. By sitting behind a desk, rather than standing in front of it, Eastwood reveals his desire to be in the background rather than the forefront. This theme would dominate *Unforgiven* and *A Perfect World*, two films in which Eastwood is a passive and reluctant participant. In *Unforgiven*, Munny remains in the periphery until he is resurrected into a diabolical version of the Man with No Name.

Veteran grand-theft auto cop Nick Pulovski (Clint Eastwood) balks at having to team up with a new partner and protegé, David Ackerman (Charlie Sheen), a hapless twentysomethinger. With *The Rookie*, Eastwood thumbs his nose at the *Dirty Harry* series by appropriating the absurd, ultra-violent conventions of the *Die Hard/Lethal Weapon* films.

In *A Perfect World*, Red Garnett bides his time in the hopes that the manhunt he is supposed to be leading comes to an uneventful end. During the sequence in which David races into his home on a motorcycle to save his wife, Sarah (Lara Flynn Boyle), Eastwood can be seen directing a shot, a technical gaffe that reveals, if anything else, that Eastwood the director is more ubiquitous than Eastwood the actor in *The Rookie*, *Unforgiven*, and *A Perfect World*.

    Nick is anything but indestructible or omniscient. When he is held at gunpoint by Strom, he looks weak and defenseless. Earlier in the film, after surviving a freeway melee, Nick crawls out of the wreckage, asks for a light, and falls unceremoniously on his face. Nick, despite his braggadocio, is refreshingly vulnerable. When he finally kills Strom and leans against a baggage carousel, he is a pitiable sight. His face is smeared with blood and his clothes are dirty and wrinkled. Nick divides a cigar in half, gives the other piece to David, and asks for a light (a running gag in the film). David searches his pockets, but fails to find one. Nick spits the torn cigar out of his mouth, mumbles, "the story of my life," and passes out, his head resting on David's shoulder. Instead of standing over Strom's corpse with a stoic expression (a staple of the Dirty Harry series), Nick loses consciousness and crumples into a frail, withered heap. As with *White Hunter, Black Heart*, Eastwood shows the limitations of masculinity and the realities of aging. Nick cannot be young and reckless, just as John Wilson cannot be a successful bare-knuckle fighter. For Wilson, masculinity is a concept, an ideal he must live up to at all times. It is his role, his artistic armor. Nick, though steadfastly masculine, does not feel the need to prove himself physically. His moment of truth comes when he is seduced and sexually assaulted by Liesl, who warns him, "I hate anything useless. When something is no good to me, I just cut it off and throw it away." Nick has to maintain an erection if he is to keep his manhood. His masculinity is subverted. To survive intact, Nick must be passive and compliant while being erect and sexually aroused. Liesl, with her sexual aggressiveness, and Nick, with his passive compliance, erase preconceived notions of masculinity and femininity, making us wonder if the phallus is just a penis with little significance when a woman demands that it be locus of a man's virility and identity. Nick preserves his masculinity (literally!) by adjusting to the situation and bringing Liesl to orgasm. His willingness to switch roles with Liesl, let go of his masculinity, and enter an ambiguous world of power and desire deconstructs the traditional divisions between male and female sexuality. By displaying a video recording of the event several minutes later, Eastwood exposes it not as a traumatic loss of masculinity, but a kinky rethinking of gender and sexuality.

Eastwood's treatment of violence in *The Rookie* is cavalier — it does no discernible psychological or physical damage to Nick or David. In fact, violence enables Nick to achieve his career goal (get Strom) and David to confront his past, overcome his fears, and improve his self-esteem. In both *The Gauntlet* and *Sudden Impact*, Eastwood places us in the midst of violence and asks us to identify with the protagonists. Not so in *The Rookie*, which wants us to observe, rather than participate in the violence. Its violence is not intrinsic; it happens outside of the characters, and thus, has none of the immediacy of *The Gauntlet* or *Sudden Impact*. Instead of building mood, suspense, or character, *The Rookie* raises violence to the level of empty spectacle. During the high-speed chase on the L.A. Freeway that opens the film, Eastwood does not keep the mise-en-scène and the montage balanced so that we can identify with Nick or participate in the violence. Eastwood cuts to superfluous four-car collisions and pile-ups that distance us from Nick and Strom and slow down the tension and anxiety of the chase. He prevents us from participating by dispersing time and space and depriving *The*

Rookie of any momentum. Without any visual or thematic link between Nick and Strom, this scene and many to follow (including a gratuitous, poorly composed collision between two airplanes) lack any significance whatsoever. In *The Gauntlet*, Eastwood comments on the depersonalization of late 20th-century America by having hordes of policemen in sunglasses open fire on a bus driven by Ben Shockley and Gus Mally. In *Sudden Impact*, he journeys into Jennifer Spencer's psyche to show us the gruesome legacy of rape. The violence in *The Rookie* does not have the absurd, silent comedy overkill of *The Gauntlet* or the psychopathic menace of *Sudden Impact*. It is without humor, suspense, or context.

After the freeway chase, *The Rookie* falls into a 45-minute lull that is not broken until Nick is taken hostage and David is left to confront his fears. After savagely head-butting a mirror, David tells his wife, "It's time for me to stop being scared and for other people to start." He then goes on an indefensible rampage that glorifies violence as a rite of manhood and adulthood. When David terrorizes a bar full of Latino bikers, it is hard to tell if Eastwood is parodying violence or exploiting it. The climax does not resolve, but instead intensifies this dilemma. Suddenly, as if he awoke from a cinematic slumber and realized that his film has been glorifying and trivializing violence, Eastwood arranges a last-minute series of shots that call attention to the film's lack of morality or restraint. Nick looks down at us from a high angle, his gun pointed directly at the lens. Strom looks up at us, his face registering disbelief and horror. Nick snarls, "There's got to be a hundred reasons why I don't blow you away, but right now I can't think of one." He then fires his weapon, a red filter momentarily filling the screen as the bullet finds its mark. By suddenly bringing us into the montage via point of view shots and low and high angle close-ups, Eastwood rediscovers the moral and personal ramifications of violence. For a brief moment, we sympathize with Strom as he emits a final, feral cry of panic and helplessness. We also sympathize with Nick as he straggles out of the frame, weakened by the bullet lodged in his chest and the realization of how brutal and tragic violence truly is. Why does Eastwood bring us into the violence so late in the film? Is this a last-minute rejection of *The Rookie*, or a sly, momentary return to the ambivalence of *The Gauntlet* or *Sudden Impact*? By absolving himself of moral responsibility or a visual schemata that explores the ramifications of violence, Eastwood ends up with a film that is both morally irresponsible and visually uninvolving. The last-minute insertion of identificatory montage and Nick-Eastwood's retirement do not salvage, but merely call attention to, the film's visual and thematic flaws, not to mention the lapses of judgment that make the film a perplexing and troublesome experience.

Unforgiven, 1992

Play a psychopathic killer someday? Sure, why not. That might be
interesting [Guerif, p. 180].

Hampered by lax construction and an iconic vacuum, *Sudden Impact*
and *Pale Rider* were ample proof that Eastwood was tired of his persona and
the formulaic restrictions it placed on his work. Eastwood tried to sidestep
his persona with *Bird* and *White Hunter, Black Heart*, but to maintain his
box-office standing he had no choice but to churn out *The Dead Pool* and
direct another pair of Dirty Harry-Man with No Name films. With *The
Rookie* and *Unforgiven*, Eastwood decided to retire his persona and make the
violent content of his films more ambiguous. Overcrowded with scenes of
excessive mayhem, *The Rookie* proved to be a flippant and desultory dis-
missal of the Dirty Harry mythos and Eastwood's modern persona — not
until Nick Pulovski fires pointblank into the lens does Eastwood ponder the
ambiguity or intimacy of violence. *Unforgiven* takes the penultimate scene
between Nick and Strom and broadens it into an entire narrative. William
Munny (Clint Eastwood), the troubled protagonist-antagonist of the film,
levels a rifle at Little Bill Dagget's (Gene Hackman) head and fires, but this
scene — another series of tense, cheek by jowl close-ups and low and high
angle point of view shots — is not a belated recognition of the moral consequences of violence in an otherwise amoral film, but a thematic and graphic
conclusion to a film that accepts violence as a natural, but nevertheless nau-
seating, phenomenon.

Unforgiven* is Eastwood's valediction to the Man with No Name, a film
that deconstructs and then reincarnates Eastwood's 30-year-old persona
into a mythic, yet malefic, archangel-antihero. The ease with which the
Stranger, Josey Wales, and the Preacher resort to violence turns into a fatal
flaw in *Unforgiven*, an Achilles' heel that pushes Munny toward madness and
homicidal fury. Munny lacks the moral superiority of the Stranger and the
Preacher or Wales' noble suffering. He does not have their control over violence — violence controls him. Munny's use of violence is so virulent, it
obscures the fact that he is doing the Lord's bidding and restoring order to
Big Whiskey. Munny does not just defeat Little Bill and his deputies — he
butchers them. The Stranger and the Preacher spare the weak and shoot the
wicked; Munny opens fire on both. Wales is a victim of fate; tragedy turns
him into an outlaw and gunfighter. Munny is a victim of his own past, a
past that is much more disturbing than the memories that Wales represses.
He does all he can to remain pious and secluded, but is tormented by man

(Little Bill) and nature (rain, pigs, horses) until he can no longer resist temptation or restrain his destructive impulses. Although he is the sine qua non of the film, Eastwood uses a large group of supporting characters (Ned Logan [Morgan Freeman], the Schofield Kid [Jaimz Woolvett], Little Bill Dagget, W. W. Beauchcamp [Saul Rubinek], English Bob [Richard Harris], Strawberry Alice [Francis Fisher], and Delilah Fitzgerald [Anna Thompson]), a dovetailed narrative, parallel cutting, and the kaleidoscopic properties of the widescreen to decentralize his performance and persona. Eastwood is part of an ensemble until the climax, when he metamorphoses into the Man with No Name and the film's *deus ex machina*.

Unforgiven begins and ends in Big Whiskey but is framed by a panoramic prologue and epilogue to give the film a timeless mystique similar to that of the end credit landscapes in *White Hunter, Black Heart*. *Unforgiven* continues *White Hunter, Black Heart*'s practice of delaying the front credits until the end of the film so that Eastwood can quickly establish the coexistence of a mythic and the material world (an extension of Eastwood's mortal-mythic persona) and cut directly to the event that sets the narrative into motion: Quick Mike's (David Mucci's) cutting of Delilah, a senseless and barbaric act that leads to Little Bill's undoing and Munny's anti-resurrection.

The prologue and epilogue is set in a spiritual world that is removed from human affairs. Photographed in long shot and silhouetted by the setting sun, the prologue and epilogue's lone image is that of Munny burying his wife underneath a tree. The juxtaposition of the tree and the grave signifies the harmony of life and death, existence and eternity. To emphasize the contrast between the mythic (prologue and epilogue) and material world (Big Whiskey), Eastwood cuts from the postmeridian beauty of the prologue and epilogue to the claustrophobic immorality of Big Whiskey. Big Whiskey takes us out of nature and into a man-made world beset by sin, self-interest, and sadism. It is a corrupt shantytown, a dark and foreboding place besieged by rain and misery. Munny's inner conflict — the struggle between the holy and the profane, the spirit and the flesh, conscience and cruelty — is symbolized by the juxtaposition of the two worlds. Munny is associated with the natural order of the prologue/epilogue, but he is also infected by Big Whiskey's moral leprosy. He yearns to be a good Christian, but is distracted by temptation, economic hardship, and the ghosts of the past. Claudia is Munny's godsend; alcohol his *bête noire*. Eastwood reverses the redemptive progress of *The Outlaw Josey Wales* by having Munny lose his faith and sobriety and return to his former self — "a man of notoriously vicious and intemperate disposition." Both human and inhumane, sickening and sympathetic, Munny represents the best and worst aspects of human nature. His inner conflict is an epic struggle between the Id (violence) and the superego (faith); his faith and love for Claudia his only defense against chaos and carnage. Ironically, Munny's faith and allegiance to Claudia prove to be a stumbling block when he is summoned to be the Lord's executioner. Before Munny can vanish into the horizon and be reunited with Claudia, he must revisit his past and serve as a ruthless example of the Lord's wrath. To be saved, Munny must become the ultimate sinner. Through Munny, Eastwood examines No Name's eschatological control of violence, and his pathological ability not to feel fear or remorse. He shows us the human and the inhuman sides of the Man with No Name.

A film noir western, *Unforgiven* is a conscious rejection of the studio westerns of the post war era (*Duel in the Sun* [King Vidor, 1946], *Unconquered* [Cecil B. DeMille, 1947], *The Big Country* [William Wyler, 1958], *How the West Was Won* [John Ford, Henry Hathaway, George Marshall, 1962]), the very westerns Eastwood pigeonholed with *A Fistful of Dollars* and the Man with No Name in the mid-1960s:

> I remember those high-gloss Technicolor Westerns I saw as a kid. All that light and those saturated colors. I never liked it. Some of them are called classics but they were too artificial and unreal. My approach to *Unforgiven* and to *Pale Rider* and *Bird* before it was to forget that we were shooting in color. It is as if we were shooting in black-and-white and getting the kind of look you saw in something like John Ford's *My Darling Clementine*. I told the production designer and the art decorator and the costume people to keep muted tones to everything. Not everybody likes that, but that's the way I wanted it [Tibbetts, 1993, pp. 16-17].

Unforgiven is more austere than Eastwood's other westerns. It does not have the audacity of *High Plains Drifter* or the communal spirit of *The Outlaw Josey Wales*. Nature is mercurial and dyadic — it is not *High Plains Drifter*'s elemental diorama or *Pale Rider*'s majestic overseer. In *The Outlaw Josey Wales*, nature reflects Wales' spiritual collapse and regeneration. The color filters and terrain change as Wales makes his way to the Crooked River Ranch. In *Unforgiven*, nature is a reflection of Munny's dichotomous personality and the chaos that rules Big Whiskey. Until Munny confronts his true self, he is out of sync with and at the mercy of nature — Munny is tormented by rain, pigs, fever and an inhospitable landscape. Except for the prologue and epilogue, several bridging shots of Munny and Ned Logan following the Schofield Kid's trail and the snowfall that follows Munny's resurrection, Eastwood de-emphasizes light and color in order to give the film a sober, melancholy tone. A film of shadows and imminent darkness, *Unforgiven* is an elegy, a sad and uncompromising farewell to a persona that has bedeviled Eastwood for 30 years.

Little Bill Dagget (Gene Hackman), a corrupt sheriff who wants to be the next Wyatt Earp, meets a real legend, William Munny (Clint Eastwood), a devout pig farmer who is one whiskey bottle away from becoming a sinister incarnation of the Man with No Name.

Like Lago in *High Plains Drifter*, Big Whiskey is a town in need of deliverance; it has no church or courthouse, just a spacious whorehouse-saloon named Greely's and a corrupt sheriff who sees himself as a lawman, carpenter, and gunfighter, all three of which he is not. Most of the scenes set in and around Big Whiskey seem to take place underneath a grey sky or at night. Rarely is the weather complaisant — more often than not, it is raining and thundering whenever Eastwood stages a scene inside Greely's, Little Bill's do it yourself home, or Little Bill's jail (a far less cozy jail than Sheriff John T. Chance's in *Rio Bravo* [Howard Hawks, 1959]). Eastwood breaks the serenity of the prologue by cutting to an ominous establishing shot of Big Whiskey that is similar to the introductory shots of LaHood in *Pale Rider* — in both, a mountain range looms overhead, a reminder of God and nature's imminence. He then narrows the camera's perspective and cuts to a nocturnal rainstorm, an anthropomorphic sign of God's disapproval and Big Whiskey's moral lassitude. After tracking through the muddy center of town, Eastwood gives us another sign of Big Whiskey's sinfulness by moving inside Greely's, where Davey Bunting (Rob Campbell) is having workmanlike sex with veteran prostitute Strawberry Alice. Big Whiskey is literally a hotbed of vice and cruelty. Next door, Quick Mike is lunging at Delilah with a knife for innocently giggling at his diminutive genitalia. After blood is drawn, Davey comes to his senses and tries to stop Mike, but the grisly assault does not end until Skinny DuBois (Anthony James), the proprietor of Greely's, puts a pistol to Mike's head.

Quick Mike's act of impotent rage is absolutely repugnant, but Little Bill's response to Mike's felonious act is even more loathsome. Because Delilah is a prostitute under contract to Skinny, Little Bill sees her as an investment of capital rather than a full-fledged human being. Instead of hanging or at least bullwhipping Quick Mike and Davey, Bill rules that they should compensate Skinny for his losses. As Little Bill reaches his verdict, Eastwood uses the anamorphic lens, a shallow focus, and reverse masters to keep Strawberry Alice and the other prostitutes blurry and in the background — a visual approximation of their second-class status. Their exclusion from the male domain of law and commerce causes a gender rift, a sociopolitical tug of war between Strawberry Alice and Little Bill that escalates into a bloodbath after Munny arrives in town. Alice wants Quick Mike and Davey hanged, not so much because of Delilah's disfigurement, but because she and the other prostitutes have been victimized and marginalized for too long. As she sees it, "Just because we let those smelly fools ride us like horses don't mean we got to let them brand us like horses." Her act of defiance, the whores' gold — a $1000 reward for the murder of Quick Mike and Davey — turns a travesty of justice into a vendetta and a moral quagmire that cannot be resolved without William Munny's anti-resurrection and recidivism. When Quick Mike and Davey return in the springtime to compensate Skinny, Davey offers Delilah his best pony, a genuine act of remorse that is rejected by Alice, who snarls, "She ain't got no face left, and you're going to give her some goddamn mangy pony?" While the whores pelt the two cowboys with cow chips, Delilah watches pensively and passively, her face covered with scars, regret, and sorrow. Unlike Alice, Delilah is not consumed by indignation. She is willing to forgive Davey, something Alice cannot or will not do.

The lure of the whore's gold takes us to the frontier and Munny's godforsaken, threadbare household, a homestead that bears little resemblance to the silhouette in the prologue or Wales' Edenic home in *The Outlaw Josey Wales*. Munny does not have Wales' close relationship with the earth or his two children, Will (Shane Meier) and Penny (Aline Leuasseur); he has no aptitude for pig farming or single parenting. Munny is neither a sentinel (*High Plains Drifter, Pale Rider*) nor the salt of the earth (*The Outlaw Josey Wales*). He is a haunted, impoverished man who is at odds with nature and himself, an unshaved and disheveled man knee-deep in muck and misfortune. When Eastwood makes his first appearance in *High Plains Drifter* and *Pale Rider*, he gives himself slow, progressive coverage until he rides dramatically into close-up; in *The Outlaw Josey Wales,* Eastwood introduces Wales in a bucolic setting, framed by nature and his close-knit family. In *Unforgiven*, Eastwood introduces Munny as he is jostled and thrown to the ground by a bunch of feverish, unruly pigs. The animals hog the foreground, obstructing and ruining Munny's cinematic entrance. Munny finally rises in front of the camera when the Schofield Kid introduces himself off screen with the line, "You don't look like no rootin' tootin' sonuvabitch, cold-blooded assassin." Perched on a horse and framed by the horizon, the Schofield Kid has a distinct spatial advantage over Munny, who is trapped inside his makeshift pig pen. By the end of the film the roles will be reversed: Munny takes control of the frame and the landscape, while the Kid lies crumpled against a tree, devastated by Quick Mike's murder.

The Schofield Kid tries to coax Munny into becoming his partner, having heard that Munny was at one time "as cold as the snow" and had "no weak nerve or fear." Will declines the Kid's offer, insisting, "I ain't like that anymore, kid. Whiskey done it as much as anything else. I ain't had a drop in ten years. My wife, she cured me of that. Cured me of drink and wickedness." Munny's resolve weakens, however, when his feverish pigs send him writhing in the mud for the umpteenth time. Munny rises from the muck and watches the Schofield Kid ride into the distance — the difference between the Schofield Kid's extreme long shot and the medium close-up of Munny resting against his weather-beaten fence is that of freedom and entrapment; opportunity and impoverishment. The Kid is young and eager for adventure; Munny is old and covered in excrement, a man who is so deep in debt that he is desperate enough to abandon his children and jeopardize his faith in return for several hundred dollars in blood money. Munny's decision to desert his children and homestead and join the Schofield Kid sets up an identity crisis and a rendezvous with a past that Claudia helped him repress, but never forget. Eastwood suggests Munny's inner conflict by showing him pick up his wife's daguerreotype before retrieving his pistols. Prior to his resurrection, Munny has none of the qualities associated with the Man with No Name. En route to Big Whiskey, Munny is either a comic figure given to pratfalls or a sentimental figure given to moments of nostalgia and self-reflection. Instead of a paladin (*A Fistful of Dollars, High Plains Drifter, Pale Rider*) or a seasoned professional (*The Outlaw Josey Wales*), Munny is a has-been, a schmuck who cannot shoot a canister 20 yards away or mount a horse without being thrown to the ground.

To emphasize Munny's lifelong attachment to Claudia, Eastwood cuts to a long shot of him, before he embarks on his faithful journey, visiting her grave beneath the tree that appears in the prologue and epilogue. Munny's devotion to Claudia is the most positive element in the film, a love that survives intact even after he loses his sobriety and reverts to his former self. Munny's inner struggle is not with the flesh, but a deep-seated evil so ferocious that it threatens to rob him of his superego and humanity. Munny tells Ned that it "ain't right buying flesh"— his marriage to Claudia is sacrosanct, a vow that goes beyond the grave. Claudia is more than just a memory, she is an inspiration, a spiritual force that Munny relies on for strength and support (prior to his departure, Munny tells his children, "You remember how the spirit of your dear, departed mother watches over you"). In *Unforgiven*, a no man's land exists between the mythic and the mundane. Eastwood never tells us whether Claudia is a distant memory or a living essence, or whether Munny's struggle is a product of divine intervention or human frailty.

Before leaving Kansas and intercepting the Schofield Kid, Munny visits Ned, an old comrade and fellow ex-outlaw who functions as a bridge to Munny's past. Located in a picturesque valley, Ned's home is not isolated and dilapidated like Munny's. Ned is in sync with nature. His home does not detract from the landscape. As Will rides toward Ned's home, Eastwood contrasts Munny's dual nature (has-been and legend) by varying the distance between Munny and the lens. At first, Munny resembles the Man with No Name as he crosses a stream in long shot, but as he approaches Ned's homestead and the camera, he loses his composure and nearly falls from his horse. Unlike Will, Ned has surmounted his past, married an Indian woman, Sally Two Trees (Cherrilene Cardinal), and eked out a comfortable living as a farmer. Ned reminds Will, "If Claudia was alive, you wouldn't be doing this," but Munny recants, asserting, "Just because we're going on this killing don't mean I'm going back to the way I was. I just need the money to get a new start for them youngsters." He insists, "I'm just a fellow now, I ain't no different from anyone else no more," but according to Eastwood, "Munny has been protesting all the time that he has changed, but maybe he's been protesting too much" (Tibbetts, pp. 16–17).

In *Unforgiven*, Eastwood complements his triadic persona (mortal-legend-myth) with a trio of gunfighters (English Bob, Little Bill, and William Munny) who form a hierarchy when they come into contact with journalist and dime novelist W. W. Beauchcamp. English Bob and Little Bill vie for Beauchcamp's attention. Both want to cultivate an image and become part of the burgeoning mythology of the West. When we first meet W. W., he has written a novelization of English Bob's career titled *The Duke of Death*. The stories that make up the dime novel are all erroneous and exaggerated— products of the same rumor mill that magnify Delilah's facial lacerations into genital mutilation. A notorious wastrel and braggart who is more agile with his mouth than his gun hand, English Bob is a pretender. His gunfights are mere chance encounters that Bob wins because of blind, drunken luck. Such luck does not sustain English Bob when he enters the city limits of Big Whiskey without registering his firearm, a mistake that turns the Duke into a dead duck. English Bob and Little Bill's public confrontation is not a Fordian conflict between civilization and chaos, but an ugly and self-indulgent battle of egos, a media event duly witnessed and recorded by Beauchcamp. Little Bill not only beats and imprisons English Bob—he robs him of his image and "biographer" (Beauchcamp), and consigns him to obscurity. While English Bob is a charlatan, Little Bill is more of a full-fledged gunfighter. What separates Little Bill from English Bob is not just ability, but a badge, a professional code, and a desire for power. English Bob has no ambition past being a minor celebrity; Little Bill wants to be the next Wyatt Earp. The main tenet of Little Bill's code is "a man who will keep his head and not get rattled under fire, like it or not, he will kill you," a thesis he proves when he hands English Bob a loaded pistol and gives him a chance to fire, a challenge Bob sheepishly declines. Bob then leaves Big Whiskey in disgrace.

Disenchanted with English Bob, Beauchcamp attaches himself to Little Bill, whom he regards as an authentic Western legend, a man whose deeds are grounded in fact rather than fiction. W. W. urinates in his pants the first time he is held at gunpoint. He grows less squeamish when Bill introduces him to a pistol and the exciting possibilities of a gunfight. W. W. moves into Little Bill's house and faithfully records all of his sayings and anecdotes, failing to notice that he is as flawed as his poorly constructed home. Despite his Hawksian code, Little Bill relies too heavily on his badge and his cadre of deputies to outnumber his adversaries. Instead of preserving civilization, Little Bill jeopardizes it by using the law to prey on the hapless (English Bob) and the helpless (William Munny). After Little Bill beats Munny and lynches Ned, Munny is unable to maintain his self-control and restrain his Id, a force more terrifying than Little Bill's ego.

Unlike English Bob and Little Bill, Munny has no desire to capitalize on his legendary past and be part of western lore. His marriage to Claudia and his out of the way pig farm in Kansas are genuine attempts to escape the past and replace it with a life of industry and contemplation. A congenital gunfighter, Munny has no code, just an innate ability to survive a gunfight. Like Ransom Stoddard (James Stewart) in John Ford's *The Man Who Shot Liberty Valance,* Munny is a prisoner of his legendary past. In Ford's film, Tom Doniphon's (John Wayne) sacrifice gives Stoddard a terminal case of guilt. When he visits Doniphon's casket, Stoddard feels unworthy and ashamed. Ford shows us the true circumstances behind Valance's death, even as newspaper publisher Dutton Peabody (Edmond O'Brien) proclaims, "This is the West ... When the legend becomes fact, print the legend." *Unforgiven* plays the same games with truth and fiction: with English Bob and Little Bill, Eastwood dismantles the heroic conventions of the western, but he also reaffirms the mythic roots of his own persona. Eastwood demolishes then reanimates the Man with No Name — Munny is both everyday and extraordinary. He parodies and pays homage to his persona. *Unforgiven* has the revisionist streak of such westerns as *McCabe and Mrs. Miller* (Robert Altman, 1971) and *The Missouri Breaks* (Arthur Penn, 1976), but it also preserves the decalogue of *A Fistful of Dollars, The Good, the Bad, and the Ugly, High Plains Drifter*, and *Pale Rider*. While *The Outlaw Josey Wales* can be seen as a homage to John Ford and Howard Hawks' epic westerns, *Unforgiven* takes Ford and Hawk's antiheroes one step further. Munny is more ambiguous than Ethan Edwards in *The Searchers* or Tom Dunston in *Red River*. His fate is less certain (redemption or damnation) and his exit lacks closure (does Munny disappear into darkness or fade into a sunset?).

En route to Big Whiskey, Munny tries to revisit his past with Ned and take responsibility for his sins but is thwarted by the Schofield Kid, who is only interested in the sensational highlights of Munny's violent career. Big Whiskey exerts a sinister hold over Munny — the closer he gets to Little Bill's lair, the more his vicious disposition resurfaces. Immediately before Ned, Munny, and the Schofield Kid approach the city limits, English Bob is banished in disgrace from Big Whiskey. He issues a vehement curse that is given extra significance when Strawberry Alice looks up at the overcast, rumbling sky and remarks, "Rain's coming." That rain becomes a deluge as the train taking English Bob out of town passes by Ned, Will, and the Schofield Kid. The rain — a natural occurrence and/or divine arrangement — drenches Munny and makes him feverish, intensifying his struggle with the past and his alter ego. Because of the rain and darkness, Munny's posse does not see the town ordinance requiring all visitors to register their firearms with the sheriff's office, the same ordinance Little Bill used as a pretext to beat and imprison English Bob. When they reach Greely's, Eastwood moves inside the salon with a thunderclap-cut, shooting Munny through a staircase to suggest his inner turmoil and psychological distress. While waiting for Ned and the Schofield Kid to negotiate terms for the whore's gold, Munny's is confronted by a bottle of whiskey left by Ned in the foreground. With his remaining strength Munny pushes the whiskey away and wraps himself in his coat. No longer clean-shaven or lucid, and wracked with chills and shakes, Munny begins to hallucinate, coming face to face with his mangled, bloodstained victims. The fever tests his sanity and resolve.

By making Munny sick, bewildered, and helpless, Eastwood subverts his persona and sets up Munny as a victim-aggressor, an antichrist who will usurp Little Bill and undergo a relapse-resurrection. Isolated in the back of the saloon, Munny is an object of curiosity for everyone present, particularly Delilah, who watches him with an empathetic gaze. Delilah takes an instant interest in Munny's welfare — he is the other victim of Big Whiskey's immorality and Little Bill's cruelty, a kindred spirit she can communicate with and understand. With Beauchcamp in tow, Little Bill strides into Greely's and wants to make an example of Munny, another victim to be hounded and publicly humiliated. When Little Bill accosts Munny and demands that he surrender his firearm, all Munny can do is reply, "I ain't drunk," an indication that his real adversary is not Little Bill, but the foregrounded bottle of whiskey. Unmoved by Munny's declaration of sobriety, Little Bill gives him the same scourging Dirty Harry receives in *Sudden Impact*— a series of vicious kicks and blows that force him to crawl ignominiously out of Greely's and into the street. Like Harry, Munny collapses into the elements: Harry plummets into the bay; Munny rolls in the wet mud. Both Harry and Munny emerge from the elements and undergo a physical change, a metamorphosis from man to myth, individual to icon (Wales has a link with the earth, but he is never resurrected from the elements). By beating Munny, a weak and delirious man, Little Bill shows what little respect he has for the law or humanity. His lack of restraint alienates Beauchcamp and arouses the Lord's wrath. After being told by Strawberry Alice that "you just kicked the shit out of an innocent man," Little Bill retorts, "Innocent? Innocent of what?" Bill is right and wrong at the same time: Munny is both a victim and an aggressor; the most guilty man alive, yet one of the most righteous as well; a man who is both Lot and Leviathan.

As Ned stitches Will's face back together and administers to his fever, the Schofield Kid loses faith in Munny's abilities and dismisses him as a liability: " We don't need him, he ain't nothing but a broken-down pig farmer." Scorned and rejected, Munny begs Ned not to "tell my kids none of the things I have done," and embarks on a symbolic journey to the underworld. He crosses the river Lithe, encounters the angel of death, and gazes upon Claudia's worm-ridden corpse. By breaking down and confronting death face to face, Munny reaches a tentative state of grace and self-understanding. Three days later, he is resurrected. After his fever breaks, the first person he sees is Delilah, whom he mistakes for an angel, another synthesis of the material and the spiritual. In *Unforgiven*, only Munny and Delilah are capable of transcending Big Whiskey and the world around them — it is significant that their scene is set on a mountain range high above the town. Set in the high country, with the snow providing a brightness and contrast lacking in the rest of the film (a sign of grace or piety perhaps; innocence in spite of their sins?), Munny and Delilah's scene is the emotional heart of the film, a scene of reconciliation and rebirth in which he professes his love for Claudia and heals Delilah of her spiritual wounds. Although both Munny and Delilah have been marred by the past, he convinces her that he is the truly disfigured one, that the scars crisscrossing his soul are far uglier than the scars that can be seen on her face. By mistaking her for an angel and declining her generous offer of a "free one," Munny helps Delilah regain her confidence and self-worth. Munny's devotion to Claudia inspires Delilah, who, surrounded by lust and greed, meets a man whose love for his wife is so strong and pure that it persists after death. Eastwood inserts this poignant scene to complicate our identification with Munny: how can he be so despicable if he is capable of such warmth and pathos?

All of the men responsible for Delilah's suffering (Davey, Quick Mike, Skinny, Little Bill, and his deputies) suffer in return when Munny regains his strength and rejoins Ned and the Schofield Kid. The aggressors become the victims. Munny's transformation into the Man with No Name does not happen instantly — he still has difficulty mounting a horse and firing a rifle, but when he learns that Ned has been lynched, he takes a swig of whiskey and transforms into a merciless incarnation of the Man with No Name. He escalates *Unforgiven*'s violence to a catastrophic level. Without Munny, Ned and the Schofield Kid lack the resolve to kill Davey and Quick Mike. Neither has the knack for killing: the Schofield Kid's eyesight is so poor he cannot see far enough to shoot; Ned discovers that he can no longer kill a man for profit. Despite his own misgivings, Munny has to wrest the Spenser rifle from Ned's paralyzed hands and shoot Davey before he scrambles out of range. Davey's slow demise highlights the pain and sadness of death. Davey is the least deserving of Munny's victims, the only aggressor who tries to apologize to Delilah and atone for his sins. With Davey's tragic and unnecessary death, Eastwood establishes the sanguineous link that exists between a killer and his or her victim. In *Unforgiven*, murder is unconscionable. It wounds the soul. Both Munny and Ned suffer debilitating pangs of guilt and shame as they wait for Davey to bleed to death. Davey's cries of anguish become so unbearable that Munny orders that water be taken to Davey to alleviate his suffering. Davey's death is so harrowing that Ned deserts the group immediately afterwards. Only the Schofield Kid — still eager to make his first kill — does not share in the general suffering.

With Ned's disappearance, Will grows more stern and silent. He encourages the Schofield Kid to ambush and kill Quick Mike in an outhouse. Mike's murder lacks the pathos of Davey's slow and excruciating death. Instead of a long and drawn-out death, Mike is shot pointblank while going to the bathroom. By staging Mike's death on the toilet, Eastwood associates him with excrement — he is one of the few people in *Unforgiven* who actually deserve to be shot. The importance of Mike's murder is not the act itself but the profound effect it has on the Schofield Kid. The Kid goes into shock right after killing Quick Mike. He is wracked with guilt. The enormity of death is too much for him to bear. He loses his fascination with becoming a gunfighter. Both he and Munny experience an epiphany as they wait underneath a tree for the arrival of the whore's gold — the same tree of life and death that casts a shade over Claudia's grave and appears in the prologue and epilogue. Munny stands stock-still and peers into the distance as a gray, portentous cloud creeps slowly behind him. The Schofield Kid sits underneath the tree, sipping whiskey for consolation and support as he wrestles with the murder he has just committed. The roles are reversed: instead of writhing in pig excrement, Munny towers over the Schofield Kid, Big Whiskey, and the surrounding landscape. After nearly two hours of being marginalized and deconstructed, the Man with No Name takes full control of the narrative and the frame. While the Kid is repulsed by death, Munny meets it (and metes it) with a stoic tranquillity. Free of illusions or self-righteousness, Munny tells the Kid, "It's a hell of a thing killing a man. You take away all he's got and all he's ever going to have," reminding him that no matter what the circumstances, "we all got it coming kid."

As they wait for a faraway figure on horseback to climb the hill, Munny confesses to the Kid that his past is an alcoholic melange, a blur that cannot be recalled except for several random, senseless acts of violence that he cannot account for or explain. The past comes more into focus, however, when the whore's gold arrives and Munny discovers that Ned has been captured and killed in retaliation for Quick Mike's murder. The prostitute delivering the reward money recoils from Munny, having learned that he is "the same William Munny that dynamited the Rock Island and Pacific in '69, killing women and children and all." No longer willing or able to hide from his past, Munny reaches for the Kid's bottle of whiskey and refreshes his memory. What was once a business venture becomes a personal vendetta, a blood feud that goes far beyond No Name's climactic showdown with Rojas in *A Fistful of Dollars.* Unlike David Ackerman in *The Rookie,* the Kid chooses not to be Munny's protégé. The disdain and scorn that the Schofield Kid felt for the ailing Munny changes to fear when Munny demands that the Kid hand over his pistol. The Kid hesitates until Munny reassures him, "Don't worry kid, I won't kill you. You're the only friend I've got." Preferring to be "blind and ragged rather than dead," the Schofield Kid rejects his portion of the whores' gold and distances himself from Munny's macabre legacy. He leaves with his conscience intact. Girded by whiskey, Munny has no fears or reservations. Munny — the ostensible protagonist of *Unforgiven,* the impoverished widower whom Little Bill beats and humiliates — becomes a remorseless killing machine, an automaton without thought or feeling. By reuniting with his former self and falling off the wagon, does Munny become God's emissary or merely the bastard he once was? Does Munny transform into the Man with No Name or does he merely degenerate into the man whom Claudia spent years rehabilitating? Is Munny resurrected into a mythic, moral force, or reduced to a pathetic, mean-spirited drunkard?

Day turns into night. The rain returns, soaking the earth and turning Big Whiskey into a cesspool. After being pelted by rainstorms and bewitched by alcohol, Munny returns to Greely's to do the Lord's bidding, avenge Ned (whose body has been desecrated and displayed in front of the saloon), and redefine the false mythology of the gunfighter propagated by English Bob, Little Bob and W. W. Beauchamp. As Munny rides into Big Whiskey alone and inebriated, Eastwood recreates the evening of Delilah's assault and brings *Unforgiven* full circle, giving it a concentric structure similar to *Play Misty for Me* (prologue–Big Whiskey; order-chaos; Big Whiskey–epilogue; chaos-order). *High Plains Drifter*'s final judgment comes in the form of fire; *Unforgiven*'s deliverance comes in the form of water and whiskey. Munny and the elements that overpower Big Whiskey blend, much like the Stranger and the flames that consume Lago. In both films, the elements take on greater importance as Eastwood grows closer to completing his appointed task. Munny enters Greely's and the frame surreptitiously, his rifle protruding into the foreground, a sign of his omniscience and control over space. The first time Munny visited Greely's, a blast of thunder signaled his powerlessness and delirium. The second time Munny enters Greely's, Eastwood shifts to a menacing reverse master of Munny emblazoned by a fierce blast of thunder. The second blast serves as a clarion call, a trumpet blow from the heavens. Eastwood alternates between a series of angle-reverse angle shots and reverse masters to separate Munny and Little Bill into two distinct spatial arenas — Munny stands alone in front of the entrance, framed by the wind, the rain, and the darkness; Little Bill stands in the rear of Greely's, surrounded by his many retainers. Eastwood preserves the archetypal roots of No Name by keeping Munny isolated in the frame — he is separated from mankind, a grim and unyielding extension of the tree that watches over Big Whiskey.

In *Unforgiven*, God's existence is suspect. Absolutes do not exist. Forgiveness is in short supply, as is faith or charity. Eastwood encourages us to doubt whether a moral order exists, even as Munny punishes Little Bill for his rampant misuse of violence and authority. Violence is not redemptive in *Unforgiven* — the climactic showdown in Greely's lacks the closure of *High Plains Drifter* or *The Outlaw Josey Wales*. Munny has no qualms over shooting an unarmed or a mortally wounded opponent. His use of violence supersedes that of English Bob and Little Bill — while they enjoy taunting and embarrassing their victims, Munny massacres them with little warning or fanfare. Munny turns Greely's into a slaughterhouse, blurring the line between heroism and madness, justice and lawlessness. In both *High Plains Drifter* and *The Outlaw Josey Wales*, the Man with No Name has an immoral exterior but a moral core. Munny is much more complex — he is both good and evil, a round and a flat character, a rejection and a restoration of the No Name mythos, a reverse Christ figure who degenerates from piety to barbarism. Like Harry in *Sudden Impact*, Munny's resurrection takes him outside of the law and human affairs. When he swallows a shot of whiskey and sees his reflection in the mirror, Munny is taken aback — like Harry, he has changed into an abstract and indefinite entity, a mythic-daemonic force in human form. Unlike Ben Shockley in *The Gauntlet*, Munny does not refrain from the bottle when events spin out of control — he goes on a drinking binge that quickly degenerates into a killing spree. Because of that, Munny's use of violence does not have the redemptive qualities of *High Plains Drifter*, *The Outlaw Josey Wales*, *The Gauntlet*, or even *Sudden Impact*, despite the fact that he restores order and (perhaps) morality to Big Whiskey. With Munny, Eastwood throws the triadic structure of his persona into disarray. He highlights the troubling aspects of his persona by combining all its elements into one imperfect protagonist-antagonist. Munny does not have the Stranger or the Preacher's moral authority. He lacks Wales' righteous anger. What he has is an enormous capacity for violence.

Little Bill cannot rely on his badge, code, or band of deputies to intimidate Munny. Frozen with fear and disgust, Little Bill exclaims, "You be William Munny out of Missouri, killed women and children," to which Munny replies, "That's right. I've killed women and children, killed just about everything that walks or crawled at one time or another. And I'm here to kill you, Little Bill, for what you did to Ned." Unlike No Name and Rojas in *A Fistful of Dollars* or the Preacher and Stockburn in *Pale Rider*, Munny does not challenge Little Bill to a ritualistic duel. He aims his rifle at Little Bill and fires. Only a misfire keeps Little Bill from being eviscerated. Despite the setback, Munny manages to pull out the Schofield Kid's pistol and shoot Little Bill and most of his deputies without receiving any of their return fire.

Munny's spectacular show of force captivates W. W. Beauchamp. After enduring English Bob's rodomontade and Little Bill's self-serving egotism, W. W. witnesses a true legend in action — a legend, however, who has no interest in retaining W. W. as his personal biographer. W. W. recoils from Little Bill when he is forced to take notes during Ned's "interrogation." He shows no concern or sympathy for Bill, who lies bleeding on the floor. His attention is focused instead on Munny and the legendary gunfight that has just unfolded. When W. W. points out to Munny that he has killed five men single-handedly, Will responds with a hollow, melancholy "yeah." Munny is not proud of his achievement. W. W. tries to inquire further, convinced that Munny must have a code, a technique that gives him a decided advantage in a gunfight. When he asks, "Who did you kill first? When confronted by superior numbers, an experienced gunfighter will always fire on the best shot first. Little Bill told me that," he is disappointed to learn that Munny has no *modus operandi,* just the uncanny ability to kill and not be killed: "I was lucky in the order, but I've always been lucky when it comes to killing folks." W. W. is confronted by a strange mixture of the mythic and the mundane: Munny is the quintessential gunfighter, but his lack of personality and style nullifies the very elements that constitute the mythology of the West. Contrary to English Bob and Little Bill, Munny does not appreciate W. W.'s company; when W. W. tries to get Munny to tell him whom he killed first, Munny angles his shotgun toward W. W. and growls, "All I can I tell you is who's going to be last." W. W. scurries away, rejected by the very person he has journeyed west to find and immortalize.

Eastwood ends the scene, and the film, with a climactic act of violence that is both purgative and objectionable — a vivid, personal exchange of camera angles and vantage points that complicate, rather than conclude, *Unforgiven*'s study of violence and culpability. Mortally wounded, Little Bill tries to shoot Munny, but is confronted instead by Ned's rifle several inches above his face. Bemoaning, "I don't deserve to die like this," Little Bill is met with Munny's cryptic response: "Deserve's got nothing to do with it," a remark identical to "We all have it coming, kid." As with *The Rookie,* Eastwood cuts back and forth from the low-angle shots of Munny pointing his weapon to the high angle shot of Little Bill anxiously awaiting his death to force us to identify with the victim and the aggressor and question the efficacy of violence. Even though Little Bill is a wicked man, he does not deserve to be decapitated by a shotgun blast. Seconds before his death, Little Bill tells Munny that he will see him in hell, another concatenation of the real and the supernatural that is joined together by another of Munny's empathetic "yeahs," one that can be interpreted literally or figuratively. Munny destroys Little Bill's ego in the most literal sense — he blows it to smithereens, a gratuitous act that calls into question Munny's spatial and moral superiority and the expectations an audience brings to an Eastwood film. By pulling the trigger, is Munny executing God's will or committing a moral outrage? Either the God that works through Munny is the same unforgiving Lord who consigns Lago to flames in *High Plains Drifter,* or God is dead, and there is no good and evil, just pain, regret, and suffering.

Unforgiven is wish fulfillment gone sour — instead of bombarding the audience with violence until it becomes risible (*The Rookie*), Eastwood makes the violence so vivid and personal that it cannot be dismissed or applauded. With the climax, Eastwood seems to be saying to his audience: "So you want me to be No Name again, despite the fact that I am a sexagenarian? So you want me to be ruthless and indestructible? Well, I'll be more than that. I'll be psychotic. I'll outdo the Terminator. I'll turn the standard western shoot out into a mini-Holocaust. I'll make violence so palpable and unnerving, you will not get some cheap, vicarious thrill out of watching Munny kill Little Bill. The rifle is pointed at you, but you are also pulling the trigger."

Munny's exit from Greely's and Big Whiskey preserves Munny's dual nature — it has elements of both truth and fiction. Munny is half serious when he bellows, "Any sonuvabitch who takes a shot at me, not only am I going to kill him, I'm going to kill his wife, all his friends, burn his damn house down." He uses this ambiguity to bluff his way out of Big Whiskey. Munny mounts his horse and warns that if Ned is not buried properly or if any other whore is harmed again, "I'll come back and kill every one of you sons of bitches." From Beauchcamp and the remaining townspeople's perspective, Munny resembles the Preacher or the Stranger, but up close we see the tears swell in Munny's eyes as he views Ned for the last time. As he rides out of town, everyone runs for cover except Delilah, who watches Munny leave with an angelic expression. Despite the carnage, Delilah's subtle smile suggests that Munny might be redeemed, that God has tested him like Lot, and found him to be worthy.

Eastwood does not show Big Whiskey the morning after Munny's visit — he returns instead to the mythic, allegorical world of the epilogue, where Munny's silhouette contemplates Claudia's grave and then disappears. In a postscript, Eastwood tells us that rumor has it that Munny migrated to the West Coast and prospered in dry goods, but what he actually tells us with the closing shot is that Munny has become part of nature and faded into a beautiful obscurity. The prologue and epilogue suggest that a natural, divine order exists, but the grisly showdown in Greely's makes us wonder if Munny is little more than an aberration. Munny's struggle with his past and preternatural Id is a profound recognition of how tenuous morality is and how difficult it is for us to transcend our primal impulses. In Eastwood's words:

> We all hope we change for the good, and we hope Will Munny
> has at least changed for the good. But sometimes you wonder if
> we aren't really just going in circles, chasing our tails. And
> Munny does at the end revert back to what he's been, doesn't he?
> Maybe he hasn't really learned anything [Tibbetts, p. 17].

When *Unforgiven* was released in the summer of 1992, many critics praised Eastwood for finally taking responsibility for the violent themes in his work. *Unforgiven* was seen as an apology, a *mea culpa* in which Eastwood repudiates his persona and the violent legacy of his work. Eastwood does not turn his back on the Man with No Name in *Unforgiven*, nor does he disavow the use of violence in such films as *High Plains Drifter* or *Sudden Impact*.

With *Unforgiven*, Eastwood further complicates his persona by making it as fascinating and frightening as violence itself. Munny can be seen as a sad commentary on the human condition or a grave warning that God is indeed watching us, that he is ready to send forth men such as Munny to do his dirty work. *Unforgiven* brings together Eastwood's western and genre exercises and makes them more complex, more realistic, and yet, more mythic than ever before. Instead of discarding the modern legend of Dirty Harry by planting Nick Pulovski behind a desk, Eastwood preserves the central appeal of his persona by ridding it of any boundaries — in the end, Munny is just a man, yet so much more.

A Perfect World, 1993

I know you are a good man.
No, I ain't a good man. I ain't the worst neither. I'm just a breed apart.—Butch Haynes, *A Perfect World*

Near the end of *A Perfect World*, Philip Perry (T. J. Lowther) asks Butch Haynes (Kevin Costner), the fugitive who has kidnapped and befriended him, "You're not bad, are you Butch?" Butch answers with the same enigmatic "yeah" that William Munny uses in *Unforgiven*, a yeah full of irony and ambiguity. Like Munny, Butch is a antagonist-protagonist who represents the best and worst aspects of human nature. He is Eastwood's quintessential antihero, a loner without a home or a family whose idea of nirvana is "time traveling through Texas" in a stolen Ford. Most of *A Perfect World* is set inside a moving vehicle — while Butch abducts Phil and takes him on a statewide joy ride, Texas Ranger Red Garnett (Clint Eastwood) and his associates (Tom Adler [Leo Burmester], Sally Gerber [Laura Dern], and Bobby Lee [Bradley Whitfield]) pursue him in a state of the art "headquarters on wheels." In Eastwood's road films (*The Gauntlet, Bronco Billy, Honkytonk Man*), characters reveal their hopes, memories, and dreams while riding in a car. Eastwood stays inside the confines of an automobile for most of *A Perfect World*, creating a phenomenological atmosphere in which conversations and character interaction are more important than car chases or last-minute escapes. For a convict on the run film, *A Perfect World* is surprisingly relaxed and low-key. Eastwood withholds the suspense until late in the film, when Butch reaches the end of his abortive journey.

A Perfect World is essentially a film of two spaces: the close interior of an automobile and the open expanse of nature. Locked up in prison for most of his adult life, Butch has an innate need to be free and in motion. Butch sees the automobile as an almost magical creation, a "time machine" that allows him to rush forward into the future. Eastwood manipulates the widescreen to set up a clear dichotomy between Butch and Phil's private space and the world outside of their windshield. To bring us into Butch and Phil's space, Eastwood circumscribes the widescreen by emphasizing close-ups, angle reverse-angle shots, and character development. The world inside the automobile is embryonic — when Butch leaves the comfort and security of his "time machine" and follows Phil on foot, Eastwood makes full use of the anamorphic frame and switches to shots of greater distance and depth. He uses reverse masters in the climax to suggest real time and a panoramic sense of space. He then eliminates the action axis with a circular pan and an aerial pullback shot that lifts *A Perfect World* into the heavens. For Bronco Billy, the road offers an escape from a drab and monotonous existence. The automobile offers Butch solace, but not salvation. The road leads everywhere and nowhere — Butch's destination turns out to be an anonymous meadow and a dogleg tree, the same tree that watches over the prologue and epilogue and Big Whiskey in *Unforgiven*; the same tree that forces Butch and Munny to look within and accept the truth of their existence.

In both *Unforgiven* and *A Perfect World*, the past is a millstone, a sinister force that cannot be repressed or exorcised. For Munny, the past is a melange of rotting skulls, bloody corpses, and gunfire. For Butch, the past is much more alive and everlasting. Raised in a New Orleans whorehouse, the son of a career criminal and a prostitute, Butch has more quirks and neuroses than Tippi Hedron in *Marnie* (Alfred Hitchcock, 1964). At the age of eight, Butch kills a man who tries to molest his mother — like Marnie, he remains in an arrested state of development, unable and/or unwilling to transcend his traumatic past. Butch's misfortune does not end there — not long afterwards, his mother succumbs to late-stage syphilis and commits suicide, forcing him to relocate to Texas with his father, who is as reprehensible as Huck's father in Mark Twain's *The Adventures of Huckleberry Finn*. While in Texas, Butch becomes a juvenile delinquent. At the bequest of then-sheriff Red Garnett, who is convinced that the boy would be better off separated from his father, Butch spends four years at the Gatesville Juvenile Detention Center. To Red's eventual disappointment and dismay, Butch's four-year stint at Gatesville turns him into a sociopath and a carbon copy of his father.

Although Munny cannot alter his past, he makes a valiant effort to become a devout Christian and control his impulses. Butch, handicapped by a chaotic and traumatic childhood, does not have Munny's guilty conscience or self-awareness. He is unable to distance himself from the past.

Instead of rejecting his father and breaking the cycle of abuse, Butch keeps a dog-eared postcard his father sent him years ago. Butch clings to the fantasy that he will be reunited with his father in Alaska, and that all will be forgiven. Munny understands what he is capable of if liquor touches his lips; Butch has no idea what he is capable of or who he truly is. Because of his arrested development, Butch cannot control his feelings or impulses. Whenever he witnesses a child being abused or intimidated, Butch flashes back to the past and loses his self-control and sanity. When he learns that Terry Pugh (Keith Szarabajka), his fellow escapee, has tried to harm Phil, he has no qualm with putting a bullet in Pugh's forehead. Later, while riding in Bob Fielder's (John M. Jackson's) station wagon to avert a roadblock, Butch's ire is raised when Bob's wife (Connie Cooper) browbeats her children for spilling soda in the car. Butch prepares to lash out, but refrains from doing so when Bob turns to his daughter and soothes, "It's OK, sugar. Daddy still loves you." Instead of causing grievous physical harm as he did with Pugh (Eastwood makes Pugh so reprehensible, we tacitly approve of Butch's lethal use of force), Butch steals the family's station wagon. Minutes later, Butch admits to Phil that he does not have full control over his actions: "Bob did the right thing. What if he put up a fight? I might have had to shoot him. Where would that family have been then? Bob's a good family man, that's about the best thing a man can be."

Butch's misguided attempts to break the cycle of criminality, abuse, and neglect he inherited from his parents backfire when he kills or assaults those who abuse, threaten or mishandle children — when he erupts in front of Mack (Wayne Dehart) , Lottie (Mary Alice) and Cleve (Kevin Woods), a black sharecropping family, he mixes empathy and pathology and crosses the line between healer and torturer. When Mack slaps his grandson one time too many, Butch pounces on him and forces him at gunpoint to tell Cleve, "I love you." Butch tries to fulfill a fantasy that he has had all his life — to be held and loved — but his past is too vile, the influence of his father too strong. He cannot revisit the past without replaying it. Phil has no choice but to shoot Butch with his own gun to prevent him from torturing and killing Mack and his family. Eastwood makes it ambiguous for most of the film whether Butch is capable of murder — he deliberately makes it unclear if Butch killed Larry (Mark Vogel), the guard he and Pugh take hostage when they escape from Huntsville. Butch does not reveal to Phil that "I've only killed two people in my whole life: one hurt my mama, one hurt you" until late in the film. As he caresses his gunshot wound and follows Phil into the meadow, Butch admits that he could have killed Mack, Lottie, and Cleve, an ambiguity that is given a humorous twist earlier in the film when Red discovers Larry's body and quips, "Nice to know the boy's in good hands."

Both Butch and Phil are outsiders — Phil is a misunderstood Jehovah's

Kevin Costner as the definitive Eastwoodian anti-hero, Butch Haynes. Much like William Munny in *Unforgiven*, Haynes is a protagonist-antagonist who represents the complexities and contradictions of human nature.

Witness, Butch a condemned sociopath. Products of broken families, both lack a father figure or a healthy outlet for their fears and frustrations. To establish a link between Butch and Phil, Eastwood introduces both of them in confinement — Butch is incarcerated in prison; Phil is trapped inside his house, pressed up against a window as a group of neighborhood kids pelt him with water balloons (because of his mother's religion, Phil is a social outcast). By kidnapping Phil, Butch liberates him from an inhibitive

After witnessing the death of Butch Haynes (Kevin Costner), Texas Ranger Red Garnett (Clint Eastwood) confesses to Sally Gerber (Laura Dern) that, "I don't know one thing, not one damn thing."

household dominated by females. (Eastwood goes to great lengths, however, not to demonize Phil's mother, who, though somewhat dogmatic in her faith, is still a loving mother.) What Phil needs is a model of masculinity and nonconformity, a person who will make him feel gifted and needed. Butch sees Phil as a kindred spirit. He tells Phil, "Me and you got a lot in common. Both of us is handsome devils, we both like RC Cola and neither of us got an old man worth a damn ... Guys like us Phil, we gotta be on our own, seek foolish destiny, that sort of thing." Butch takes Phil under his wing and builds his self-esteem over the course of two days. He includes Phil in his activities and encourages him to make up a list of all the things he has ever wanted to do (because of his religion, Phil cannot trick or treat, ride a roller coaster, or eat cotton candy). Butch even assuages Phil's fear — implanted by Pugh — that his penis is "puny." He offers to take a peak and informs Phil that he is of a "right fine size for a boy your age."

Butch and Phil's relationship is defined by the central motif of the pistola, a symbol of masculinity and maturity. When they first meet, Butch encourages Phil to pick up the pistola, point it at him, and repeat, "Stick 'em up." Phil is not confident or mature enough to wield the gun. He dutifully hands it back to Butch. By the end of the film, Phil is no longer intimidated by the gun — after being told by Butch that he is old enough to think for himself, Phil takes the pistol and shoots Butch before the latter massacres Mack and his family. Throughout the film, Phil has to predict whether Butch's actions will be life affirming or life threatening. Phil keeps Butch balanced — he anticipates Butch's mood swings and does what he can to curb any potential violence. When Butch steals a farmer's automobile, Phil bites the farmer's hand so that Butch cannot shoot him. At Mack's, Phil has no recourse but to pull the trigger before Butch goes on a murderous rampage. Butch does not resent Phil for shooting him in the chest. In fact, he seems almost relieved and thankful — he congratulates Phil for his bravery and his sound judgment, observing, "That was a hell of a thing to do, Philip. You're a hero. Probably be in all the papers tomorrow, how you saved those folks ... Never been shot before ... Truth is, if it had to happen, I'm glad it was you as opposed to someone I didn't know." Just before Red and a convoy of squad cars arrive, Butch peers into the distance and muses, "All things considered, I feel pretty good."

Although he takes a paternal interest in Phil, Butch resists the boy's efforts to hold his hand. Like Dave Garver in *Play Misty for Me*, Frank Harmon in *Breezy*, Ben Shockley in *The Gauntlet* and Tom Highway in *Heartbreak Ridge*, Butch is not in touch with his feelings. He must break out of his protective shell if he is to comprehend the meaning of love or forgiveness. For Butch, befriending Phil is a form of therapy — he revisits himself 30 years earlier and tries to undo all the damage done to him as a child. Butch gives Phil the encouragement and attention he never received. In return, Phil gives Butch the unconditional love he has been lacking his entire life. Phil does not abandon Butch when they reach the meadow. Instead of walking toward Red and the authorities, Phil runs back to Butch and gives him a hug, perhaps the first embrace Butch has received in his entire life. Afraid that Butch will be slaughtered by the FBI agents perched on the ridge, Phil guarantees Butch's safety by staying close to him. Touched by Phil's concern and affection, Butch is able to take his hand and walk toward the authorities. Instead of bargaining for his own freedom, Butch ensures that Phil will live a normal existence and not be isolated from his peers. He makes Phil's mother promise that the boy will be allowed to trick or treat, eat cotton candy, and ride roller coasters. As a parting gesture, Butch gives his cherished postcard to Phil, a sign that he has begun to free himself of his past. The postcard is mistaken for a gun and Butch is killed just as he reaches a pivotal moment in his life. Like Red in *Honkytonk Man*, Butch's finest moments are his last. Eastwood uses those precious moments as a linking device, an impressionistic vortex the film emerges from and returns to prior to the closing credits.

In *Unforgiven*, Munny and the world he inhabits are in flux: nature is both tranquil and tempestuous; God is both nonexistent and omnipresent;

Munny is sensitive and sadistic. In *A Perfect World*, it is only Butch Haynes who is in flux. There is no tug of war between the mythic and the mundane — the film's dichotomies come from within Haynes. Eastwood returns to the demythologized world of *The Gauntlet*, a world of endless highways and burgeoning technology (the governor's headquarters on wheels, Butch's time machine), of impending disaster and disillusionment (the film is set in 1963, several weeks before President Kennedy's assassination). Nature has a subtler role in the film — it is removed from human affairs, much like Africa and the elephants in *White Hunter, Black Heart*. Eastwood waits until the end of the film to foreground nature; once he takes us to the meadow and underneath the dogleg tree, the earth and the sky are as compelling as Butch's death.

In *White Hunter, Black Heart*, Eastwood postpones the credits to establish Wilson's conflict with nature and himself; in *Unforgiven*, Eastwood juxtaposes the prologue and the epilogue with the rest of the film to give the film a concentric structure and a mythic-material duality. Following the pattern of *White Hunter, Black Heart* and *Unforgiven*, Eastwood truncates *A Perfect World*'s credits to a lone title, postponing the front credits until the end of the film. He forgoes the credits by plunging directly into the narrative and beginning the film with a series of images that establish a centrifugal sense of time and place — although *A Perfect World* covers a lot of terrain over a span of several days, it derives its structure and pathos from the meadow and Butch's dying moments. The first two and the final 20 minutes of *A Perfect World* are the backbone of the film and the purest example of Eastwood's love of phenomenology, circular construction, and unobtrusive location shooting. Shot on location in Texas, *A Perfect World* resembles *Bronco Billy* and *Honkytonk Man* in their extensive use of natural and rural settings, but instead of a 1 to 1:85 aspect ratio, Eastwood uses the rectangular width of the anamorphic lens to give *A Perfect World* a much greater sense of depth and spatial contrast to stress the dichotomy between inside-intimate space and outside-natural space. Although Butch has no real destination (Alaska is a pipe dream), the film does — in the climax, Eastwood takes the camera out of the confines of the automobile and to a plain where time, nature, and space are as immediate as the Monterey Jazz Festival in *Play Misty for Me* and as elemental as the flames in *High Plains Drifter* or the rain in *Unforgiven*. By rooting the film in a fixed location after two hours of non-stop movement and shifting to shots of greater depth and contrast (he cuts from close two-shots to far shots to point of view and over the shoulder shots without losing a panoramic sense of space), Eastwood succeeds in capturing the same phenomenological illusion of time and space that Antonioni achieves in *l' avventura* (1959) and *la notte* (1961). Instead of using an aerial shot to frame the film and provide it with closure (*Play Misty for Me, The*

Gauntlet, Bronco Billy, Sudden Impact), Eastwood progresses from a close-up (the first image of the film) to a vast aerial pullback shot. The film starts out with Butch's face and ends with a majestic bird's-eye shot that takes us outside of human affairs and into the firmament.

The only time Eastwood gives us Butch's point of view is in the prologue — we experience Butch's death firsthand, two hours before the camera provides us with a more expansive view of the event. The recurring images of the beginning and end — the Casper mask, the dollar bills fluttering in the wind, the medium close-up of Butch lying in the grass watching the helicopter hovering overhead — serve as a vortex and give the film a centrifugal sense of déjà vu. The initial shots of Butch's death are languid and dream-like. As "Big Fran's Baby" — a Cajun waltz that Butch plays on Mack's phonograph before and after his homicidal seizure — is heard dolefully and almost inaudibly in the background, Butch watches a bird glide into the sun. Eastwood uses close-ups, slow motion, and vivid color (the grass is almost too green) to make it appear as if Butch is daydreaming rather than dying. The prologue is microcosmic. Space is de-emphasized. Our sole frame of reference is Butch, who is barely conscious. We do not see the meadow or the dogleg tree. As with *Bird, White Hunter, Black Heart*, and *Unforgiven*, Eastwood gives us a brief but highly privileged and subjective introduction to his lead character that serves as a springboard for the rest of the film. During the climax, Eastwood takes us out off Butch's private universe (the prologue), widens the visual field, foregrounds nature, and brings the film's characters together to make Butch a part of a macrocosm. The airborne shot that pulls back into the sky and closes the film can be seen as a rocket ship taking Phil to a newer, more fulfilling world, or Butch's soul following the bird into the sun. By rising so far into the sky and so far away from Butch's final resting place, does Eastwood want us to experience freedom or entrapment? Are we reminded of our terrestrial link to the earth or are we lifted into a spiritual realm, free of pain and suffering? Is Butch's death an end or a beginning?

With *A Perfect World*, Eastwood brings the third phase of his career to a gratifying close by appearing as a supporting actor in his own film. After playing a movie director in *White Hunter, Black Heart* (the self-reflective apex of the artistic cycle), and retiring his persona in *The Rookie* and *Unforgiven*, Eastwood did not want to be *A Perfect World*'s raison d'être. Instead of redefining and playing hide and go seek with his persona, Eastwood evades it altogether by playing Red Garnett, a Texas Ranger with a guilty conscience. In many ways, *A Perfect World* is Eastwood's third non-starring film, one in which his physical presence is evident but not essential. To make Butch as complex and beguiling as William Munny, Eastwood relies on Kevin Costner's affable features and personality to make us identify with an antagonistic protagonist. Like Eastwood, Costner's acting style is reserved and reminiscent of Gary Cooper. When Butch loses control, Costner's change in demeanor and behavior is as jarring as Munny's reunion with the bottle in *Unforgiven*. A worthy successor to Munny and the many misfits and malcontents found in Eastwood's work, Butch is an enigma — a man-child who has no control over his volcanic impulses. Butch does not have Munny's lethal grace; when he goes berserk, it is a coin toss whether he will butcher Mack and his family or thank them for their hospitality. Eastwood shows us a human being with a fractured ego: in several seconds, Butch can change from a Southern gentleman to a heartless killer. Eastwood does not downplay Butch's dark side — when enraged, Butch is possessed by a hostile, malevolent force that knows no mercy or restraint. Phil has to shoot Butch to repair his ego. With the character of Haynes, Eastwood is able to go beyond his own persona and create a character who is substantially different in appearance and manner from his own antiheroes (although he is a prison escapee, Butch bears little resemblance to Eastwood's cool and resourceful Frank Norris in Siegel's *Escape from Alcatraz*). Because Butch is much more personable than Munny, his breakdown is all the more frightening. Costner's bravura performance is ample proof that Eastwood can continue to make Eastwoodian films without having to be their star.

During their joyride through Texas, Butch teaches Phil that there is always an exception to the rule: "Stealing's wrong, except if you need something really bad." The same principle applies to Red Garnett — a by the book lawman, Red sidestepped the law to have Butch sent to Gatesville for a minor offense, a ploy to protect him from his abusive father. Of all the people pursuing Butch, Red is the most compassionate and understanding. A benign version of Little Bill Dagget, Red shows more interest in tater tots than in hunting or apprehending Butch. His guilty conscience prevents him from being vindictive or self-righteous. Unlike Little Bill, who relishes pain and suffering, Red has no desire to harm Butch. Red confirms this when Tom asks him, "If they get a clean shot, should they take it?" and he responds, "No, I don't want any half-ass Sgt. York to take a potshot at him." Red is almost relieved when the headquarters on wheels crashes into a thicket. He prefers to stay still, hoping out loud that Butch will make it out of the state so that the FBI will have to take over the case. For the first half of the film, Sally, the criminal psychologist assigned to Red's team, denigrates Red as a Hillbilly Sherlock Holmes and a member of the old boy's club (Red is first shown chatting with the governor [Dennis Letts] on the phone). To her surprise, Red turns out to be a mild and gentle man who is wracked with guilt (he cringes when Butch's stay at Gatesville is mentioned and Tom blurts out, "That's where the sonuvabitch learned how to be a criminal") and willing to admit his mistakes. Eastwood sums up Red's ambivalent feelings about

Butch, Gatesville, and his assignment (the governor wants to exploit Butch's capture for political purposes) with a marvelous split-screen shot of Red walking away from the disabled headquarters on wheels. He pauses and spits a wad of tobacco in the foreground, isolated from the members of his team. The disparity in space and the lack of a middle ground suggest Red's guilty conscience and his misgivings about having to chase a man he may very well have turned into a disturbed convict.

Red, in keeping with his ambivalent feelings about Butch, is inactive during most of the film — he sips on Geritol (Eastwood's nod to old age) and nurses his guilty conscience until all the principal characters congregate at the meadow. Caught in a tense hostage situation, Red goes to great lengths to placate Butch and avoid any unnecessary bloodshed — when Butch demands that Phil be allowed to trick or treat, Red orders all the patrolmen and FBI agents to empty out their pockets and put any candy or gum they have into his hat. As a final gesture of good will, Red takes the gun out of his holster and ventures forth to negotiate with Butch, but can only watch helplessly as Butch is shot handing his father's postcard to Phil. His only aggressive act is to punch Bobby Lee, the FBI sharpshooter who cannot wait to kill Butch. As in *Unforgiven*, the true villains in *A Perfect World* are the people who knowingly cause grief and suffering. Red is partly responsible for Butch's condition, but Eastwood does not condemn him for his misguided attempts to rehabilitate Butch, just as he cannot condemn Butch for lashing out against child abuse. The end of *A Perfect World* subverts the prison breakout genre — there is no heated pursuit, threat of capture, or clear division of right and wrong, just guilt and memory and dreams and emotions. Red hides in his headquarters on wheels, silenced and immobilized by guilt and indecisiveness; Butch pushes on the accelerator, refusing to look back or too far into the future. In the end, the only thing real and lasting is the meadow, the dogleg tree, the blood flowing from Butch's gunshot wound, and Red's admission that "I don't know nothing, not one damn thing."

A Perfect World uses Eastwood's venerable aesthetic — virtually unchanged since the mid-1970s — to place us in a micro- and macrocosmic world devoid of absolutes or archetypes, just people trying to make sense of their lives and their uncertain destinies. When Red admits that he knows nothing, Eastwood reaches a critical stage in his career and achieves a cinematic epiphany in which he acknowledges the mysteries of his own existence, rather than those of Dirty Harry or the Man with No Name. As with *Unforgiven*, Eastwood leaves the Manichean world of right and wrong and leads the audience into a world where good and evil are sometimes indistinguishable. Eastwood asks many questions: Is Butch evil? Or is he a victim who cannot be held accountable for his actions? If Butch is innocent, how can his behavior at Mack's be rationalized? Butch is a clear threat to society, but he is Phil's godsend. He does not deserve to be blown away, and yet, the authorities cannot be blamed for being trigger happy. Butch's death is tragic, but unavoidable.

From the beginning of his career, Eastwood has tried to sustain a balance between mise en scene and montage, sunlight and shadow, narrative and phenomenology, men and women, personal freedom and responsibility, and his persona and his personal projects while also widening the scope of his cinema. With *A Perfect World*, Eastwood achieves a tangible sense of time and place and a magical convergence of man, nature, and eternity — although he stands out in the meadow with his bloody T-shirt, Butch eventually lies down in the grass and becomes one with the earth and the sky. The bird's-eye shot that closes *A Perfect World* forms a continuum with *Play Misty for Me*, but it also opens up new horizons in Eastwood's work, allowing him to hone his technique without losing the basic elements of his style.

6

Fourth Phase, 1995–

It's inevitable that one day the public will stop wanting to see me, and when that day comes I expect to hang it all up. Not that I think about it too much, but I'm a realist and I know that such a day will come and hopefully by then I'll be able to either direct some films and still be involved with the business, or else hang it up completely and do other things ... like chase squirrels or pick up golf balls [Munn, 1992, p. 175]!

I never second-guess audiences because many times they're just so much farther ahead of you. And then sometimes, they miss what you think you've been explaining so simply. So, you can't second guess. All you can do is build on your own instinctive reactions. That tells you what to do. You do it the best way you know how, and hope, of course, that somebody likes it [Thompson p. 177].

As he enters his fourth (and by no means final) phase, Eastwood will be the first starteur to bid Godspeed to his on-screen persona without compromising his presence or aesthetic. In *A Perfect World*, Eastwood was ready to move toward a cinema of phenomenology and human experience. Red Garnett's closing observation — "I don't know nothing, not one damn thing" — serves as a epigrammatic prelude to Eastwood's next phase, one that focuses upon mortality, the vicissitudes of existence, and the complexities of time, space, and human consciousness. In *The Bridges of Madison County* Eastwood brings us closer to his character's impressions and feelings and the details and sensations of everyday life by tapering his style down to three key elements: mood, space, and character.

Over the last several years, Eastwood has been showered with Academy Awards and accepted into the Hollywood establishment on his own terms.

This has not kept him from tinkering with his style, adopting new genres, and expanding the scope of his cinema. If he continues to make films into the next millennium, Eastwood will easily overstep Charlie Chaplin, who went into retirement after the ill-conceived and ill-received *A Countess From Hong Kong* (1967). As a starteur, Eastwood's only competition may be Woody Allen, who seems to have regained his footing with *Husbands and Wives* (1992), *Shadows and Fog* (1992), *Manhattan Murder Mystery* (1993), *Bullets Over Broadway* (1994), and *Mighty Aphrodite* (1995). Whatever course he takes, it can be guaranteed that Eastwood will continue to re-define his work and to reveal just how disingenuous his statement — "To me what a Clint Eastwood picture is, is one that I'm in" (Johnstone, p. 138) — truly is.

The Bridges of Madison County, 1995

> The book is very simple, and I didn't want to veer from that ...
> You got the house, a little bit of Winterset, the bridge, some
> country roads — and that's it. It's like an old-fashioned movie,
> just telling a story. No special effects, no matte shots or superim-
> positions — nothing fancy like that [Dowling, 1995, p. 116].

> Where great passion leaves off and mawkishness begins, I'm not
> sure. But our tendency to scoff at the possibility of the former
> and to label genuine and profound feelings as maudlin makes it
> difficult to enter the realm of gentleness required to understand
> the story of Francesca Johnson and Robert Kincaid [Waller, 1991,
> p. xii].— Robert James Waller

In *A Perfect World*, Eastwood examines the mystery of existence by opening the film with a close-up of Butch Haynes gazing into the sun and closing it with an aerial pullback of Butch taking his last breath. Eastwood frames *A Perfect World* with the subjective viewpoint of a dying man and an objective bird's-eye view of the same moment and event to give us a holistic view of humankind and its standing in the universe — in the end, Butch is no more significant than the bird that glides across the sun. With *The Bridges of Madison County*, Eastwood continues to deliberate upon the mystery of human existence and consciousness, but he does so not by foregrounding nature and space, but by tightening his spatiotemporal coverage to bring us inside the psyche of Francesca Johnson (Meryl Streep) and the love she shares with Robert Kincaid (Clint Eastwood). Instead of racing across the state of Texas and partitioning the screen into multiple spatial zones, Eastwood keeps the camera fixed inside Francesca's farmhouse and focused on the intimate details of Francesca and Robert's four-day romance.

Although *The Bridges of Madison County* has a linear plot and a circular construction, it is primarily a film of casual dialogue, meaningful silences, facial expressions, and subtle body language — Eastwood resists the overwrought prose style of Robert James Waller's source novel by patiently observing the nuances of everyday life. Eastwood has been moving toward a cinema of phenomenology ever since the Monterey Jazz Festival scene in *Play Misty for Me*; he gives us the illusion of uninterrupted time and space that characterizes the Italian neo-realist cinema of Michelangelo Antonioni (*l'avventura*), Vittorio De Sica (*umberto D*, 1953), Roberto Rosselini (*Voyage to Italy*, 1953), and Lucino Visconti (*la terra trema*, 1948). *The Bridges of Madison County* is a film of close interiors and private conversations. Most of the film occurs inside Francesca's kitchen and living room. To stress this reduction of space and scope, Eastwood returns to the 1:85 to 1 aspect ratio of *Play Misty for Me*, *Breezy*, *Bronco Billy*, *Honkytonk Man*, *Bird*, and *White Hunter, Black Heart*. In *A Perfect World*, Eastwood uses the anamorphic frame to make space metaphysical and multidimensional. *The Bridges of Madison County* does not have such spatial diversity — although the film is shot outside on location, nature does not play an animistic role in the narrative. The exterior shots do not contrast with the scenes set inside Francesca's home. Nature serves as a backdrop, much like the landscapes in *Bronco Billy* or *Honkytonk Man*. The automobile — so crucial to *A Perfect World*— does not divide space into private and public zones. In *Bird*, Eastwood uses the emancipatory powers of montage and bebop jazz to transcend time and space and take us inside Charlie Parker's turbulent psyche. Eastwood commutes through time and space in *The Bridges of Madison County*, but he preserves the spatiotemporal continuity that brings *A Perfect World* to a topological close. He relies on long takes and the spatiotemporal consistency of mise-en-scène to give the film a cogent sense of time and place.

In keeping with *White Hunter, Black Heart*, *Unforgiven*, and *A Perfect World*, *The Bridges of Madison County* begins without any front credits. The first shot of the film is a rack focus that pans from a close-up of a mailbox to a long shot of Francesca's farmhouse. Eastwood gives the film a circular construction by opening the film in the present as Francesca's adult children, Michael (Victor Slezak) and Caroline (Annie Corley), gather to read their mother's will. Francis' diary links two generations and serves as a gateway to the past and Francesca's feelings and memories. Eastwood uses point of

Francesca Johnson (Meryl Street) shares a poignant moment with her soul mate Robert Kincaid (Clint Eastwood). Eastwood keeps the camera inside Francesca's farmhouse for extended periods of time to give *The Bridges of Madison County* a phenomenological mystique.

view shots from Francesca's perspective to identify her as the subject of the film and to denote Robert as an object of feminine desire. When Robert asks Francesca for directions to the Rosemont Bridge, Eastwood keeps distance between the two by using angle-reverse angle shots and reflective montage. Robert breaks the spatial ice by reaching into his glove compartment and brushing against Francesca's legs. Francesca strolls inside the covered bridge to gaze at Robert as he sets up his equipment and plans his *National Geographic* shoot. In *The Bridges of Madison County*, Francesca is the voyeur — we see Robert from afar as he photographs the bridge and washes up before dinner. Eastwood does not give Robert the same coverage. (There are only two scenes in the film in which Eastwood is alone and the focus of the frame: the brief scene in which Robert begins his photo shoot and discovers Franesca's note, and the scene in which Robert eats lunch at a cafe and witnesses how intolerant Francesca's community can be toward women who commit adultery). He does, however, eliminate the distance between Robert and Francesca by having Robert appear in front of the bridge and surprise Francesca with a bouquet of wild flowers. For the rest of the film, Robert and Francesca share the same physical and emotional space.

After he sets up Francesca's voyeuristic interest in Robert and develops their relationship, Eastwood builds the chemistry between them by setting a majority of their scenes inside Francesca's home. The long scenes of Robert and Francesca talking, dancing, and making love are the core of the film; they are an exercise in phenomenology that layers detail upon detail. Eastwood keeps sentimentality in check by developing the relationship with subtle and progressive brush strokes. Eastwood concentrates on details such as the weather or the time of day to influence and heighten Francesca and Robert's moods and actions. For Robert and Francesca, the four days that they share together are insulated from the rest of the world — to achieve this intimacy, Eastwood moves from lunch-time banter in the kitchen to intense declarations of love over a candlelight dinner. The bond between Robert and Francesca becomes so strong that when he waits for one last glimpse of her in the rain, they achieve a sublime intimacy, even though they do not appear in the same frame. Distance is no longer voyeuristic — it is a transcendent meeting of two souls. The climactic shots of Robert hanging Francesca's cross on his rearview mirror are as intimate and romantic as the scenes in which they lie nude or dance to the radio. Physical contact is no longer necessary. Francesca does not have to be in the same frame to know what Robert is thinking or feeling. This intimacy is carried over into the later scenes of an aging Francesca opening the package containing Robert's possessions — even after death, she still has a profound connection to him — this is confirmed by the dispersal of her ashes in front of the bridge where she met Robert, her kindred soul. Eastwood does not cut to a saccharin shot of Robert; we never see his or Francesca's face again. We are left with the phenomenological afterglow of the farmhouse.

Eastwood concludes *The Bridges of Madison County* with an end credit montage of rural Ohio, but the images are unrelated to the rest of the film, unlike the African landscapes that bring *White Hunter, Black Heart* to a majestic close. The ground-level shots of Robert's truck navigating Winterset's country roads and the aerial shots of the covered bridges are a pleasant postscript to the dispersal of Francesca's ashes, but they do not have a direct link to the rack focus that opens the film. The bird's-eye shots that glide over Winterset are not as schematic or significant as the airborne pullback that brings *A Perfect World* to a magnanimous close. As with *Bird*, memory and experience give *The Bridges of Madison County* its structure; once we leave Charlie Parker or Francesca's consciousness, the film has no identity or purpose. All things considered, *The Bridges of Madison County* is a transitional work in which Eastwood wrestles with the incompatibility of narrative and phenomenology, character and exposition. His future work may be defined by this struggle.

Neither Francesca nor Robert are a by-product of Eastwood's mythic or contemporary persona. Neither are scarred or bedeviled by the past. When they part ways, Francesca and Robert are not crippled by heartbreak or longing. Both accept life's restrictions and the ravages of time without losing their *joie de vivre*. Robert Kincaid is a nomadic artist, but he does not have Red Stovall, Charlie Parker, or John Wilson's propensity for self-destructiveness. For Robert, art is not an addiction or a defense mechanism. He is a creative person who has no illusions about his livelihood and the perils of pursuing art for art's sake; as he sees it, "I don't think obsessions have reasons, that's why they're obsessions." Robert does not need Francesca to revitalize him (*Bronco Billy*) or mend his ego (*The Gauntlet*). Quite the contrary — it is Robert who imbues Francesca with his love and devotion. Francesca does commit adultery, but her desire for Robert is so genuine, it cannot be dismissed as a mere affair. A proud and gracious woman, Francesca does not let Robert compromise her sense of duty or decorum. Her allegiance to her husband, Richard (Jim Haynie), and children prevents her from roaming the earth with Robert and behaving like Marlene Dietrich in *Morocco* (Joseph Von Sternberg, 1931). Francesca sleeps with Robert, but she never leaves Richard's side — she remains faithful to both men.

Despite its theme of adultery, *The Bridges of Madison County* is a tribute to family and marriage — Francesca's decision to remain with Richard is not presented as a cop-out or the wrong choice. Francesca declares in her diary that "we are the choices that we have made." However strong her passion for Robert may be, Francesca cannot break the bonds of matrimony and family. The film's circular narrative — as opposed to the crazy-quilt construction of Waller's novel — turns life into a cycle and time into a surreal entity that gives human experience its importance and meaning. Eastwood does not avoid the reality of death. The throwing of Francesca's ashes — a minor event in the novel — is the climax of the film; a moving and vivid reminder that all of us share the same fate *The Bridges of Madison County* gives Eastwood the opportunity to deal with mortality without the violent catharsis of *The Rookie, Unforgiven,* and *A Perfect World.* Francesca does not point a gun in our face — death gives the film its meaning and structure, but it is not a savage bullet to the head. Eastwood manages to make the normal extraordinary, turning a brief encounter into a profound study of love, desire, and sacrifice.

Of all the characters that he has played over the last 40 years, Eastwood has admitted that he feels closest to Robert Kincaid:

> For the first time in my life, I feel like I'm just portraying myself. I like Robert Kincaid because he is his own person. He's independent and creative, but he goes about his life quietly. He enjoys who he is and what he does without being irresponsible. He has integrity [Dowling, p. 120].

In many ways, Robert Kincaid is an ideal role for Eastwood: he is a Man of the West, a successful commercial artist, a jazz aficionado, and a rustic wanderer. Eastwood could have easily turned *The Bridges of Madison County* into the sixth installment of the artistic cycle, but he chose not to be focus of the film (a pattern set by *Unforgiven* and *A Perfect World*). As with *Sudden Impact,* Eastwood steps back and lets a woman define and determine the course of the narrative. Kincaid exists within Francesca's memories and writings — without her guiding hand, he has no being or place in the film. Much like Dave Garver in *Play Misty for Me,* Robert is the object of a woman's desire. In Waller's novel, Kincaid is an autonomous character. There is no central narrator. For several chapters, we sit in the front seat of Robert's truck and dawdle alongside him as he does his photo shoot for *National Geographic.* Eastwood and screenwriter Richard LaGravenese turn *The Bridges of Madison County* into Francesca's story by taking the second to the last chapter, which features Caroline and Michael reading Francesca's diary, and expanding it into a framing device.

With the exception of Marsha Mason in *Heartbreak Ridge,* Eastwood's third phase is bereft of strong female leads. There are steely and determined women in *Bird* (Chan Parker), *The Rookie* (Liesl), *Unforgiven* (the spirit of Munny's deceased wife, Delilah, and Strawberry Alice), and *A Perfect World* (Sally Gerber), but they do not dominate or define the narrative (Chan is important to *Bird*, but it is Parker who gives the film its ebb and flow). Eastwood's third phase is full of male characters in need of catharsis and redemption. To find release, Thomas Highway, Charlie Parker, John Wilson, William Munny, and Butch Haynes must confront their inner demons and/or the horror of violence. *The Bridges of Madison County* is conspicuously absent of violence or antagonism. There are no firearms. There is none of the sexual animosity of *Play Misty for Me* or the male-female wrangling of *The Gauntlet*, *Bronco Billy*, or *Heartbreak Ridge*. Eastwood has shared the screen with many well-known actresses over the years, but *The Bridges of Madison County* marks the first time he has costarred with a full-scale female star who can relate to the camera as well as he does. Despite her plucky and appealing performances in *The Gauntlet*, *Every Which Way But Loose*, *Bronco Billy*, and *Sudden Impact*, Sondra Locke has always been considered to be a Malpaso player. At this point in his career, Eastwood can de-emphasize his own presence and defer to a star like Meryl Streep.

For Eastwood, *The Bridges of Madison County* was the first opportunity for him to play a man of feeling and understanding who does not need to be civilized or browbeaten by a woman of superior intelligence and discipline. Unlike Dave Garver in *Play Misty for Me*, Bronco Billy in *Bronco Billy*, Red Stovall in *Honkytonk Man*, or John Wilson in *White Hunter, Black Heart*, Robert has no inner conflict that hinders his career or relationships with others. Because of this, *The Bridges of Madison County* does not belong to the artistic cycle; Eastwood does not make Kincaid the film's reference point — no longer constrained by the limited legacy of the Man with No Name, Eastwood has no need or desire to be the film's *raison d'etre*. In the 1970s and early 1980s, Eastwood's physique made up a substantial part of his appeal and screen presence — he appeared shirtless at least once in every Malpaso film (*Every Which Way But Loose* and *Any Which Way You Can* derive their blue-collar aesthetic from Eastwood's bare-chested frame). In the late 1980s, Eastwood seemed to become self-conscious about doing partial nudity — he does not take off his shirt in *Heartbreak Ridge*, *White Hunter, Black Heart*, *The Rookie* (Nick Pulovski keeps his shirt on when Liesl "rapes" him), *Unforgiven*, and *A Perfect World*. Eastwood lets it all hang out in *The Bridges of Madison County*. He removes his T-shirt in front of the camera, revealing his aging physique. Backlighting does not make Eastwood mythical — it makes him look fragile and endearingly human. As Kincaid, Eastwood enjoys playing an old man who has not lost his love and lust for life. In *The Bridges of Madison County*, age is a state of mind, not body. Eastwood plays on the contrast (for many people) of being a robust 65-year-old man — while his face is full of wrinkles, Eastwood has not lost his athletic stature.

Although *A Perfect World* and *The Bridges of Madison County* are both structured around the death of its protagonists, mortality is treated differently

For over 25 years, Clint Eastwood has filmed on location to give his films a distinct mood and atmosphere. Here he gives *The Bridges of Madison County* its relaxed and rural tone by placing the camera in an Iowa corn field.

in each film — in the former, death gives the film closure, but it does not resolve the circumstances leading up to Butch's death. Red Garnett's confession ("I don't know one thing, not one damn thing.") is similar to Marlene Dietrich's eulogy ("What can you say about people? He was some kind of man.") at the end of *Touch of Evil* (Orson Welles, 1958): death does not disentangle the imbroglio of existence; no one is right or wrong, just alive or dead. In *The Bridges of Madison County*, death does not confound Michael and Caroline Johnson — it renews their lives and encourages them to reevaluate their priorities and give thanks to their loved ones. Death is a conundrum in *A Perfect World*, a cruel dilemma that is left unresolved when Butch collapses to the ground and watches Phil ascend into the sky. Death is a serene mystery in *The Bridges of Madison County*, a beautiful enigma that ends quietly with Francesca's final blessing. As with Red Stovall in *Honkytonk Man*, Francesca's death gives her life context and consanguinity — the spreading of her ashes next to the Rosemont Bridge is a glorious moment, a tribute to the inescapable choices and sacrifices that we all must make over the course of our lives.

Except for *The Rookie* and his non-directorial efforts (*The Dead Pool*, *Pink Cadillac*, *In the Line of Fire*), Eastwood chose in the late 1980s and the first half of the 1990s to set five of his last six films in the past. *The Bridges of Madison County* takes place during the same era as *A Perfect World*, a time before American society went haywire and Dirty Harry became emblematic of a nation in crisis. In the post-modern age, American filmmakers such as Katherine Bigelow (*Strange Days*, [1995], Terry Gilliam (*Brazil* [1985], *The Fisher King* [1991], *12 Monkeys* [1995]), and Oliver Stone (*Natural Born Killers*) have popularized a new strain of mega-montage that knocks down the fourth wall of spectatorship and calls attention to the excesses and lost souls of an alienated, media-obsessed culture. Eastwood has not been influenced by the cross-flow of the information age. By setting films in the past, Eastwood is able to preserve the deliberate pace of his films and maintain his commitment to phenomenology and character. As he grows older, Eastwood seems to be less interested in alienation and more interested in the links between people and the contradictions that make up personality and character. While many directors such as David Lynch (*Wild at Heart* [1988]) and Quentin Tarantino (*Reservoir Dogs* [1992], *Pulp Fiction* [1994]) have embraced chic nihilism, Eastwood has overcome his persona and widened his iris to include all of humanity. With *The Bridges of Madison County*, Eastwood acknowledges the inevitability of death to make us all appreciate the miracle of life and love. Francesca and Robert may be dead, but their ashes and artifacts resonate with life.

Appendix:
The Malpaso Crew
Participation in
Eastwood Films

Malpaso Productions grew out of Clint Eastwood's frustration with Hollywood, which was (and still is) rife with waste and mismanagement. In the late 1960s, Eastwood assembled Malpaso, a hand-picked production crew known for their speed and efficiency. By the early 1970s, Malpaso developed into a loyal group of cast and crew members that would reappear and remain with Eastwood over several decades. Eastwood has rewarded his crew's loyalty and hard work by promoting them to the status of director (James Fargo, Buddy Van Horn), cinematographer (Jack N. Green), or producer (David Valdes). All of Eastwood's Malpaso films are listed to stress the continuity of the Malpaso crew, which has contributed to the consistency of Eastwood's style and direction.

Upper case letters indicate a film directed by Clint Eastwood.

Hang 'Em High (1967). Pat Hingle (Performer).
Coogan's Bluff (1968). Alexander Golitzen (Art Director). Lalo Schifrin (Music). Albert Popwell (Performer). Bruce Surtees (Camera Operator).
Two Mules for Sister Sarah (1970). Bruce Surtees (Camera Operator).
The Beguiled (1971). Alexander Golitzen (Art Director). Bruce Surtees (Director of Photography). Carl Pingitore (Editor). Lalo Schifrin (Music).
PLAY MISTY FOR ME (1971). Alexander Golitzen (Art Director). Bruce Surtees (Director of Photography). Carl Pingitore (Editor). Jennings Lang/Robert Daly (Executive Producer/Producer). Dee Barton (Music). Jack Ging, James McEachin (Performers). Jack Green (Aerial Camera). Rexford Metz (2nd Unit Camera).

Dirty Harry (1971). Bruce Surtees (Director of Photography). Carl Pingitore (Editor). Robert Daly (Executive Producer/Producer). Lalo Schifrin (Music).John Mitchum, Woodrow Parfrey, Albert Popwell, John Vernon (Performers). Rexford Metz (Aerial & 2nd Unit).

Joe Kidd (1972). Henry Bumstead/Alexander Golitzen (Art Directors). Bruce Surtees (Director of Photography). Ferris Webster (Editor). Robert Daly (Executive Producer/Producer). Lalo Schifrin (Music). Gregory Walcott (Performer). James Fargo (Assistant Director).

HIGH PLAINS DRIFTER (1973). Henry Bumstead (Art Director). Bruce Surtees (Director of Photography). Ferris Webster (Editor). Jennings Lang/ Robert Daly (Executive Producer/Producer). Dee Barton (Music). Walter Barnes, Verna Bloom, Jack Ging, Geoffrey Lewis, John Mitchum, William O'Connell, John Quade, Dan Vadis (Performers). James Fargo (Assistant Director).

BREEZY (1973). Alexander Golitzen (Art Director). Frank Stanley (Director of Photography). Ferris Webster (Editor). Robert Daly (Executive Producer/ Producer). Michael Legrand (Music). James Fargo (Assistant Director).

Magnum Force (1973). Frank Stanley (Director of Photography). Ferris Webster (Editor). Robert Daly (Executive Producer/Producer). Lalo Schifrin (Music). John Mitchum, Albert Popwell (Performers). Buddy Van Horn (2nd Unit Director).

Thunderbolt & Lightfoot (1974). Tambi Larsen (Art Director). Frank Stanley (Director of Photography). Ferris Webster (Editor). Robert Daly (Executive Producer/Producer). Dee Barton (Music). George Kennedy, Geoffrey Lewis, Bill McKinney, Gregory Walcott (Performers).

THE EIGER SANCTION (1975). Aurelio Crugnola/George Webb (Art Directors). Frank Stanley (Director of Photography). Ferris Webster (Editor). David Brown/Robert Daly (Executive Producers/Producers). John Williams (Music). George Kennedy, Gregory Walcott (Performers). James Fargo (1st Ass't Director). Rexford Metz (Aerial Camera).

THE OUTLAW JOSEY WALES (1976). Tambi Larsen (Art Director). Bruce Surtees (Director of Photography). Ferris Webster (Editor). Robert Daly (Executive Producer/Producer). Jerry Fielding (Music). Sam Bottoms, Matt Clark, Sondra Locke, Doug McGrath, Bill McKinney, John Mitchum, William O'Connell, Woodrow Parfrey, John Quade, John Russell, John Vernon (Performers). Joel Cox (Associate Editor). James Fargo (Associate Producer/Assistant Director). Fritz Manes (Assistant to Producer).

The Enforcer (1976). Allen E. Smith (Art Director). Ferris Webster/Joel Cox (Editor). Robert Daly (Executive Producer/Producer). Jerry Fielding (Music). Michael Cavanaugh, Bradford Dillman, John Mitchum, Albert Popwell (Performers). James Fargo (Director). Fritz Manes (Ass't to Producer). Rexford Metz (Aerial & 2nd Unit).

THE GAUNTLET (1977). Allen E. Smith (Art Director). Rexford Metz (Director of Photography). Ferris Webster/Joel Cox (Editor). Robert Daly (Executive Producer/Producer). Jerry Fielding (Music). Michael Cavanaugh, Pat Hingle, Roy Jenson, Sondra Locke, Dough McGrath, Bill McKinney,

William Prince, Dan Vadis (Performers). Jack Green (Aerial Camera). Fritz
Manes (Associate Producer).

Every Which Way But Loose (1978). Rexford Metz (Director of Photography).
Ferris Webster/Joel Cox (Editor). Robert Daly (Executive Producer/Producer). Steve Dorff (Music). Walter Barnes, Roy Jenson, Geoffrey Lewis,
Sondra Locke, James McEachin, Bill McKinney, William O'Connell, Joan
Quade, Dan Vadis, Gregory Walcott, Hank Worden (Performers). James
Fargo (Director). Jack Green (Camera Operator). Fritz Manes (Associate
Producer).

Escape from Alcatraz (1979). Bruce Surtees (Director of Photography). Ferris Webster (Editor). Robert Daly (Executive Producer/Producer). Jerry Fielding
(Music). Joel Cox (Assistant Film Editor). Fritz Manes (Associate Producer).

BRONCO BILLY (1980). Gene Lourie (Art Director). David Worth (Director of
Photography). Ferris Webster/Joel Cox (Editor). Robert Daly/Dennis
Dobrofsky, Dennis Hacklin (Executive Producer/Producers). Steve Dorff
(Music). Walter Barnes, Sam Bottoms, Geoffrey Lewis, Sondra Locke,
Dough McGrath, Bill McKinney, Woodrow Parfrey, William Prince, Dan
Vadis, Hank Worden (Performers). Jack Green (Camera Operator). Fritz
Manes (Associate Producer).

Any Which Way You Can (1980). David Worth (Director of Photography). Ferris Webster/Ron Spang (Editor). Robert Daly (Executive Producer/
Producer). Steve Dorff (Music). Michael Cavanaugh, Barry Corbin, Michael
Currie, Roy Jenson, Geoffrey Lewis, Sondra Locke, Bill McKinney, William
O'Connell, John Quade, Dan Vadis (Performers). Buddy Van Horn (Director). Jack Green (Camera Operator). Fritz Manes/David Valdes (2nd Assistant Directors).

FIREFOX (1981). Elayne Ceder/John Graysmark (Art Directors). Bruce Surtees
(Director of Photography). Ferris Webster/Ron Spang (Editor). Fritz
Manes/Clint Eastwood (Executive Producer/Producer). Maurice Jarre
(Music). Michael Currie (Performer). Jack Green (Camera Operator).
David Valdes (2nd Assistant Director).

HONKYTONK MAN (1982). Edward Carfagno (Art Director). Bruce Surtees
(Director of Photography). Ferris Webster/Joel Cox/Michael Kelly (Editors). Fritz Manes/Clint Eastwood (Executive Producers/Producers). Steve
Dorff (Music). Verna Bloom, Matt Clark, Barry Corbin, John Russell (Performers). Jack Green (Camera Operator).

SUDDEN IMPACT (1983). Edward Carfagno (Art Director). Bruce Surtees
(Director of Photography). Joel Cox (Editor). Fritz Manes/Clint Eastwood
(Executive Producers/Producers). Lalo Schifrin (Music). Bradford Dillman, Michael Currie, Pat Hingle, Sondra Locke, James McEachin, Albert
Popwell (Performers). Jack Green (Camera Operator). David Valdes (1st
Assistant Director).

Tightrope (1984). Edward Carfagno (Art Director). Bruce Surtees (Director of
Photography). Joel Cox (Editor). Fritz Manes/Clint Eastwood (Executive
Producers/Producers). Lennie Niehaus (Music). Jack Green (Camera Operator). David Valdes (1st Assistant Director).

City Heat (1984). Edward Carfagno (Art Director). Fritz Manes (Executive Producer/Producer). Lennie Niehaus (Music). David Valdes (1st Assistant Director).

PALE RIDER (1985). Edward Carfagno (Art Director). Bruce Surtees (Director of Photography). Joel Cox (Editor). Fritz Manes/Clint Eastwood (Executive Producers/Producers). Lennie Niehaus (Music). Doug McGrath, John Russell (Performers). Jack Green (Camera Operator). David Valdes (Associate Producer).

HEARTBREAK RIDGE (1986). Edward Carfagno (Art Director). Jack N. Green (Director of Photography). Joel Cox (Editor). Fritz Manes/Clint Eastwood (Executive Producers/Producers). Lennie Niehaus (Music). Arlen Dean Snyder (Performer).

BIRD (1988). Edward Carfagno (Art Director). Jack N. Green (Director of Photography). Joel Cox (Editor). David Valdes/Clint Eastwood (Executive Producers/Producers). Lennie Niehaus (Music). Arlen Dean Snyder, Anna Thompson (Performers).

The Dead Pool (1989). Edward Carfagno (Art Director). Jack N. Green (Director of Photography). Joel Cox/Ron Spang (Editors). David Valdes (Executive Producer/Producer). Lalo Schifrin (Music). Michael Currie (Performer). Buddy Van Horn (Director).

Pink Cadillac (1989). Edward Carfagno (Art Director). Jack N. Green (Director of Photography). Joel Cox (Editor). David Valdes (Executive Producer/Producer). Steve Dorff (Music). Francis Fisher, Geoffrey Lewis, Bill McKinney (Performers). Buddy Van Horn (Director).

WHITE HUNTER, BLACK HEART (1990). John Graysmark (Art Director). Jack N. Green (Director of Photography). Joel Cox (Editor). David Valdes/Clint Eastwood (Executive Producers/Producers). Lennie Niehaus (Music).

THE ROOKIE (199). Judy Cammer (Art Director). Jack N. Green (Director of Photography). Joel Cox (Editor). David Valdes/Howard Kazanjian, Steve Siebert (Executive Producers/Producers). Lennie Niehaus (Music).

UNFORGIVEN (1992). Henry Bumstead (Art Director). Jack N. Green (Director of Photography). Joel Cox (Editor). David Valdes/Clint Eastwood (Executive Producers/Producers). Lennie Niehaus (Music). Francis Fisher, Anthony James, Anna Thompson (Performers).

A PERFECT WORLD (1993). Henry Bumstead (Art Director). Jack N. Green (Director of Photography). Joel Cox/Ron Spang (Editors). David Valdes/Clint Eastwood (Executive Producers/Producers). Lennie Niehaus (Music).

THE BRIDGES OF MADISON COUNTY (1995). Jeannine Oppewall (Art Director). Jack N. Green (Director of Photography). Joel Cox (Editor). Kathleen Kennedy/Clint Eastwood (Executive Producer/Producer). Lennie Niehaus (Music).

Filmography

Play Misty for Me (1971). Universal, 102 minutes. *Director*: Clint Eastwood. *Producer*: Robert Daley. *Screenplay*: Jo Heims, Dean Riesner. *Director of Photography*: Bruce Surtees. *Art Director*: Alexander Golitzen. *Editor*: Carl Pingitore. *Music*: Dee Barton. *Cast*: Clint Eastwood (Dave Garver); Jessica Walter (Evelyn Draper); Donna Mills (Tobie Williams); John Larch (Sgt. McCallum); James McEachin (Al Monte); Clarice Taylor (Birdie); Don Siegel (Murphy); Jack Ging (Frank).

High Plains Drifter (1973). Universal, 105 minutes. Panavision. *Director*: Clint Eastwood. *Producer*: Robert Daley. *Executive Producer*: Jennings Lang. *Screenplay*: Ernest Tidyman. *Director of Photography*: Bruce Surtees. *Production Designer*: Henry Bumstead. *Editor*: Ferris Webster. *Music*: Dee Barton. *Cast*: Clint Eastwood (the Stranger); Billy Curtis (Mordecai); Verna Bloom (Sarah Belding); Marianna Hill (Callie Travers); Mitchell Ryan (Dave Drake); Jack Ging (Morgan Allen); Ted Hartley (Lewis Belding); Geoffrey Lewis (Stacey Bridges); Anthony James (Cole Carlin); Dan Vadis (Dan Carlin); Stefan Gierasch (Mayor Jason Hobart); Walter Barnes (Sheriff Sam Shaw); Robert Donner (Preacher); William O'Connell (Barber); John Quade (Jake Ross); John Hillerman (Bootmaker); Reid Cruikshanks (Gunsmith); Scott Walker (Bill Borders); Paul Brinnegar (Luthe Naylor); Richard Bull (Aba Goodwin); John Mitchum (Warden); Clint Eastwood/Buddy Van Horn (Marshal Jim Duncan).

Breezy (1973). Universal, 106 minutes. *Director*: Clint Eastwood. *Producer*: Robert Daley. *Executive Producer*: Jennings Lang. *Screenplay*: Jo Heims. *Director of Photography*: Frank Stanley. *Production Designer*: Alexander Golitzen. *Editor*: Ferris Webster. *Music*: Michel LeGrand. *Cast*: William Holden (Frank Harmon); Kay Lenz (Breezy); Roger Carmel (Bob Henderson); Marj Dusay (Betty Tobin); Joan Hotchkis (Paula Harmon); Jamie Smith Jackson (Marcy); Dennis Olivieri (Bruno).

The Eiger Sanction (1975). Universal, 125 minutes. Panavision. *Director*: Clint Eastwood. *Producer*: Robert Daley. *Executive Producer*: Richard D. Zanuck, David Brown. *Screenplay*: Hal Dresner, Warren B. Murphy, and Rob Whitaker. Based on Trevanian's novel *The Eiger Sanction*. *Director of Photography*: Frank Stanley. *Production Designer*: George Webb and Aurelio Crugnola. *Editor*: Ferris Webster. *Music*: John Williams. *Cast*: Clint Eastwood (Jonathon Hemlock); George Kennedy (Ben Bowman); Vonetta McGee (Jemima Brown); Jack Cassidy (Miles Mellough); Thayer David (Dragon); Reiner Schoene (Freytag); Michael Grimm (Meyer); Jean-Pierre Bernard (Montaigne); Gregory Walcott (Pope); Heidy Bruhl (Mrs. Montaigne); Brenda Venus (George); Walter Kraus (Kruger).

The Outlaw Josey Wales (1976). Warner Brothers, 135 minutes. Panavision. *Director*: Clint Eastwood. *Producer*: Robert Daley. *Screenplay*: Phil Kaufman and Sonia Chernus. Based on Forrest Carter's novel *Gone to Texas*. *Director of Photography*: Bruce Surtees. *Production Designer*: Tambi Larsen. *Editor*: Ferris Webster. *Music*: Jerry Fielding. *Cast*: Clint Eastwood (Josey Wales); Chief Dan George (Lone Watie); Sondra Locke (Laura Lee); Bill McKinney (Terrill); John Vernon (Fletcher); Paula Trueman (Grandma Sarah); Sam Bottoms (Jamie); Geraldine Keams (Little Moonlight); Will Sampson (Ten Bears); Woodrow Parfrey (Carpetbagger); William O'Connell (Sim Carstairs); John Quade (Comanchero Leader); Doug McGrath (Lige); John Russell (Bloody Bill Anderson); John Mitchum (Al); Matt Clerk (Kelly); Joyce Jameson (Rose); Sheb Wooley (Travis Cobb); Royal Dano (Ten Spot); Frank Schofield (Senator Lane); Madeline T. Holmes (Granny Hawkins); Cissy Wellman (Josey's Wife).

The Gauntlet (1977). Warner Brothers, 111 minutes. Panavision. *Director*: Clint Eastwood. *Producer*: Robert Daley. *Screenplay*: Michael Butler and Dennis Schryack. *Director of Photography*: Rexford Metz. *Production Designer*: Allen E. Smith. *Editor*: Ferris Webster and Joel Cox. *Music*: Jerry Fielding. *Cast*: Clint Eastwood (Ben Shockley); Sondra Locke (Gus Mally); William Prince (Blakelock); Pat Hingle (Josephson); Bill McKinney (Constable); Michael Cavanaugh (Feyderspiel); Doug McGrath (Bookie); Samantha Doane (Biker); Roy Jenson (Biker); Dan Vadis (Biker).

Bronco Billy (1980). Warner Brothers, 116 minutes. *Director*: Clint Eastwood. *Producer*: Dennis Hackin and Neal Dobrofsky. *Executive Producer*: Robert Daly. *Screenplay*: Dennis Hackin. *Director of Photography*: David Worth. *Production Designer*: Gene Lourie. *Editor*: Ferris Webster and Joel Cox. *Music*: Steve Dorff. *Music Supervisor*: Snuff Garrett. *Cast*: Clint Eastwood (Bronco Billy); Sondra Locke (Antoinette Lily); Geoffrey Lewis (John Arlington); Scatman Crothers (Doc Lynch); Bill McKinney (Lefty LeBow); Sam Bottoms (Leonard James); Dan Vadis (Chief Big Eagle); Sierra Pecheur (Lorraine Running Water); Walter Barnes (Sheriff Dix); Woodrow Parfrey (Dr. Canterbury); Beverlee McKinsey (Irene Lily); William Prince (Edgar Lipton); Doug McGrath (Lt. Wiecker); Mitzi (Tessa Richarde); Hank Worden (Station Mechanic).

Firefox (1981). Warner Brothers, 136 minutes. Panavision. *Director-Producer*: Clint Eastwood. *Executive Producer*: Fritz Manes. *Screenplay*: Alex Lasker and Wendell Wellman. Based on Craig Thomas' novel *Firefox*. *Director of Photography*:

Bruce Surtees. *Production Designer*: John Graysmark and Elayne Ceder. *Editor*: Ferris Webster and Ron Spang. *Music*: Maurice Jarre. *Cast*: Clint Eastwood (Mitchell Gant); Kai Wulff (Lt. Colonel Voskov); Freddie Jones (Kenneth Aubry); David Huffman (Buckholz); Warren Clarke (Pavel Upenskoy); Ronald Lacey (Semlowsky); Kenneth Colley (Colonel Kontarsky); Klaus Lowitsch (General Vladimirov); Nigel Hawthorne (Pyetr Baranovich); Stefan Schnabel (First Secretary); Michael Currie (Captain Seerbacker); Alan Tilvern (Air Marshall Kutuzov); Barry Houghton (Boris Glazunov).

Honkytonk Man (1982). Warner Brothers, 122 minutes. *Director-Producer*: Clint Eastwood. *Executive Producer*: Fritz Manes. *Screenplay*: Clancy Carlile, based on his own novel. *Director of Photography*: Bruce Surtees. *Production Designer*: Edward Carfagno. *Editor*: Ferris Webster, Michael Kelly, and Joel Cox. *Music*: Steve Dorff. *Music Supervisor*: Snuff Garrett. *Cast*: Clint Eastwood (Red Stovall); Kyle Eastwood (Whit); John McIntire (Grandpa); Alexa Kenin (Marlene); Verna Bloom (Emmy); Matt Clark (Virgil); Barry Corbin (Armspringer); Jerry Hardin (Snuffy); Tim Thomerson (Highway Patrolman); Macon McCalman (Dr. Hines); Joe Regalbutto (Henry Axle); Gary Grubbs (Jim Bob); Bette Ford (Lulu); Rebecca Clemons (Belle); Johnny Gimble (Bob Wills); Linda Hopkins (Flossie); Tracey Walter (Pooch); John Russell (Jack Wade); Marty Robbins (Smoky).

Sudden Impact (1983). Warner Brothers, 117 minutes. Panavision. *Director-Producer*: Clint Eastwood. *Executive Producer*: Fritz Manes. *Screenplay*: Joseph C. Stinson. *Director of Photography*: Bruce Surtees. *Production Designer*: Edward Carfagno. *Editor*: Joel Cox. *Music*: Lalo Schifrin. *Cast*: Clint Eastwood (Harry Callaghan); Sondra Locke (Jennifer Spencer); Paul Drake (Mick); Audrie J. Neenan (Ray Parkins); Jack Thibeau (Kruger); Pat Hingle (Chief Jennings); Bradford Dillman (Captain Briggs); Michael Currie (Lt. Donnelly); Albert Popwell (Horace King); Mark Keyloun (Officer Bennett); Kevin Major Howard (Hawkins); Bette Ford (Leah); Nancy Parsons (Mrs. Kruger); Russ McCubbin (Eddie); Robert Sutton (Carl); Carmen Argenziano (D'Ambrosia); Liza Britt (Elizabeth); James McEachin (Detective Barnes).

Pale Rider (1985). Warner Brothers, 116 minutes. Panavision. *Director-Producer*: Clint Eastwood. *Executive Producer*: Fritz Manes. *Screenplay*: Michael Butler and Dennis Shryack. *Director of Photography*: Bruce Surtees. *Production Designer*: Edward Carfagno. *Editor*: Joel Cox. *Music*: Lennie Niehaus. *Cast*: Clint Eastwood (Preacher); Michael Moriarty (Hull Barrett); Carrie Snodgrass (Sarah Wheeler); Sidney Penny (Megan Wheeler); John Russell (Stockburn); Coy LaHood (Richard Dysart); Josh LaHood (Christopher Penn); Doug McGrath (Spider Conway); Charles Hallahan (McGill); Richard Kiel (Club); Marvin J. McIntyre (Jason Marvin); Fran Ryan (Ma Blankenship); Richard Hamilton (Jed Blankenship); Chuck LaFont (Eddie Conway); Jeffrey Weissman (Teddy Conway); S. A. Griffin (Deputy Folke); Jack Radosta (Deputy Grissom); Robert Winley (Deputy Kobold); Billy Drago (Deputy Mather); Jeffrey Josephson (Deputy Sedge); John Dennis Johnston (Deputy Tucker).

Heartbreak Ridge (1986). Warner Brothers, 130 minutes. *Director-Producer*: Clint Eastwood. *Executive Producer*: Fritz Manes. *Screenplay*: Jim Carabatsos. *Director of Photography*: Jack N. Green. *Production Designer*: Edward Carfagno. *Editor*: Joel Cox. *Music*: Lennie Niehaus. *Cast*: Clint Eastwood (Sgt. Tom Highway); Marsha Mason (Aggie); Mario Van Peebles (Stitch Jones); Arlen Dean Snyder (Choozoo); Everett McGill (Major Powers); Moses Gunn (Sgt. Webster); Eileen Heckart (Little Mary); Bo Svenson (Roy Jennings); Boyd Gaines (Lt. Ring); Vincente Irizarry (Fraggetti); Ramon Franco (Aponte); Tom Villard (Profile); Mike Gomez (Quinones); Rodney Hill (Collins); Peter Koch ("Swede" Johnson); Richard Venture (Colonel Meyers); Peter Jason (Major Devin); Nicholas Worth (Jail Binger); Timothy Fall (Kid in Jail).

Bird (1988). Warner Brothers, 161 minutes. *Director-Producer*: Clint Eastwood. *Executive Producer*: David Valdes. *Screenplay*: Joel Oliansky. *Director of Photography*: Jack N. Green. *Production Designer*: Edward Carfagno. *Editor*: Joel Cox. *Music-Music Supervisor*: Lennie Niehaus. *Cast*: Forest Whitaker (Charlie "Bird" Parker); Diane Venora (Chan Parker);. Michael Zelnicker (Red Rodney); Samuel E. Wright (Dizzy Gillespie); Keith David (Buster Franklin); Michael McGuire (Brewster); James Handy (Esteves); Hamilton Camp (Mayor of 52nd St.); Arlen Dean Snyder (Dr. Heath); Jason Bernard (Benny Tate); Audrey (Anna Levine (Thompson)); Diane Salinger (Baroness Nica); Bill Cobbs (Dr. Caulfield); Joey Green (Gene); John Witherspoon (Sid); Tony Todd (Frog); Damon Whitaker (Young Bird); Morgan Nagler (Kim); Jo DeWinter (Mildred Berg); Richard Zavaglia (Ralph the Narc); Sam Robards (Moskowitz); Owner, Three Deuces (Al Pugliese); Ann Weldon (Violet Wells).

White Hunter, Black Heart (1990). Warner Brothers, 112 minutes. *Director-Producer*: Clint Eastwood. *Executive Producer*: David Valdes. *Screenplay*: Peter Viertel, James Bridges, and Burt Kennedy. Based on Viertel's novel *White Hunter, Black Heart*. *Director of Photography*: Jack N. Green. *Production Designer*: John Graysmark. *Editor*: Joel Cox. *Music*: Lennie Niehaus. *Cast*: Clint Eastwood (John Wilson); Jeff Fahey (Peter Verrill); George Dzundra (Paul Landers); Alun Armstrong (Ralph Lockheart); Boy Mathias Chuma (Kivu); Conrad Asquith (Oglivy); Geoffrey Hutchings (Alec Lang); Clive Mantle (Harry); Marisa Berenson (Kay Gibson); Richard Vanstone (Phil Duncan); Jamie Koss (Mrs. Duncan); Charlotte Cornwell (Miss Wilding); Edward Tudor Pole (Reissar); Roddy Maule-Roxby (Thompson); Richard Warwick (Basil Fields); Catherine Nelson (Irene Saunders); Christopher Fairbank (Tom Harrison).

The Rookie (1990). Warner Brothers, 121 minutes. Panavision. *Director*: Clint Eastwood. *Producers*: Howard Kazanjian, Steven Siebert, and David Valdes. *Screenplay*: Boaz Yakin and Scott Spiegel. *Director of Photography*: Jack N. Green. *Production Designer*: Judy Cammer. *Editor*: Joel Cox. *Music*: Lennie Niehaus. *Cast*: Clint Eastwood (Nick Pulovski); Charlie Sheen (David Ackerman); Raul Julia (Strom); Sonia Braga (Liesl); Tom Skerrit (Eugene Ackerman); Lara Flynn Boyle (Sarah); Pepe Serna (Lt. Ray Garcia); Marco Rodriguez (Loco); Pete Randall

(Cruz); Tony Plana (Morales); Donna Mitchell (Laura Ackerman); Xander Berkeley (Blackwell); David Sherrill (Max); Hal Williams (Powell); Jordan Lund (Bartender); Paul Butler (Captain Hargate); Roberta Vasquez (Heather Torres).

Unforgiven (1992). Warner Brothers, 131 minutes. Panavision. *Director-Producer*: Clint Eastwood. *Executive Producer*: David Valdes. *Screenplay*: David Webb Peoples. *Director of Photography*: Jack N. Green. *Production Designer*: Henry Bumstead. *Editor*: Joel Cox. *Music*: Lennie Niehaus. *Cast*: Clint Eastwood (William Munny); Gene Hackman (Little Bill Dagget); Morgan Freeman (Ned Logan); Richard Harris (English Bob); Jaimz Woolvett (The Schofield Kid); Saul Rubinek (W. W. Beauchcamp); Francis Fisher (Strawberry Alice); Anna Thompson (Delilah Fitzgerald); David Mucci (Quick Mike); Rob Campbell (Davey Bunting); Anthony James (Skinny DuBois); Tara Dawn Frederick (Little Sue); Beverley Elliot (Silky); Lisa Repo-Martell (Faith); Josie Smith (Crow Creek Kate); Shane Meier (Will Munny); Aline Leuasseur (Penny Munny); Cherrilene Cardinal (Sally Two Trees); Robert Koons (Crocker); Ron White (Clyde Ledbetter); Mina E. Mina (Muddy Chandler); Henry Kope (German Joe Schultz); Jeremy Ratchford (Deputy Andy Russell); John Pyper-Ferguson (Charley Hecker); Jefferson Mappin (Fatty Rossiter); Walter Marsh (Barber); Garner Butler (Eggs Anderson); Larry Reese (Tom Luckinbill); Blair Haynes (Paddy McGee).

A Perfect World (1993). Warner Brothers, 138 minutes. Panavision. *Director*: Clint Eastwood. *Producers*: Mark Johnson and David Valdes. *Screenplay*: John Lee Hancock. *Director of Photography*: Jack N. Green. *Production Designer*: Henry Bumstead. *Editor*: Joel Cox and Ron Spang. *Music*: Lennie Niehaus. *Cast*: Kevin Costner (Butch Haynes); Clint Eastwood (Red Garnett); T. J. Lowther (Philip Perry); Laura Dern (Sally Gerber); Keith Szarabajka (Terry Pugh); Leo Burmester (Tom Adler); Paul Hewitt (Dick Suttle); Bradley Whitford (Bobby Lee); Ray McKinnon (Bradley); Jennifer Griffin (Gladys Perry); Linda Hart (Eileen); Wayne Dehart (Mack); Mary Alice (Lottie); Kevin Woods (Cleveland); Leslie Flowers (Naomi Perry); Belinda Flowers (Ruth Perry); Mark Voges (Larry); James Jeter (Oldtimer); Ed Geldart (Fred Cummings); Bruce McGill (Paul Saunders); George Haynes (Farmer); Rodger Boyce (Mr. Wilitts); Lucy Lee Flippin (Lucy); Elizabeth Ruscio (Paula); Dennis Letts (Governor); John M. Jackson (Bob Fielder); Connie Cooper (Bob's Wife); Cameron Finley (Bob Fielder, Jr.); Katy Wottrich (Patsy Fielder); Tony Frank (Arch Andrews); Woody Watson (Lt. Hendricks).

The Bridges of Madison County (1995). An Amblin/Malpaso Production. Warner Brothers, 135 minutes. *Director*: Clint Eastwood. *Producers*: Clint Eastwood and Kathleen Kennedy. *Screenplay*: Richard LaGravenese Based on the novel by Robert James Waller. *Director of Photography*: Jack N. Green. *Editor*: Joel Cox. *Music*: Lennie Niehaus. *Cast*: Meryl Streep (Francesca Johnson), Clint Eastwood (Robert Kincaid), Jim Haynie (Richard Johnson), Annie Corley (Caroline Johnson), Victor Slezak (Michael Johnson), Sarah Schmidt (Young Caroline), Chris Koon (Young Michael), Michelle Benes (Lucy Redfield).

Bibliography

Achteneier, Paul J., General Editor. *Harper's Bible Dictionary*. San Francisco: Harper & Row, 1985.

Andrew, Dudley. *The Major Film Theories*. New York: Oxford University Press, 1976.

Andrew, Dudley. *Concepts in Film Theory*. New York: Oxford University Press, 1984.

Biskind, Peter. "Any Which Way He Can." *Premiere*. April, 1993: 53-60.

Breskin, David. "Clint Eastwood." *Rolling Stone*. September 17, 1992: 66-9, 108, 110.

Buscombe, Edward, Editor. *The BFI Companion to the Western*. New York: DaCapo Press, 1988.

Cahill, Tim. "Clint Eastwood." *Rolling Stone*. July 4, 1985: 18-23.

Calhoun, James F., Coordinating Author. *Abnormal Psychology: Current Perspectives*. Second Edition. New York: Random House, 1977.

Campbell, Joseph. *The Hero with a Thousand Faces*. New York: Princeton University Press, 1949.

Carr, Patrick, Editor. *The Illustrated History of Country Music*. Garden City: Doubleday, 1979.

Clinch, Minty. *Clint Eastwood*. London: Hodder & Stoughton, 1994.

Combs, Richard. "Shadowing the Hero." *Sight and Sound*. October, 1992: 12-16.

Cook, David A. *A History of Narrative Film*. Second Edition. New York: W. W. Norton & Company, 1990.

Coursodon, Jean-Pierre, Editor. *American Directors Volume II*. New York: McGraw Hill, 1983.

Cumbow, Robert C. *Once Upon a Time: The Films of Sergio Leone*. Metuchen: The Scarecrow Press, Inc., 1987.

Douglas, Peter. *Clint Eastwood, Movin' On*. Chicago: Henry Regnery Company, 1974.

Dowling, Claudia Glenn. *The Bridges of Madison County: The Film*. New York: Warner Books, 1995

Eastwood, Clint. "Don Siegel, the Padron." *Film Comment*. September/October, 1991: 35-6.

Everson, William K. *The Hollywood Western.* New York: Carol Publishing Group, 1992.

Fine, Marshall. *Bloody Sam.* New York: Donald I. Fine, 1991.

Fischoff, Stuart. "Clint Eastwood and the American Psyche — A Rare Interview." *Psychology Today.* January/February 1993: 38-41, 75-79.

Frank, Alan. *Clint Eastwood.* New York: Exeter Books, 1982.

Frayling, Christopher. *Spaghetti Westerns.* London: Rutledge & Kegan Paul, Ltd., 1981.

Frayling, Christopher. "Unforgiven." *Sight and Sound.* October, 1992: 58.

Gallafent, Edward. *Clint Eastwood: Filmmaker and Star.* New York: Continuum Publishing Company, 1993.

Gallagher, Tag. *John Ford: The Man and His Films.* Berkeley: University of California Press, 1986.

Gentry, Rick. "Clint Eastwood: An Interview." *Film Quarterly.* Spring 1989: 12-23.

Giddins, Gary. *Celebrating Bird: The Triumph of Charlie Parker.* New York: William Morrow, 1987.

Guerif, Francois. *Clint Eastwood.* New York: St. Martin's Press, 1986.

Hamill, Pete. "Once Upon a Time in America." *American Film.* June, 1984: 20-6.

Hammen, Scott. *John Huston.* Boston: Twayne Publishers, 1985.

Hemingway, Ernest. *The Short Stories of Ernest Hemingway.* New York: Macmillan Publishing Company, 1938.

Hentoff, Nat. "Flight of Fancy." *American Film.* September, 1988: 24-7.

Jameson, Richard T. "Deserve's Got Nuthin' to Do with it." *Film Comment.* September/October, 1992: 12-4.

Johnstone, Iain. *The Man with No Name.* New York: Morrow Quill Paperbacks, 1981.

Kaminsky, Stuart M. *Don Siegel: Director.* New York: Curtis Books, 1974.

Kehr, Dave. "A Fistful of Eastwood." *American Film.* March, 1985: 63-7.

Keogh, Peter. "Ghostly Presences." *Sight and Sound.* October, 1992: 15.

Konigsberg, Ira. *The Complete Film Dictionary.* New York: Meridian, 1987.

Lee, Spike and Jones, Lisa. *Mo' Better Blues.* New York: Simon and Schuster, 1990

Leeming, David Adams. *The World of Myth.* New York: Oxford University Press, 1990.

Lenihan, John H. *Showdown: Confronting Modern America in the Western Film.* Illinois: University of Illinois Press, 1980.

Lowell, Alan. *Don Siegel.* London: British Film Institute, 1975.

McBride, Joseph. *Hawks on Hawks.* Berkeley: University of California Press, 1982.

McDonald, Archie P., Editor. *Shooting Stars: Heroes and Heroines of Western Film.* Indiana: Indiana University Press, 1987.

Mast, Gerald and Kawin, Bruce F. *A Short History of the Movies.* Fifth Edition. New York: Macmillan Publishing Company, 1992.

Megill, Donald D. and Devlory, Richard S. *Introduction to Jazz History.* Englewood Cliffs: Prentice-Hall, 1984.

Munn, Michael. *Clint Eastwood: Hollywood Loner*. London: Robson Books, 1992.

Myers, Allen C., Editor. *The Eerdman's Bible Dictionary*. Grand Rapids: William B. Eerdman's Publishing Company, 1987.

Nachbar, Jack, Editor. *Focus on the Western*. New Jersey: Prentice-Hall, Inc, 1974.

Pilkington, William T. and Graham, Don, Editors. *Western Movies*. New Mexico: University of New Mexico Press, 1979.

Plaza, Fuensanta. *Clint Eastwood/Malpaso*. Carmel Valley: Ex Libris, 1991.

Rayns, Tony. "Clint at Claridges." *Sight and Sound*. Spring, 1985:83.

Reisner, Robert George. *Bird: The Legend of Charlie Parker*. New York: DaCapo Press, 1962.

Sarris, Andrew. "Don Siegel, the Pro." *Film Comment*. September/October, 1991: 34-38.

Schatz, Thomas. *The Genius of the System*. New York: Pantheon Book. 1988.

Schatz, Thomas. *Hollywood Genres*. Philadelphia: Temple University Press, 1981.

Shapiro, Nat and Hentoff, Nat, Editors. *The Jazz Makers*. New York: DaCapo Press, Inc., 1957.

Sheehan, Henry. "Dark Worlds." *Sight and Sound*. June, 1991:28-30.

Sheehan, Henry. "Scraps of Hope, Clint Eastwood and the Western." *Film Comment*. September/October, 1992: 17-27.

Siegel, Don. *A Siegel Film*. London: Faber and Faber, 1993.

Smith, Paul. *Clint Eastwood, A Cultural Production*. Minneapolis: University of Minnesota Press, 1993.

Studlar, Gaylyn and Desser, David, Editor. *Reflections in a Male Eye: John Huston and the American Experience*. Washington: Smithsonian Institution Press, 1993.

Suid, Lawrence H. *Guts & Glory: Great American War Movies*. Reading: Addison-Wesley Publishing Company, 1978.

Thomas, Craig. *Firefox*. New York: Bantam Books, 1978.

Thompson, Douglas. *Clint Eastwood: Riding High*. Chicago: Contemporary Books, 1992.

Thompson, Richard and Hunter, Tim. "Clint Eastwood, Auteur." *Film Comment*. January/February, 1978: 24-32.

Thomson, David. "Cop on a Hot Tightrope." *Film Comment*. September/October, 1984: 64-73.

Tibbetts, John C. "Clint Eastwood and the Machinery of Violence". *Literature Film Quarterly*. Vol 21, No 1. 1993: 10-17.

Trevanian. *The Eiger Sanction*. New York: Avon Books, 1972.

Verniere, James. "Clint Eastwood Stepping Out." *Sight & Sound*. September, 1993: 6-10.

Viertel, Peter. *Dangerous Friends*. New York: Doubleday, 1992.

Viertel, Peter. *White Hunter, Black Heart*. New York: Dell Publishing, 1953.

Waller, Robert James. *The Bridges of Madison County*. New York: Warner Books, 1991.

Zmijewsky, Boris and, Lee. *The Films of Clint Eastwood*. New York: Carol Publishing Group, 1993.

Index